THE UN CONVENTION ON THE RIGHTS OF PERSONS WITH DISABILITIES AND THE EUROPEAN UNION

Ten years ago, the European Union made a historic accession to the UN Convention on the Rights of Persons with Disabilities (CRPD). This book analyses the impact of the CRPD on EU non-discrimination law and governance to date, and explores whether the theory has been put into practice.

To understand if the CRPD is living up to its full potential to substantially improve the protection of the rights of persons with disabilities in the EU, this book brings together the practices of the European Court of Justice (CJEU) with regard to disability discrimination in the workplace. Additionally, it investigates whether the governance mechanisms underlying the EU Framework for promoting, protecting, and monitoring the CRPD are effectively fostering the implementation of the CRPD and the role of civil society.

This book will be of interest to academics, law students, and legal practitioners working in the field of EU non-discrimination and equality law.

Volume 109 in the Series Modern Studies in European Law

Modern Studies in European Law

Recent titles in this series:

The Juridification of Individual Sanctions and the Politics of EU Law
Eva Nanopoulos

Sixty Years of European Integration and Global Power Shifts:
Perceptions, Interactions and Lessons
Edited by Julien Chaisse

Fundamental Rights and Mutual Recognition in the Area of
Freedom, Security and Justice: A Role for Proportionality?
Ermioni Xanthopoulou

Law and Judicial Dialogue on the Return of Irregular Migrants from the European Union
Edited by Madalina Moraru, Galina Cornelisse and Philippe De Bruycker

Framing Convergence with the Global Legal Order: The EU and the World
Edited by Elaine Fahey

EU Citizenship at the Edges of Freedom of Movement
Katarina Hyltén-Cavallius

The Internal Market 2.0
Edited by Sacha Garben and Inge Govaere

New Directions in European Private Law
Edited by Mateja Durovic and Takis Tridimas

Standing to Enforce European Union Law before National Courts
Hilde Ellingsen

The Relative Authority of Judicial and Extra-Judicial Review:
The EU Courts, the Boards of Appeal and the Ombudsman
Michal Krajewski

Responsive Human Rights: Vulnerability and the ECtHR
Corina Heri

The Architecture of Fundamental Rights in the European Union
Šejla Imamovic

The EU and its Member States' Joint Participation in International Agreements
Edited by Nicolas Levrat, Yuliya Kaspiarovich, Christine Kaddous and Ramses A Wessel

The UN Convention on the Rights of Persons with Disabilities and
the European Union: The Impact on Law and Governance
Carmine Conte

For the complete list of titles in this series, see
'Modern Studies in European Law' link at
www.bloomsburyprofessional.com/uk/series/modern-studies-in-european-law

The UN Convention on the Rights of Persons with Disabilities and the European Union

The Impact on Law and Governance

Carmine Conte

•HART•

OXFORD • LONDON • NEW YORK • NEW DELHI • SYDNEY

HART PUBLISHING

Bloomsbury Publishing Plc

Kemp House, Chawley Park, Cumnor Hill, Oxford, OX2 9PH, UK

1385 Broadway, New York, NY 10018, USA

29 Earlsfort Terrace, Dublin 2, Ireland

HART PUBLISHING, the Hart/Stag logo, BLOOMSBURY and the Diana logo are trademarks of Bloomsbury Publishing Plc

First published in Great Britain 2022

A catalogue record for this book is available from the British Library.

A catalogue record for this book is available from the Library of Congress

ISBN: HB: 978-1-50994-514-6
ePDF: 978-1-50994-516-0
ePub: 978-1-50994-515-3

Typeset by Compuscript Ltd, Shannon
Printed and bound in Great Britain

FOREWORD

Dr Carmine Conte's book, based on the PhD thesis he brilliantly defended at Middlesex University London in 2018, sets out to analyse the impact of the UN Convention on the Rights of Persons with Disabilities (CPRD) on EU law and governance. For Dr Conte, the CRPD not only represents the most recent human rights treaty introduced at international level, but also encompasses important legal developments concerning the model of equality. This book's primary objective, however, is not to focus on these two aspects but rather to critically examine the complicated relationship between the CRPD and the EU governance framework and legal systems.

More specifically, Dr Conte examines how the innovative provisions of the CPRD may impact on EU equality law, and EU governance structures insofar as they concern disability-related issues – and also analyses whether the functioning of EU law and governance in this context reflects the values of substantive equality and participative democracy that underpin the CRPD. The book thus covers plenty of ground and as you would expect, is well written, well argued and well referenced. Amongst its many noteworthy findings, one may in particular mention the author's compelling demonstration that 10 years after its ratification by the European Union, the CJEU is yet to apply the 'human rights' model of disability enshrined in the CRPD with the Court's understanding of multiple and intersectional discrimination in line with the substantive and inclusive model of equality. As Dr Conte put it, disapprovingly, the CJEU is still embracing a 'protectionist' and 'minimalist' approach with regard to the status of the CRPD in the EU legal order. When it comes to the impact of the CPRD on EU governance, this book persuasively highlights a number of flaws such as a deficient 'reporting and benchmarking' process, an excessively fragmented monitoring EU independent framework, a marginalised European Parliament and the insufficient involvement of civil society organisations. To remedy the gaps and shortcomings identified, Dr Conte positively offers multiple concrete suggestions which will helpfully be taken on board by relevant stakeholders so as to unleash the CRPD's full potential in order to achieve its ambitious goal to effectively foster equality for persons with disabilities in the EU legal framework. To that end, I can only but agree with the author's appeal directed at EU policymakers and judges. The time has come to transpose the human rights model of disability and the inclusive approach towards equality into concrete legal and judicial practices.

My congratulations therefore to Dr Carmine Conte for his first scholarly book. It has been a pleasure supervising his doctoral research and it is heartening to see him continuing to produce excellent research while trying to make the world a better place in his current capacity as Legal Policy Analyst for Migration Policy Group.

Last but not least, I would like to take this opportunity to thank Professor Colm O'Cinneide (UCL) and Dr Shivaun Quinlivan (NUI Galway) for acting as external examiners at the time of Dr Conte's viva and providing him in the process with generous and extremely helpful feedback, the end result of which is this great book.

Professor Laurent Pech
August 2021

ACKNOWLEDGEMENTS

This book is based on the PhD thesis that I defended at the Middlesex University of London in February 2018. I had the unique opportunity to pursue my PhD under the precious and expert supervision of professor Laurent Pech, who gave me all the necessary support and advice to realise my academic potential.

The core arguments of the book have developed in the years since then, and have been updated with more recent judgments from the European Court of Justice, taking into account the dynamic legal academic and policy debate on anti-discrimination and disability. During this time, I have also been working at the European Disability Forum and the Migration Policy Group, where I have gained more practical experience and knowledge relating to anti-discrimination law and policy.

I would also like to thank Sinead Moloney, Sasha Jawed and the excellent team at Hart Publishing for all their work with the publication of this book, and Professor Colm O'Cinneide (UCL) and Dr Shivaun Quinlivan (NUI Galway) for their constructive feedback during my PhD viva.

Special thanks go to my family and soul mate; I am very lucky for your presence in my life.

CONTENTS

Foreword ... *v*
Acknowledgements ... *vii*
Abbreviations ... *xv*
Table of Cases ... *xvii*
Table of Legislation and Statutory Materials ... *xxi*

1. Introducing the CRPD: A New Approach to Equality and Non-Discrimination? ... **1**
I. Introductory Remarks ... 1
II. Equality and Non-Discrimination: A New Approach for Disability Rights ... 2
III. The Complex and Intriguing Evolution of the Right to Equality in International Law ... 4
A. The Controversial 'Sameness' Model ... 5
B. Embracing the Symmetrical Approach at International Level ... 6
C. Is the Formal Approach Adequate to Combat Discrimination? ... 8
i. The Shift Towards Substantive Equality: Acknowledging the Diversity ... 9
ii. Substantive Equality Jurisprudence ... 9
iii. Affirmative Actions as Special Measures to Achieve Equality ... 10
D. Beyond Differences: Time to Recognise Social Barriers and Positive Duties ... 12
E. The Prohibition of Discrimination under the CRPD: A New Inclusive Model ... 14
i. The Case of *HM versus Sweden* ... 16
ii. The Substantive Content of the Non-Discrimination Requirement ... 17
F. Defining the Concept of Multiple and Intersectional Discrimination ... 19
i. The Unsatisfactory One-Dimensional Approach to Discrimination ... 21
ii. Intersectional Equality under the CRPD: Women and Children with Disabilities ... 22
IV. The CRPD's Model of Disability: From a Social Construct Towards a Human Rights Approach ... 24

V. Reconceptualising the Human Rights Dichotomy 26
A. Disability Rights are Universal and Indivisible: Do Civil and Political Rights also Demand Economic Resources? 28
B. Disability Rights as (Quasi)-Justiciable Rights 29
i. The Right to Control One's Own Financial Affairs 30
ii. Debunking the Argument of the 'Progressive Realisation of Socio-Economic Rights' 32
iii. The Peculiar Case of Accessibility: A Bridge between Civil-Political and Socio-Economic Rights? 33

2. The New Role for Civil Society under the CRPD 35
I. The Rise of Civil Society in Global Governance 35
A. Participatory Democracy and Global Governance 37
B. Opening Up the Decision-Making Process 37
C. Ensuring Transparent Procedures 38
II. Mainstreaming Disability in the International Agenda 39
A. 'Nothing about us without us': A Commitment to Participatory Democracy 40
i. The Participation of Persons with Disabilities in the Ad Hoc Committee 40
ii. The Working Group on the Convention: Mixing State Delegates and Stakeholders 42
iii. Civil Society's Main Achievements 43
III. Civil Society's Role in Implementing the CRPD at National Level 44
A. Institutionalising Civil Society 45
B. Awareness-Raising: A Synergetic Action between States Parties and NGOs 47
IV. Participatory Democracy in the EU: From the White Paper to the Lisbon Treaty 48
A. The Inclusive Process of the EUCFR's Adoption: The 'Convention' Method 50
B. How to Improve EU Participatory Democracy? The Good Practice of the CRPD 52

3. Ten Years after EU Accession to the CRPD: From Theory to Reality 55
I. An Overview of the Prohibition of Discrimination under EU Law 55
A. The EU Charter of Fundamental Rights 56
B. The Convention for the Protection of Human Rights and Fundamental Freedoms 57
II. Disability Rights in the EU 58

III. The EU Anti-Discrimination Framework: Directive 2000/78/EC 60
  A. Exploring the Meaning of Direct Discrimination 60
  B. Introducing the Concept of Indirect Discrimination 61
  C. Reasonable Accommodation: The Paramount Obligation 62
IV. Filling in the Gap: The Evolving Concept of Disability 63
  A. The EU Approach to Disability 63
    i. A First Controversial Approach of the CJEU 65
    ii. *Chacón Navas*: A Missed Opportunity 66
  B. An Intriguing Evolution: The Case of *Ring and Skouboe Werge* 67
    i. Facts and Questions 68
    ii. Defining Disability and the Personal Scope of the Directive 69
    iii. Reasonable Accommodation as Adaptation of Working Hours? 70
    iv. Addressing Indirect Discrimination: Legitimate Aim, Necessity and Proportionality 71
    v. A Significant, but Incomplete, Development for EU Equality Law 73
  C. Obesity and Disability: The Case of *Kaltoft v Municipality of Billund* 76
    i. The Prohibition of Discrimination on Grounds of Obesity 77
    ii. The Prohibition of Discrimination in the Labour Market: The CJEU's Minimalist Approach 77
    iii. Is Obesity a Disability under the Equality Framework Directive? 78
    iv. Should Obesity be Considered a Disability? 80
  D. The Case of *Daouidi:* Clarifying the Long-Term Nature of the Impairment 81
  E. Absence from Work on Grounds of Sickness: The Case of *Ruiz Conejero* 83
    i. Factual Background and CJEU Key Findings 83
    ii. Drawing the Line between Illness and Disability 84
  F. Defining Disability beyond the Labour Market: The Case of *Glatzel* 85
    i. The Problematic CJEU Assessment 86
    ii. The Role of the CRPD: A Confusing Approach 87
    iii. The EU Charter of Fundamental Rights: A Narrow Interpretation 88
  G. Is the CJEU Still a Real Promoter of Disability Rights? 89

4. The EU Legal Framework: Associative and Intersectional Discrimination ... 91
I. Discrimination by Association on Grounds of Disability ... 91
A. The *Coleman* Case: Factual Background ... 91
B. The Advocate General's Opinion ... 92
C. Analysis of the Judgment: Who Falls under the Protection of Discrimination by Association? ... 94
D. The Controversial Nature of Reasonable Accommodation ... 95
E. Concluding Remarks: A Shift Towards Substantive Equality ... 96
II. Why Does Multiple and Intersectional Discrimination Matter? ... 97
III. The *Odar* Case: Disability and Age Discrimination ... 99
IV. *Surjit Singh Bedi v Bundesrepublik Deutschland*: Collective Agreement and Intersectional Discrimination ... 101
V. The Case of *Z v A Government Department*: Gender and Disability ... 102
A. The Court's Findings ... 103
B. How to Deal with Multiple and Intersectional Discrimination under EU Law ... 104
C. The Failure to Apply the Human Rights Model of Disability ... 106
D. The Complex Interplay between International Law and EU Law ... 106
E. The Incongruous CJEU Reasoning: Time for a Change ... 108

5. EU Governance and the Framework for Monitoring the CRPD ... 111
I. Ratifying and Implementing the UN Convention: Winners and Losers in the EU Institutional Game ... 111
II. The Negotiations of the CRPD and the EU ... 112
A. The Commission's Contribution to the Drafting of the CRPD ... 113
B. Ensuring Coordination between Various EU Actors ... 114
C. The Commission and the Union's External Policy Representation ... 115
III. Monitoring the CRPD's Implementation: New Governance Mechanisms ... 116
A. The Experimentalist Paradigm ... 117
B. The Open Method of Coordination (OMC) ... 118
C. The Focal Point ... 120
D. Coordination Mechanism between the EU and the Member States ... 121

IV. The EU Framework for Promoting, Protecting and Monitoring the CRPD 123
A. The Commission's Experimentalist Approach 125
B. The European Parliament and the Protection of Disability Rights 126
i. The PETI's Main Tasks and Achievements 128
ii. The Disability Intergroup of the European Parliament 130
C. The European Ombudsman 130
i. The Ombudsman's Own Initiatives 131
ii. The Ombudsman's Limited Mandate 132
D. The Monitoring Role of the EU Agency for Fundamental Rights 133
E. The EDF's Challenge to Open Up the EU Decision-Making Process 135
F. Focal Point and Coordination Mechanism: Innovative or Inefficient Practices? 138
V. Light and Shadow in the EU Independent Framework 139
A. The Commission's Withdrawal from the Framework: What Next? 139
B. Is the European Parliament Marginalised? 141
C. Is the OMC Appropriate? 144
i. An Overview of the Reporting Mechanism 144
ii. Enhancing the EU Independent Framework: Some Suggestions 146
iii. Proposal to Upgrade and Simplify the EU Independent Framework to Implement the CRPD 148

6. Conclusion: Time to Unleash the CRPD's Full Potential 150
I. The EU Legal Framework: Main Findings 150
A. The Definition of Disability: A Missed Opportunity 150
B. The Legal Gaps in Addressing Multiple and Intersectional Discrimination 152
C. Indirect Discrimination and Reasonable Accommodation: Towards a Better Judicial Interpretation? 153
D. The Inclusive Equality Paradigm under the CRPD 155
E. The Complicated Relationship between the CRPD and the EU Legal System 155
F. Key Recommendations for Improving the Interpretation of EU Equality Norms 156

II. EU Governance: Main Findings 158
A. The Importance of Reforming the EU Independent Framework 159
B. Key Recommendations for Improving EU Governance Mechanisms 160
C. Good Governance and Participatory Democracy: The CPRD's Positive Practice 160
III. Time to Unleash the CRPD's Full Potential 161

Bibliography *162*
Index *173*

ABBREVIATIONS

CEDAW	UN Convention on the Elimination of All Forms of Discrimination Against Women
CESCR	Committee on Economic, Social and Cultural Rights
CJEU	Court of Justice of the European Union
COHOM	Council Working Group on Human Rights
CRC	UN Convention on the Rights of the Child
CRPD	Convention on the Rights of Persons with Disabilities
CSO	civil society organisation
DPO	disabled people's organisation
EC	European Community
ECHR	European Convention on Human Rights
ECOSOC	United Nations Economic and Social Council
ECtHR	European Court of Human Rights
EDF	European Disability Forum
EEC	European Economic Community
EES	European Employment Strategy
EMPL	Committee on Employment and Social Affairs
ESI	European Structural and Investment Fund
EU	European Union
EUCFR	EU Charter of Fundamental Rights
FRA	European Union Agency for Fundamental Rights
FWCW	Fourth World Conference on Women
HLGD	High Level Group on Disability
ICCPR	International Covenant on Civil and Political Rights

ICERD	International Convention on the Elimination of all Forms of Racial Discrimination
ICESCR	International Covenant on Economic, Social and Cultural Rights
MEP	Member of the European Parliament
NGO	non-governmental organisation
NHRIs	National Human Rights Institutions
NRPs	National Reform Programmes
OJ	Official Journal of the European Union
OMC	Open Method of Coordination
PETI	European Parliament's Petitions Committee
TEU	Treaty on European Union
TFEU	Treaty on the Functioning of the European Union
UDHR	Universal Declaration of Human Rights
UNCED	United Nations Conference on Environment and Development
WTO	World Trade Organization

TABLE OF CASES

Decisions of the Committee on the Rights of Persons with Disabilities and International Case Law

UN Committee on the Rights of Persons with Disabilities, Communication No 1/2010, Views adopted in Nyusti & Takas v Hungary (15–19 April 2013) 30, 33
UN Committee on the Rights of Persons with Disabilities, Communication No 3/2010, Views adopted in HM v Sweden (6 December 2010) 16, 19
International Court of Justice, South West Africa, Ethiopia v South Africa, Second Phase [1966] ICJ Rep 6, ICGJ 158 (ICJ 1966) (18 July 1966) 6

Judgments of the European Court of Human Rights

Abdulaziz, Cabales and Balkandali v the United Kingdom, Application nos 9214/80; 9473/81; 9474/81 (28 May 1985, ECtHR) 4
Abdulaziz, Cabales and Balkandali v the United Kingdom (1985) 7 EHRR 471
Glor v Switzerland, Application no 13444/04 (30 April 2009, ECtHR) 57
Schuler-Zgraggen v Switzerland, Application no 14518/89 (24 June 1993 ECtHR) 10
Schuler-Zgraggen v Switzerland (1993) 16 EHRR 405 10

Judgments of the Court of Justice of the European Union

C-13/05 Chacón Navas v Eurest Colectividades SA [2006] ECR 1-6467 .... 63–66, 82
C-32/75 Christini [Fiorini] [1975] ECR 1085
C-68/17 IR v JQ 57
C-144/04 Werner Mangold v Rüdiger Helm [2005] ECR I-9981 56
C-152/1 Odar v Baxter Deutschland 99–100
C-175, 176, 178 and 179/08 Salahadin Abdulla and others [2010] ECR I-1493
C-211/10 Doris Povse [2010] ECR I-6673

C-249/96 Lisa Jacqueline Grant v South-West Trains Ltd [1998] ECR I-621 8
C-270/16 Carlos Enrique Ruiz Conejero v Ferroser Servicios Auxiliares SA and Ministerio Fiscal 83, 151
C-303/06 Coleman v Attridge Law and Steve Law [2008] ECR I-5603........61, 91–92, 94, 96
C-312/11 Commission v Italy [2013] ECR
C-312/17 Surjit Singh Bedi v Bundesrepublik Deutschland 101
C-335/11 and C-337/11 HK Danmark [2013] ECR 104
C-335/11 and C-337/11 HK Danmark, acting on behalf of Jette Ring v Dansk almennyttigt Boligselskab (C-335/11); HK Danmark, acting on behalf of Lone Skouboe Werge v Dansk Arbejdsgiverforening, acting on behalf of Pro Display A/S (C-337/11)........67, 134, 150
C-354/13 Fag og arbejde (FOA) v Kommunernes landsforening (KL)........76–77, 79, 151
C-356/12 Wolfgang Glatzel v Freistaat Bayern [2014] ECR 85, 88, 152
C-363/12 Z v A Government Department and The Board of Management of a Community School [2013] ECR......88, 102–04, 106–07, 152
C-366/10 Air Transport Association of America and Others [2011] ECR I-13755 ....104, 107, 109
C-395/15 Daouidi v Bootes Plus SL and Others 66, 81
C-397/18 DW v Nobel Plastiques Ibérica SA 154
C-402/05 P and C-415/05 P Kadi and Al Barakaat International Foundation v. Council and Commission [2008] ECR I–6351 107
C-403/09 Detiček [2009] ECR I-12193
C-408/92 Smith v Avdel [1994] ECR I-4435 5–6
C-414/16 Egenberger v Evangelisches Werk für Diakonie und Entwicklung eV (2018)........57
C-673/16 Relu Adrian Coman and Others v Inspectoratul General pentru Imigrări and Ministerul Afacerilor Interne (2018)........57

Opinions of the Advocates General

Opinion of AG Geelhoed delivered on 16 March 2006 in Case C-13/05 Chacón Navas v Eurest Colectividades SA [2006] ECR 1-6467 ....63–66, 82
Opinion of Advocate General Poiares Maduro delivered on 31 January 2008 in Case C-303/06 Coleman v Attridge Law [2008] ECR I-05603 ....61, 91–92, 94
Opinion of AG Sharpston delivered on 6 December 2012 in Case C-152/11 Odar v Baxter Deutschland 99–100
Opinion of Advocate General Wahl delivered on 26 September 2013 in Case C-363/12 Z v A Government Department and the Board of Management of a Community School 2013] ECR........88, 102–04, 106–07, 152

Opinion of AG Jääskinen delivered on 17 July 2014 in Case C-354/13 FOA, acting on behalf of Karsten Kaltoft v Kommunernes Landsforening (KL), acting on behalf of the Municipality of Billund 76–77, 79, 151
Opinion of Mr Advocate General Bot delivered on 18 July 2013 in Case of Wolfgang Glatzel v Freistaat Bayern [2014] ECR 85–88, 152

National Case Law

Bahl v The Law Society and others [2004] IRLR 799 CA 21
Bahl v The Law Society & Anor [2004] EWCA Civ 1070 21
Perera v Civil Service Commission (No 2) [1983] ICR 428 20

TABLE OF LEGISLATION AND STATUTORY MATERIALS

European Union

Charter of Fundamental Rights of the European Union [2000] OJ C 364/01 .... 15, 27, 50–51, 56, 78
Code of Conduct between the Council, the Member States and the Commission setting out internal arrangements for the implementation by and representation of the European Union relating to the United Nations Convention on the Rights of Persons with Disabilities (2010/C 340/08) 122–23
Code of Conduct between the Council, the Member States and the Commission setting out internal arrangements for the implementation by and representation of the European Union relating to the United Nations Convention on the Rights of Persons with Disabilities [2010] OJ C 340 (2010/C 340/08) 120
Consolidated version of the Treaty on the Functioning of the European Union [2008] OJ C115/471........ 50, 54–56, 69, 77, 79, 87, 92–93, 97–98, 106, 111, 113, 115–16, 125, 127, 130–31
Council of Europe, Protocol No 12 to the Convention for the Protection of Human Rights and Fundamental Freedoms, Explanatory Report (ETS No 177) (2000) 4, 57
Council, 'Decision (EC) on the signing, on behalf of the European Community, of the United Nations' Convention on the Rights of Persons with Disabilities' [2010] OJ L23 115
Council, 'Decision of 26 November 2009 concerning the conclusion, by the European Community, of the United Nations Convention on the Rights of Persons with Disabilities' [2010] OJ L/23/35 120
Council Decision No 252/2013/EU of 11 March 2013 establishing a Multiannual Framework for 2013–2017 for the European Union Agency for Fundamental Rights [2013] OJ L79/1 134
Council and Representatives of the Governments of the Member States, 'Equality of opportunity for people with disabilities' [1997] OJ C 12/1 65
Decision No 771/2006/EC of the European Parliament and of the Council of 17 May 2006 establishing the European Year of Equal Opportunities for All (2007) towards a just society [2006] OJ L146/1 98

European Ombudsman, 'Decision of the on own-initiative inquiry OI/3/2003/JMA concerning the European Commission', 4 July 2007 131
European Ombudsman, 'Decision of the closing her own-initiative inquiry OI/8/2014/AN concerning the European Commission', 11 May 2015 132
European Parliament, 'Resolution of 18 June 2020 on the European Disability Strategy post 2020 (2019/2975(RSP), Brussels', P9_TA-PROV (2020) 0156 146
European Parliament, 'Decision on the Regulations and General Conditions Governing the Performance of the Ombudsman's Duties (94/262/ECSC)...133
European Parliament, Disability Intergroup, 'Work Programme 2020–2022'....130
European Parliament, 'Report on the activities of the Committee on Petitions 2013' (A7-0131/2014) 128
European Parliament, Report on the activities of the Committee on Petitions 2014' (A8-0361/2015) 128
European Parliament, 'Motion for a Resolution, pursuant to Rule 216(2) of the Rules of Procedure on the ratification of the Marrakesh Treaty, based on petitions received, notably Petition 924/2011, 28.1.2016' (2016/2542(RSP) 129
European Parliament, 'Resolution of 8 July 2020 on the rights of persons with intellectual disabilities in the COVID-19 crisis' (2020/2680(RSP)), Brussels, 8 July 2020, B9-0204/2020.................................129
Explanations relating to the Charter of Fundamental Rights (2007/C 303/02) [2007] OJ C 303/17 56
Treaty on European Union [1992] OJ C 191/1...................... 48, 55–57, 77, 100, 134

Directives

Directive 2000/43/EC of the Council of 29 June 2000 implementing the principle of equal treatment between persons irrespective of racial or ethnic origin [2000] OJ L180/22 .... 59, 98, 153
Directive 2000/78/EC of the Council of 27 November 2000 establishing a general framework for equal treatment in employment and occupation [2000] OJ L303/16.........12, 59–63, 65–66, 68–75, 77–85, 89, 91–98, 102–03, 105–07, 113–15, 150, 154
Directive 2006/54/EC of the European Parliament and of the Council of 5 July 2006 on the implementation of the principle of equal opportunities and equal treatment of men and women in matters of employment and occupation (recast) [2006] OJ L204/23...........98, 102–03, 153
Directive 2006/126/EC of the European Parliament and of the Council of 20 December 2006 on driving licences [2006] OJ L403/18 ....85–88, 152
Directive (EU) 2019/882 of the European Parliament and of the Council of 17 April 2019 on the accessibility requirements for products and services [2019] OJ L151/70...136

Regulations

Council Regulation (EC) No 168/2007 of 15 February 2007 establishing a European Union Agency for Fundamental Rights [2007] OJ L53/1 133
Regulation (EU) No 1303/2013 of the European Parliament and of the Council of 17 December 2013 laying down common provisions on the European Regional Development Fund, the European Social Fund, the Cohesion Fund, the European Agricultural Fund for Rural Development and the European Maritime and Fisheries Fund [2013] OJ L347/320 132

United Nations

UN Committee on Economic, Social and Cultural Rights, General Comment No 20, Non-discrimination in Economic, Social and Cultural Rights (Art 2, para 2, of the International Covenant on Economic, Social and Cultural Rights), UN Doc E/C.12/GC/20 ...... 6–8, 22, 26
UN Committee on the Elimination of Discrimination against Women, General Recommendation No 18: Disabled Women, UN Doc A/46/38, 3 (1993), reprinted in Compilation of General Comments and General Recommendations Adopted by Human Rights Treaty Bodies, UN Doc. HRI/GEN/1/Rev.6, 243 (2003) 22
UN Committee on the Elimination of Discrimination against Women, General Recommendation No 25, Note by the Secretariat, Compilation of General Comments and General Recommendations Adopted by Human Rights Treaty Bodies, UN Doc HRI/GEN/1/Rev (2004) 13
UN Committee on the Elimination of Racial Discrimination, General Recommendation No 8, Compilation of General Comments and General Recommendations Adopted by Human Rights Treaty Bodies, UN Doc HRI\GEN\1\Rev.6, 200 (2003) 13
UN Committee on the Elimination of Racial Discrimination, General Recommendation No 25: Gender related dimensions of racial discrimination reprinted, UN Doc A/55/18, annex V, 152 (2000), reprinted in Compilation of General Comments and General Recommendations Adopted by Human Rights Treaty Bodies UN Doc HRI\GEN\1\Rev.6, 214 (2000) 22
UN Committee on the Elimination of Racial Discrimination, General Recommendation No XXIX on Article 1, Paragraph 1, of the Convention (Descent) (1 November 2002) 13
UN Committee on the Rights of Persons with Disabilities, Communication No 1/2010, UN Doc CRPD/C/9/D/1/2010 (Views adopted by the Committee at its ninth session, 15–19 April 2013).. 30, 33

UN Committee on the Rights of Persons with Disabilities, *HM v Sweden*, Communication No 3/2011, UN Doc CRPD/C/7/D/3/2011 16
UN Committee on the Rights of Persons with Disabilities, *SC v Brazil*, Communication No 10/2013, UN Doc CRPD/C/12/D/10/2013 85
UN Committee on the Rights of Persons with Disabilities, 'Concluding Observations on the Initial Report of China', Un Doc CRPD/C/CHN/CO/1 (adopted by the Committee at its eighth session, 17–28 September 2012) 28
UN Committee on the Rights of Persons with Disabilities, 'Concluding Observations on the Initial Report of the European Union', UN Doc CRPD/C/EU/CO/1 (adopted by the Committee at its fourteenth session, 17 August–4 September 2015) 137
UN Committee on the Rights of Persons with Disabilities, General Comment No 2 on Article 9: Accessibility, UN Doc CRPD/C/GC/2 (eleventh session, 30 March –11 April 2014) 34
UN Committee on the Rights of Persons with Disabilities, General Comment No 6 on equality and non-discrimination, UN Doc CRPD/C/GC/6 (adopted by the Committee at its nineteenth session, 14 February–9 March 2018) 15, 97, 154
UN, Convention on the Rights of Persons with Disabilities, UN Doc A/RES/61/106 (2007) 1, 3, 15, 28, 30, 69
UN General Assembly, 'Accreditation and participation of non-governmental organizations in the Ad Hoc Committee on a Comprehensive and Integral International Convention on Protection and Promotion of the Rights and Dignity of Persons with Disabilities', UN Doc A/RES/56/510 (2002) 41, 52
UN General Assembly, 'Participation of persons with disabilities in the Ad Hoc Committee on a Comprehensive and Integral International Convention on Protection and Promotion of the Rights and Dignity of Persons with Disabilities', UN Doc A/DEC/56/474 (2002) 41
UN General Assembly, 'Principles relating to the Status of National Institutions adopted by General Assembly Resolution 48/134 of 20 December 1993', UN Doc A/RES/48/134 .... 44, 126
UN General Assembly, 'Report of the Ad Hoc Committee Established by UNGA Res A/56/168', UN Doc A/RES/56/168 (2002) 41, 52
UN, Human Rights Committee, General Comment No 18, Compilation of General Comments and General Recommendations Adopted by Human Rights Treaty Bodies, UN Doc HRI/GEN/1/Rev.1 (1994) 9
UN, International Covenant on Civil and Political Rights was adopted and opened for signature, ratification and accession by General Assembly Resolution 2200A (XXI) of 16 December 1966 and entered into force on 23 March 1976 26

UN, Optional Protocol to the Convention against Torture and other Cruel, Inhuman or Degrading Treatment or Punishment (adopted on 18 December 2002, entered into force on 22 June 2006) 44
UN, Universal Declaration of Human Rights, adopted 10 December 1948, UNGA Res 217 A(III) 5–6

Other

Americans with Disabilities Act 1990 (ADA), as amended by the ADA Amendments Act 2008 (PL 110 325) 19
Beijing Declaration on Disabled Persons in the New Millennium, World NGO Summit on Disability (12 March 2001) 39–40
Disability Discrimination Act 1995 92
HELIOS I (Second) Community Social Action Programme for Disabled People [1988] OJ L104/38 59
HELIOS II (Third) Community Action Programme to Assist Disabled People [1993] OJ L56/30 59
Legislative Royal Decree No 1/1995 of 24 March 1995 approving the amended text of the Workers' Statute (Estatuto de los Trabajadores, BOE No 75 of 29 March 1995) 9654 64
Marrakesh Treaty to Facilitate Access to Published Works for Persons Who Are Blind, Visually Impaired, or Otherwise Print Disable, Word Intellectual Property Organization, WIPO (27 June 2013) 128
'Principles relating to the Status of National Institutions adopted by General Assembly resolution 48/134 of 20 December 1993 .... 44, 126
Treaty of Amsterdam amending the Treaty on European Union, the Treaties establishing the European Communities and certain related acts, signed in Amsterdam on 2 October 1997, entered into force on 1 May 1999 136
UK Equality Act 2006 46
UK Equality Act 2010 66
Vienna Declaration and Programme of Action, adopted by the World Conference on Human Rights in Vienna on 25 June 1993 27

1

Introducing the CRPD: A New Approach to Equality and Non-Discrimination?

I. Introductory Remarks

The UN Convention on the Rights of Persons with Disabilities (CRPD) was formally adopted by the UN General Assembly in December 2006 and entered into force in May 2008.[1] It represents the first human rights convention introduced in the new millennium and the most recent enforceable instrument provided by the United Nations in the context of international human rights protection. The Convention is also the first human treaty to be open for signature by regional integration organisations, and the European Union (EU) became a party to the CPRD in November 2009. It is worth noting that the CRPD has now been signed by 163 countries worldwide and ratified by 181.[2] This means that it is one of the most widely ratified international treaties which can effectively and positively address the rights of persons with disabilities across the globe.[3] In particular, the EU's ratification of the Convention establishes a clear obligation in law for its provisions to be taken into account in interpreting EU primary and secondary legislation.

The Convention does not introduce new rights under international human rights law, but it seeks to ensure the correct interpretation and implementation of existing human rights obligations.[4] The CRPD represents a remarkable improvement in the legal protection of the rights of persons with disabilities. It embraces a human rights approach according to which persons with disabilities are considered as rights-bearers who can enjoy all human rights and fundamental freedoms on an equal basis with others. This understanding of disability rejects

[1] UN Convention on the Rights of Persons with Disabilities, UN Doc A/RES/61/106 (2007). The Convention on the Rights of Persons with Disabilities and its Optional Protocol was adopted on 13 December 2006 at the United Nations Headquarters in New York, and was opened for signature on 30 March 2007.

[2] Data provided by the UN Division for Social Policy and Development Disability.

[3] S Quinlivan, 'The United Nations Convention on the Rights of Persons with Disabilities: An Introduction' (2012) 13 *ERA Forum* 71.

[4] G Quinn, 'The United Nations Convention on the Rights of Persons with Disabilities: Toward a New International Politics of Disability' (2009–10) 15 *Texas Journal on Civil Liberties & Civil Rights* 33.

the traditional social welfare or medical model that depicts certain categories of individuals as objects of pity and charity.[5] In order to achieve the ambitious goals of the human rights approach, the CRPD enshrines a substantive model of equality that acknowledges diversity and aims to ensure that individuals in different situations are treated differently. By doing so, it moves away from the formal concept of equality in accordance with 'things that are alike should be treated alike'.[6] This approach fails to address the concrete differences of vulnerable groups of individuals and does not confer a right or a benefit on the basis of a personal or physical characteristic.

The cornerstone of the substantive model of equality adopted by the CRPD is the obligation to provide reasonable accommodation for persons with disabilities. This duty is crucial to enable persons with disabilities to have access to, participate in, or advance in employment. It requires an adjustment or a modification of the environment to accommodate the specific needs or characteristics of persons with disabilities and eliminate such disadvantages in comparison with others.

Against this background, it may be argued that the CRPD shows the legal potential to improve the protection of persons with disabilities by clarifying and broadening the personal and material scope of the existing instruments of international human rights law. This book aims to analyse the impact of the Convention on the EU legal order and governance.

II. Equality and Non-Discrimination: A New Approach for Disability Rights

The CRPD is the most complex human rights treaty ever drafted. It mainstreams equality, intersectional diversity and inclusion. In doing so, the CRPD reflects the remarkable evolution of international human rights law with regard to the concept of equality and the prohibition of discrimination. To put it differently, the Convention may be said to crystallise the legal shift from a formal approach of equality to a substantive and asymmetrical model of equality and non-discrimination. These fundamental principles underpin the entire Convention and bring together socio-economic rights with civil and political rights.[7]

Discrimination on the basis of disability is recognised as a serious violation of the inherent dignity and worth of the human person. The legal backdrop

[5] M Stein and P Stein, 'Beyond Disability Rights' (2007) 58 *Hastings Law Journal* 1203.

[6] WD Ross (1877–1971), JO Urmson and JL Ackrill (eds), *Aristotle The Nicomachean Ethics* (Oxford, Oxford University Press, 1980).

[7] G Quinn and E Flynn, 'Transatlantic Borrowings: The Past and Future of EU Non-Discrimination Law and Policy on the Ground of Disability' (2012) 60 *American Journal of Comparative Law* 23.

delineated by the CRPD places the protection of persons with disabilities at the heart of international human rights law and definitively acknowledges disability as a ground of discrimination. The main purpose of the Convention is to promote the full and equal enjoyment of all human rights and fundamental freedoms by all persons with disabilities. To this end, states are obliged to provide general measures in order to ensure and promote the full realisation of all human rights for persons with disabilities without discrimination of any kind on the basis of disability, including the necessary legislation to modify or abolish existing laws, regulations, customs and practices that constitute discrimination against persons with disabilities.[8]

The principle of non-discrimination is embodied within the general values underlying the entire Convention:

a. respect for inherent dignity, individual autonomy including the freedom to make one's own choices, and independence of persons;
b. non-discrimination;
c. full and effective participation and inclusion in society;
d. respect for difference and acceptance of persons with disabilities as part of human diversity and humanity;
e. equality of opportunity;
f. accessibility;
g. equality between men and women;
h. respect for the evolving capacities of children with disabilities and respect for the right of children with disabilities to preserve their identities.[9]

Equality norms and the prohibition of discrimination represent essential legal tools to achieve an effective and solid framework for the protection of persons with disabilities. Normative acts and policies often trigger discrimination against particular groups of individuals. For this reason, the principle of equality includes procedural and substantive rules to prevent and address human rights violations. The principle of equality constitutes the fundamental lens through which human rights issues will be investigated in the present book. Equality is a structural principle that provides a systematic analytical framework to assess and examine the protection of human rights.[10]

[8] Art 4 CRPD demands 'the adoption of all appropriate legislative, administrative and other measures for the implementation of the rights recognised in the Convention, including the necessary legislation to modify or abolish existing laws, regulations, customs and practices that constitute discrimination against persons with disabilities'.

[9] Art 3 of the Convention on the Rights of Persons with Disabilities and its Optional Protocol (A/RES/61/106).

[10] J Clifford, 'Equality' in D Sheldon (ed), *The Oxford Handbook of International Human Rights Law* (Oxford, Oxford University Press, 2013) 421.

III. The Complex and Intriguing Evolution of the Right to Equality in International Law

International law encompasses an ever-changing and complex concept of equality, which is deeply rooted in the norms for the protection of human rights. However, equality does not find a comprehensive and clear definition in international law. As such, it has been subject to intense doctrinal debate. Theoretically speaking, the international legal order is indeed characterised by the debated coexistence of two different approaches: formal and substantive equality. According to Aristotle's notion of formal equality, 'things that are alike should be treated alike'.[11] By contrast, the substantive equalities model points out that treating individuals alike despite disadvantage or discrimination does not tackle inequality.[12] These two separate approaches entail a distinction between negative and positives duties to promote equality. On the one hand, civil and political rights merely trigger duties of restraint which prevent the state from interfering with individual freedom. On the other, socio-economic equality requires specific and positive duties on the state in order to eliminate discrimination and disadvantage.[13]

This theoretical framework shows that the concept of equality is profoundly interwoven with the prohibition of discrimination. The principle of equality demands that equal situations are treated equally and unequal situations differently. Failure to comply with this obligation will amount to discrimination unless the difference of treatment cannot be justified objectively and reasonably by a legitimate aim.[14] This implies that not every distinction or difference of treatment amounts to discrimination. For instance, the European Court of Human Rights (ECtHR), in the case of *Abdulaziz, Cabales and Balkandali v the United Kingdom*, concluded that

> a difference of treatment is discriminatory if it 'has no objective and reasonable justification', that is, if it does not pursue a 'legitimate aim' or if there is not a 'reasonable relationship of proportionality between the means employed and the aim sought to be realised'.[15]

[11] Aristotle (n 6).

[12] S Fredman, *Human Rights Transformed: Positive Rights and Positive Duties* (Oxford, Oxford University Press, 2008). See also, C Barnard and B Hepple, 'Substantive Equality' (2010) 59 *Cambridge Law Journal* 562.

[13] ibid. It is worth noting that the distinction between civil and political rights and socio-economic rights is not strictly accurate in the light of the new developments of international human rights law. The CRPD requires positive action and affirmative programmes also in relation to those civil and political rights which are merely associated with duties of restraint. For instance, the civil and political right to a fair trial for persons with disabilities would involve significant investments from the state to implement procedural accommodation, physical, informational and communicational accessibility and ensure the training of court staff, judges, police officers and prison staff.

[14] See Protocol No 12 to the Convention for the Protection of Human Rights and Fundamental Freedoms, Explanatory Report (ETS No 177) para 15.

[15] *Abdulaziz, Cabales and Balkandali v the United Kingdom*, Application nos 9214/80; 9473/81; 9474/81 (28 May 1985, ECtHR).

It is thus commonly recognised that equality and non-discrimination are positive and negative statements of the same principle.[16]

A. The Controversial 'Sameness' Model

The formal model of equality is also referred to as the 'sameness' or symmetrical approach.[17] It is based on the idea that equals have to be treated equally and unequal unequally. In doing so, it ignores the personal characteristics of an individual. The fundamental principle that sustains the entire paradigm of formal equality is the concept of equality before the law in accordance with all are equal before the law and are entitled without any discrimination to equal protection of the law.[18] The approach of de jure equality avoids conferring a right or a benefit on the basis of a personal or physical characteristic. It only forbids direct discrimination which occurs when a person is treated less favourably than another in a comparable situation on specific grounds, such as race, sex or disability.[19] In this regard, the treatment must be different in relation to a comparable circumstance or it must be similar in comparison to a different situation. However, not all the different treatments are deemed discriminatory, but only those measures which lack a legitimate purpose in light of the democratic principles that regulate the social and legal order.[20]

The idea of formal equality comprises a concept of procedural justice which does not assure the realisation of any specific result. This approach does not address the concrete differences of certain vulnerable groups of individuals and fails to ensure the effective achievement of equality. The application of a principle of equality, merely intended as consistent treatment, does not imply an assessment of the legitimacy of the law, allowing the possibility to apply equally an unfair legal act. For instance, according to Catherine Barnard, the requirement for equal treatment could also be fulfilled by depriving both the persons compared of a particular benefit as well as by conferring the benefit on them both.[21] In a famous decision of the Court of Justice of the European Union (CJEU), *Smith v Avdel*

[16] A Bayefsky, 'The Principle of Equality and Non-Discrimination in International Law' (1990) 11 *Human Rights Law Journal* 1.

[17] OM Arnardóttir, 'A Future of Multidimensional Disadvantage Equality?' in OM Arnardóttir and G Quinn (eds), *The UN Convention on the Rights of Persons with Disabilities: European and Scandinavian Perspectives* (Leiden, Martinus Nijhoff, 2009).

[18] Art 7 of the Universal Declaration of Human Rights, adopted 10 December 1948, UNGA Res 217 A(III).

[19] L Waddington and A Hendriks, 'The Expanding Concept of Employment Discrimination in Europe: From Direct and Indirect Discrimination to Reasonable Accommodation Discrimination' (2002) 18 *International Journal of Comparative Labour Law and Industrial Relations* 403.

[20] S Besson, 'The Principle of Non-Discrimination in the Convention on the Rights of the Child' (2005) 13 *International Journal of Children's Rights* 433.

[21] C Barnard, *EC Employment Law* (Oxford, Oxford University Press, 2006).

Systems Ltd, it was ruled that equalisation in pension age can be secured by either upwards or downwards equalisation (for instance increasing the women's age to that of men).[22] This judgment strictly applied the concept of equality and laid down the compatibility of the legislation raising the pension age to 65 for women. It represents a concrete implementation of the so-called principle of levelling down.[23] This canon of protection aims to remove inequality through a levelling-down process which worsens the situation of the advantaged group to the same level of the disadvantaged one.[24] Consequently, this approach merely risks perpetuating unlawful discrimination and exacerbating the conditions of a particular group, instead of enhancing the real situation of those individuals who are more assailable.

B. Embracing the Symmetrical Approach at International Level

At international level, the symmetrical approach to equality and non-discrimination noticeably influenced the adoption of the first human rights treaties, such as the Universal Declaration of Human Rights (UDHR), the European Convention on Human Rights (ECHR) and the two United Nations Covenants: the International Covenant on Economic, Social and Cultural Rights (ICESCR) and the International Covenant on Civil and Political Rights (ICCPR).[25]

The UDHR expressly introduced the prohibition of non-discrimination as a fundamental clause applying to everyone, without distinction of any kind, such as race, colour, sex, language, religion, political or other opinion, national or social origin, property, birth or other status.[26] This provision acquired a significant role in the context of international law and it was acknowledged as a norm of customary international law in the Dissenting Opinion of Judge Tanaka of the International Court of Justice (ICJ).[27] Article 7 of the Declaration sets forth the right to equality, according to which 'all are equal before the law and are entitled without any discrimination to equal protection of the law. All are entitled to equal protection against any discrimination in violation of this Declaration and against any incitement to such discrimination'.

[22] Case C-408/92 *Smith v Avdel* [1994] ECR I-4435.

[23] E Howard, *The EU Race Directive: Developing the Protection against Racial Discrimination within the EU* (London, Routledge, 2010).

[24] DL Brake, 'When Equality Leaves Everyone Worse Off: The Problem of Leveling Down in Equality Law' (2004) 46 *William & Mary Law Review* 513.

[25] Arnardóttir (n 17) 47.

[26] Art 2 of the Universal Declaration of Human Rights, adopted 10 December 1948, UNGA Res 217 A(III).

[27] See Judge Tanaka, *South West Africa*, Second Phase (1966) ICJ, 293.

The same model of equality has been adopted in the ICCPR; for instance Article 26 reflects the identical words and structure of the UDHR.[28] Moreover, Article 2(2) of the ICESCR uses the same language as the ICCPR, stating that:

> States Parties to the present Covenant undertake to guarantee that the rights enunciated in the present Covenant will be exercised without discrimination of any kind as to race, colour, sex, language, religion, political or other opinion, national or social origin, property, birth or other status.

It is worth noting that these influential instruments for the international protection of human rights emphasise an open model of non-discrimination and a paradigm of formal equality. Open-ended clauses are not bound by a strict list of discrimination grounds.[29] The utilisation of the 'or other status' term means that the list of prohibited grounds of discrimination is not exhaustive but, on the contrary, is purely indicative and allows the inclusion of other grounds. The open approach does not clarify the legal standards and guidelines to assess unequal treatment.[30] As a result, the lack of a clear demarcation between unlawful discrimination and justified treatment implies 'creative' involvement of the courts, which are called upon to identify illegal conduct. This approach leaves a wide margin of discretion to the judges in interpreting the notion of reasonable justification and the set of prohibited treatments.[31] To the same extent, the leeway stemming from the open model of non-discrimination does not preclude the possibility of advancing an unlimited number of exceptions and defences for justifying differentiations. This model therefore seems highly vague and inappropriate to combat discrimination. In addition, those international provisions concerning the prohibition of discrimination and the right to equality cannot be considered as independent norms because their application is subordinated to the violations of specific rights embodied in the Treaty. This structure is also evident in the formulation of Article 14 of the ECHR which lays down that

> the enjoyment of the rights and freedoms set forth in this Convention shall be secured without discrimination on any ground such as sex, race, colour, language, religion, political or other opinion, national or social origin, association with a national minority, property, birth or other status.[32]

[28] L Weiwei, 'Equality and non-discrimination under international human rights law', Norwegian Centre for Human Rights, Research Notes 03/2004. See also Art 26 of the ICCCPR: 'All persons are equal before the law and are entitled without any discrimination to the equal protection of the law. In this respect, the law shall prohibit any discrimination and guarantee to all persons equal and effective protection against discrimination on any ground such as race, colour, sex, language, religion, political or other opinion, national or social origin, property, birth or other status'.

[29] D Schiek and V Chege, *European Union Non-Discrimination Law: Comparative Perspectives on Multidimensional Equality Law* (London, Routledge 2009) 55.

[30] T Loenen and PR Rodrigues, *Non-Discrimination Law: Comparative Perspectives* (Leiden, Martinus Nijhoff Publishers, 1999).

[31] S Fredman, *Discrimination Law* (Oxford, Clarendon Law Series, 2001).

[32] W Vandenhole, *Non-Discrimination and Equality in the View of the UN Human Rights Treaty Bodies* (Antwerp, Intersentia, 2005).

C. Is the Formal Approach Adequate to Combat Discrimination?

A significant weakness of the formal model is represented by the essential requirement of a suitable comparator for the analysis of equality. The choice of a comparator can often be challenging and problematic. This requisite implies the exclusion of discriminatory grounds such as pregnancy and disability which lack adequate comparators. In this context, individuals who suffer systematic discrimination can only claim the same treatment as the privileged group despite having different and special needs.[33] For instance, the case of *Lisa Jacqueline Grant and South-West Trains Ltd* shows the main limits of the formal approach.[34] In this case, a travel concession was denied to the lesbian partner of a female employee. The CJEU stated that the refusal of the travel concessions to Ms Grant's partner did not amount to discrimination on grounds of sex, as the rules concerning its grant applied equally to men and women. The CJEU explained that the employers' refusal to allow travel concessions to the person of the same sex with whom a worker has a stable relationship did not constitute discrimination as prohibited by Article 119 of the EC Treaty or Council Directive 75/117/EEC. The CJEU made the comparison with a hypothetical gay partner of a male employee and concluded that there was no discrimination. By contrast, whether the comparator had been a male employee of a female partner, the applicant would have benefited from the travel concession. This means that there is no violation of equality law where a contested measure lacks the necessary comparator.

To conclude, it may be said that this approach does not tackle those systemic problems which permeate the legal system and does not provide normative indicators to identify illegal differentiation. The formal conception is also strictly related to the idea according to which states have only negative obligations and must abstain from introducing positive measures to guarantee equality. Thence, the sameness model emerging from the legal text of the first human rights treaties outlines 'empty' clauses of non-discrimination and equality. International instruments such as the UDHR, ICCPR and ICESCR symbolised an outstanding step forward for the protection of human rights, but they failed to recognise and accommodate the specific characteristics of vulnerable individuals.

[33] OM Arnardóttir, *Equality and Non-Discrimination under the European Convention on Human Rights* (Leiden, Martinus Nijhoff Publishers, 2003). See also CJM Kimber, 'Equality or Self Determination' in C Gearty and A Tomkins (eds), *Understanding Human Rights* (London, Mansell Publishing, 1996).

[34] Case C-249/96 *Lisa Jacqueline Grant v South-West Trains Ltd* [1998] ECR I-621. See also, Barnard (n 21) 291.

i. The Shift Towards Substantive Equality: Acknowledging the Diversity

Substantive equality refers to the concept that individuals in different situations should be treated differently. This model includes two significant approaches: equality of results and equality of opportunity. Equality of results aims to reach equal outcomes through the adoption of specific measures in favour of marginalised groups of individuals. On the other hand, equality of opportunity seeks to guarantee an equal opportunity in order to gain access to a particular benefit, without assuring the achievement of the final result.[35]

The substantive model gradually assumed a leading role in international law and filled the legal vacuum deriving from the conception of formal equality. The adoption of the International Convention on the Elimination of Racial Discrimination (ICERD) in 1965, along with the UN Convention on the Elimination of All Forms of Discrimination against Women (CEDAW) in 1979 and the UN Convention on the Rights of the Child (CRC) in 1989, highlighted a fundamental and profound change in the approach towards equality and non-discrimination.

The new paradigm starts to take into account the concrete differences of disadvantaged persons and exceptionally establishes the conditions to accommodate specific biological and unalterable characteristics. The substantive model also refuses a passive role from the state and points out the necessity to introduce affirmative and relevant measures in the legal system for eliminating unequal treatment. This context privileges an asymmetrical approach that focuses on group characteristics and disadvantages. It sets out the requirements to assess the equality of a treatment and constitutes fertile ground to address indirect discrimination. In this way, the legal analysis aims to deal with discrimination that continues to be perpetuated despite the application of formal equality rules.

ii. Substantive Equality Jurisprudence

The main proof of this change in human rights law is represented by the revolutionary interpretation of the Human Rights Committee concerning Article 26 of the ICCPR.[36] In the view of the Committee:

> Article 26 does not merely duplicate the guarantee already provided for in Article 2 but provides in itself an autonomous right. It prohibits discrimination in law or in fact in any field regulated and protected by public authorities. Article 26 is therefore concerned with the obligations imposed on States parties in regard to their legislation

[35] Interights, *Non-Discrimination in International Law: A Handbook for Practitioners* (London, 2011).

[36] Human Rights Committee, General Comment No 18, Compilation of General Comments and General Recommendations Adopted by Human Rights Treaty Bodies, UN Doc HRI/GEN/1/Rev.1 (1994).

> and the application thereof. Thus, when legislation is adopted by a State Party, it must comply with the requirement of Article 26 that its content should not be discriminatory. In other words, the application of the principle of non-discrimination contained in Article 26 is not limited to those rights which are provided for in the Covenant.[37]

In its General Comment 18, the Committee underlined a renovated idea of equality and non-discrimination, which includes normative contents and positive duties on States Parties. The emphasis on substantive equality also has its historical explanations. Human rights advocates and civil society organisations strongly advocated for substantive equality to tackle those laws, policies and practices bringing about systematic racial and gender discrimination. Moreover, this broader interpretation was promoted by several academics and scholars who criticised the emptiness of the formal model of equality.[38]

The departure from this model is also noticed in the jurisprudence of the ECtHR. For instance, in *Schuler-Zgraggen* the Court held that denying a woman her invalidity pension, when it has been granted to men under the same circumstance, amounts to discrimination on grounds of sex.[39] The Court adopted a strict scrutiny and stressed the necessity to verify the objectiveness and reasonableness of the unequal measures. According to the Court,

> the advancement of the equality of the sexes is today a major goal in the Member States of the Council of Europe and very weighty reasons would have to be put forward before such a difference of treatment could be regarded as compatible with the Convention.[40]

This interpretation of the prohibition of discrimination on grounds of sex is in line with the substantive concept of equality that aims to concretely ensure the equal enjoyment of human rights for all groups of individuals.

iii. *Affirmative Actions as Special Measures to Achieve Equality*

The legal shift towards equality of result is also reflected in several provisions of human rights treaties such as ICERD and CEDAW.

They encompass a substantive and closed model for combating discrimination based on the identification of specific groups.[41] The closed model limits the grounds of discrimination and enshrines guidelines to identify objective justifications for certain treatments. Both Conventions use the same language and refer to

[37] ibid.

[38] P Westen, 'The Empty Idea of Equality' (1982) 95 *Harvard Law Review* 537; K Greenawalt, 'How Empty is the Idea of Equality?' (1983) 83 *Columbia Law Review* 1167.

[39] *Schuler-Zgraggen v Switzerland* (1993) 16 EHRR 405.

[40] K Dzehtsiarou et al (eds), *Human Rights Law in Europe: The Influence, Overlaps and Contradictions of the EU and the ECHR* (London, Routledge, 2014).

[41] DL Shelton, 'Prohibited Discrimination in International Law' in A Constantinides and N Zaikos (eds), *The Diversity of International Law: Essays in Honour of Professor Kalliopi K Koufa* (Leiden, Brill–Nijhoff, 2009).

the various types of discrimination which have the effect or purpose of impairing or nullifying the recognition, enjoyment or exercise, on an equal footing, of human rights and fundamental freedoms in the political, economic, social, cultural, civil or any other field.

The concept of de facto equality is the cornerstone of ICERD; the Preamble expressly refers to the goal to guarantee the enjoyment of certain rights without distinction of any kind and to prohibit discrimination between human beings on grounds of race. ICERD acknowledges the possibility to provide distinctions for the purpose of launching affirmative actions and enhancing the social development of the various ethnic, racial and national groups. In this regard, Article 2(1)(c) of the ICERD underlines the duty of states to take policy measures and to amend, rescind, or nullify any laws or regulations which have the effect of creating or perpetuating racial discrimination. This framework illustrates the legitimacy of introducing positive and affirmative actions in order to reach an effective level of equality within society, but at the same time it identifies these measures as exceptions. Article 1(4) states that:

> Special measures taken for the sole purpose of securing adequate advancement of certain racial or ethnic groups or individuals requiring such protection as may be necessary in order to ensure such groups or individuals equal enjoyment or exercise of human rights and fundamental freedoms shall not be deemed racial discrimination, provided, however, that such measures do not, as a consequence, lead to the maintenance of separate rights for different racial groups and that they shall not be continued after the objectives for which they were taken have been achieved.

According to Theodor Meron, this provision marks an exception in respect of the definition of racial discrimination and excludes affirmative actions because it allows the adoption of 'special measures' unless they bring about 'the maintenance of separate rights for different racial groups' or are 'continued after the objectives for which they were taken have been achieved'. As a result, there would be the risk of justifying discriminatory rules and excluding action programmes.[42] Moreover, Article 2(2) lays down that:

> States Parties shall, when the circumstances so warrant, take, in the social, economic, cultural and other fields, special and concrete measures to ensure the adequate development and protection of certain racial groups or individuals belonging to them, for the purpose of guaranteeing them the full and equal enjoyment of human rights and fundamental freedoms. These measures shall in no case entail as a consequence the maintenance of unequal or separate rights for different racial groups after the objectives for which they were taken have been achieved.

This provision guarantees wide margins of discretion to states in order to adopt positive measures in favour of marginalised groups by providing that, 'when the

[42] T Meron, *Human Rights Law-Making in the United Nations: A Critique of Instruments and Processes* (Oxford, Clarendon Press, 1986).

circumstances so warrant', they shall take special and concrete measures to ensure the adequate protection of certain racial groups. In addition, the provision does not set out guidelines to identify vulnerable individuals and the extent to which the social, political and economic circumstances permit the issue of affirmative measures. The same approach has also been embraced by Article 4 of the CEDAW:

> Adoption by States Parties of temporary special measures aimed at accelerating de facto equality between men and women shall not be considered discrimination as defined in the present Convention, but shall in no way entail as a consequence the maintenance of unequal or separate standards; these measures shall be discontinued when the objectives of equality of opportunity and treatment have been achieved.

In the context of CEDAW, the concept of de facto equality has been confirmed in compliance with new developments occurring in international human rights law. However, CEDAW presents the same weaknesses found in ICERD's framework and reveals a substantive model of equality in which affirmative action programmes continue to be deemed as special measures.

The approach emerging from these international instruments seems to reflect a paradigm that focuses on the biological and immutable differences of the person rather than the social barriers preventing individuals from the enjoyment of the rights.[43] The adoption of close-model discrimination clauses accelerated the process towards a broader and more effective protection of human rights, accommodating the specific diversity of disadvantaged groups of individuals.[44] Despite that, the active role of the state and the duty to provide affirmative actions for implementing the prohibition of discrimination still remain controversial issues because they are considered as exceptions to the formal equality model. All the international instruments examined above focus on 'substantive equality without forfeiting the merits of formal equality'.[45]

D. Beyond Differences: Time to Recognise Social Barriers and Positive Duties

The interpretation of human rights treaties by international courts started to reinforce the concept of equality and acknowledge those structural factors that jeopardise the concrete enjoyment of all human rights. The substantive model of equality was applied to recognise the positive role of the state to tackle those social and external barriers that lead to discrimination. For instance, the Committee

[43] Arnardóttir (n 17) 52.

[44] S Fredman and B Goldblatt, 'Gender Equality and Human Rights' (July 2015) Discussion Paper, UN Women.

[45] M De Vos, *Beyond formal equality: Positive action under Directive 2000/43/EC and Directive 2000/78/EC* (Luxembourg, Office for Official Publications of the European Communities, European Commission, 2007).

on the Elimination of Discrimination against Women pointed out that special measures taken under Article 4, paragraph 1, by States Parties should aim to accelerate the equal participation of women in the political, economic, social, cultural, civil or any other field. The Committee expressly considered

> the application of these measures not as an exception to the norm of non-discrimination, but rather as an emphasis that temporary special measures are part of a necessary strategy by States Parties directed towards the achievement of *de facto* or substantive equality of women with men in the enjoyment of their human rights and fundamental freedoms.[46]

In the same recommendation, the Committee put the emphasis on the social meaning of gender, which is an ideological and cultural construct. In this sense, gender refers to those constructed identities, attributes and roles for women that are imposed by society.

A similar approach has been adopted by the Committee on the Elimination of Racial Discrimination in the General Comment 8. The Committee stated that the identification of an individual, as a member of a particular racial or ethnic group, should be based on self-identification by the individual concerned.[47] In line with this assumption, the Committee considered even the concept of descent as a form of social construction, strongly reaffirming that discrimination based on 'descent' includes discrimination against members of communities based on forms of social stratification such as caste and analogous systems of inherited status which nullify or impair their equal enjoyment of human rights.[48]

The significant evolution concerning equality and non-discrimination at the international level emerges also in the draft of the CRC. To give an example, Article 2 of the CRC lays down that States Parties are the main negative and positive duty-holders without referring to the adoption of any special or temporary measures:[49]

1. States Parties shall respect and ensure the rights set forth in the present Convention to each child within their jurisdiction without discrimination of any kind, irrespective of the child's or his or her parent's or legal guardian's race, colour, sex, language, religion, political or other opinion, national, ethnic or social origin, property, disability, birth or other status.
2. States Parties shall take all appropriate measures to ensure that the child is protected against all forms of discrimination or punishment on the basis of

[46] UN Committee on the Elimination of Discrimination against Women, General Recommendation No 25, Note by the Secretariat, Compilation of General Comments and General Recommendations Adopted by Human Rights Treaty Bodies, UN Doc HRI/GEN/1/Rev (2004).

[47] UN Committee on the Elimination of Racial Discrimination, General Recommendation No 8, Compilation of General Comments and General Recommendations Adopted by Human Rights Treaty Bodies, UN Doc HRI\GEN\1\Rev.6, 200 (2003).

[48] UN Committee on the Elimination of Racial Discrimination, General Recommendation No XXIX on Article 1, Paragraph 1, of the Convention (Descent) (1 November 2002).

[49] Besson (n 20) 449.

the status, activities, expressed opinions, or beliefs of the child's parents, legal guardians, or family members.

The Convention promotes the introduction of specific protection measures to repair the unlawful consequences of unequal treatment and consolidate the concept of material equality in compliance with the new legal developments of international human rights law.[50] The application of the Convention's provision cannot be made dependent 'upon budgetary resources' and the affirmative obligations are not regarded as exceptional actions.[51] In this general framework, the principle of non-discrimination gradually acquired an asymmetrical and substantive connotation. This model explicitly requires positive duties to remove social barriers that prevent the most vulnerable from the full enjoyment of their rights.

Currently, the peak of this process is mirrored by the adoption of the CRPD which aims to redress inequality and encourage real disability law reform, based on a conception of non-discrimination that goes beyond formal equality and involves a relevant category of substantive rights.[52]

E. The Prohibition of Discrimination under the CRPD: A New Inclusive Model

The CRPD not only represents the most recent human rights treaty introduced at international level, but also encompasses important legal developments concerning the model of equality. The Convention embraces an overarching concept of non-discrimination, which takes into account the specific differences of vulnerable groups and extends legal protection in favour of persons with disabilities. To this end, the Convention outlines the importance of providing affirmative action programmes and requires the active role of States Parties. The prohibition of discrimination is clearly stated under Article 5(2) of the Convention which points out that:

> States Parties shall prohibit all discrimination on the basis of disability and guarantee to persons with disabilities equal and effective legal protection against discrimination on all grounds. In order to promote equality and eliminate discrimination, States Parties shall take all appropriate steps to ensure that reasonable accommodation is provided. Specific measures which are necessary to accelerate or achieve de facto equality of persons with disabilities shall not be considered discrimination under the terms of the present Convention.

This clear-cut provision expressly introduces disability as a ground of discrimination under international human rights law. To the same extent, only the CRC and

[50] ibid, 452.
[51] ibid, 453.
[52] Quinn (n 4).

the EU Charter of Fundamental Rights (EUCFR) added disability to the potential grounds of discrimination. However, the approach of the Convention not only departs from the asymmetrical model of equality, but it formalises the increasing need to ensure a clear normative framework for the protection of persons with disabilities which, inter alia, takes into account indirect discrimination, intersectional discrimination and the duty to provide reasonable accommodation.[53] To this end, the UN Committee on the Rights of Persons with Disabilities clarified that the Convention is based on an 'inclusive' concept of equality that embraces and extends the substantive model of equality. The new *inclusive* approach to equality implies:

> (a) a fair redistributive dimension to address socioeconomic disadvantages; (b) a recognition dimension to combat stigma, stereotyping, prejudice and violence and to recognize the dignity of human beings and their intersectionality; (c) a participative dimension to reaffirm the social nature of people as members of social groups and the full recognition of humanity through inclusion in society; and (d) an accommodating dimension to make space for difference as a matter of human dignity.[54]

Furthermore, the CRPD lays down that persons with disabilities shall enjoy legal capacity on an equal basis with others in all aspects of life and have the right to recognition everywhere as persons before the law.[55] According to Article 5.1, 'States Parties recognize that all persons are equal before and under the law and are entitled without any discrimination to the equal protection and equal benefit of the law'. This provision does not replicate a simple and empty concept of equality, but it triggers the issue of legal capacity and is closely related to several provisions of the Convention.[56] It follows that, persons with disabilities are deemed as bearers of rights and responsibilities,[57] in need of special protection in case they are unable to manage their affairs independently.[58] This provision prohibits the legislator from adopting measures that set forth the legal incapacity of persons with disabilities and nullifies their capacity to take independent decisions. States Parties are instead called upon to guarantee the access of persons with disabilities to the support they may require in exercising their legal capacity.[59] Persons with disabilities are entitled to equal benefit from the law and consequently to have access to justice without encountering barriers.

[53] Arnardóttir (n 17) 60.

[54] UN Committee on the Rights of Persons with Disabilities, General Comment No 6 on equality and non-discrimination, UN Doc CRPD/C/GC/6 (adopted by the Committee at its nineteenth session (14 February–9 March 2018).

[55] Art 12 of the Convention on the Rights of Persons with Disabilities and its Optional Protocol (A/RES/61/106).

[56] A Lawson, 'New Era or False Dawn?' (2006–07) 34 *Syracuse Journal of International Law & Commerce* 562.

[57] ibid, 595.

[58] See Art 12(5) CRPD.

[59] See Art 12(3) CRPD.

This legal framework reveals an innovative agenda for assuring the highest standards of protection for persons with disabilities.

i. The Case of HM versus Sweden

The UN Committee on the Rights of Persons with Disabilities seems to adhere to the logic and scope underlying the Convention in its decisions following individual complaints. For instance, in one of its earliest decisions, the Committee held that Sweden failed to fulfil its obligations under the duty to provide reasonable accommodation of the Convention.[60]

The claimant in the case involving Sweden had suffered from chronic connective tissue disorder, which led to hypermobility, severe luxations and subluxations, fragile and easily damaged blood vessels, weak muscles and severe chronic neuralgia. For this reason, she had not been able to walk or stand for eight years. The claimant was prevented from leaving her house or being transported to hospital or rehabilitation care due to the increased risk of injuries that may be incurred due to her impairment. The only type of rehabilitation that could stop its progress was hydrotherapy, which in the claimant's circumstances would have only been practicable in an indoor pool in her house.[61] To this end, the claimant applied for obtaining permission for an extension of approximately 63 square metres to the house, but the request was rejected by the Örebro Local Housing Committee. The Administrative Court of Appeal also refused the claimant's application for planning permission. In this context, the applicant claimed that she had been discriminated against by the decisions of the State Party's administrative bodies and courts and her rights to equal opportunity for rehabilitation and improved health were violated. Furthermore, she argued that the refusals were based merely on public interest to preserve the development plan and that a specific exception to the development plan would not have jeopardised the surrounding area.[62] On the contrary, the justifications of the Swedish government reflect the obsolete approach of formal equality. The State Party emphasised that

> the relevant act in this case, the Planning and Building Act, is applied in the same way to all, whether they have disabilities or not. Nor are there any clauses in the Act that might lead indirectly to discrimination against persons with disabilities. The rejection of the application for a building permit in this case is in no way due to the author's disability, but rather consistent with practice that applies equally to all.[63]

[60] UN Committee on the Rights of Persons with Disabilities, *HM v Sweden*, Communication No 3/2011, UN Doc CRPD/C/7/D/3/2011. See also, D Ferri, 'Reasonable Accommodation as a Gateway to the Equal Enjoyment of Human Rights: From New York to Strasbourg' (2018) 6 *Social Inclusion* 40.

[61] UN Committee on the Rights of Persons with Disabilities, *HM v Sweden*, ibid, 2.2.

[62] ibid, 3.1.

[63] ibid, 4.12.

By contrast, the Committee's stance confirms the significance of the substantive model of equality and non-discrimination. The Committee asserted that:

> A law which is applied in a neutral manner may have a discriminatory effect when the particular circumstances of the individuals to whom it is applied are not taken into consideration. The right not to be discriminated against in the enjoyment of the rights guaranteed under the Convention can be violated when States, without objective and reasonable justification, fail to treat differently persons whose situations are significantly different.

In addition, the Committee observed that the prohibition of discrimination requires the implementation of the duty to provide reasonable accommodation. In this regard, the access to a hydrotherapy pool at home would have been an essential and effective means of improving the health needs of the claimant. Consequently, appropriate adjustments demanded a departure from the development plan in order to guarantee the building of a hydrotherapy pool.

With this background, the Committee affirmed that the refusal of the State Party to approve the applicant's request for a building permit constituted a failure to accommodate the specific circumstances of her case and her particular disability-related needs.[64] The Committee therefore considered the decisions of the Swedish authorities disproportionate, since they brought about a discriminatory effect that adversely affected the claimant, as a person with disability, access to the healthcare and rehabilitation required for her specific health condition. The Committee underlined that the State Party is under a specific obligation to redress the violation of the claimant's rights under the Convention, including by reconsidering her application for a building permit for a hydrotherapy pool.

The UN body stressed that the State Party has the legal obligation to prevent similar violations in the future by adopting normative rules that do not have the purpose or effect of impairing or nullifying the recognition, enjoyment or exercise of any right for persons with disabilities on an equal basis with others.[65] The decision of the Committee shows an outstanding interpretation of the prohibition of discrimination that requires the adoption of affirmative action by the State Party to advance the dignity of persons with disabilities. The equality paradigm of the CRPD crystallises the legal developments of international human rights law.

ii. The Substantive Content of the Non-Discrimination Requirement

Article 5 of the CRPD concerning equality and non-discrimination is a directly justiciable clause and it can be invoked by an individual to claim violation of his or her rights. This provision represents an autonomous clause and its application is not strictly subordinated to the breach of other rights contained in the Convention.

[64] ibid, 8.12.
[65] ibid, para 9.

It enshrines specific obligations on the State Party that has the positive duty to remedy the violation by introducing those necessary and concrete measures to implement disability rights. The State Party also has the general obligation to acknowledge the structural factors that prevent persons with disabilities from the enjoyment of their rights. The State Party has to ensure that its legislation and its application by domestic courts is consistent with the Convention's provisions.

It is noteworthy that the prohibition of discrimination triggers a dual obligation on the State Party which has the broader duty to 'prevent similar violations in the future' and eliminate the systemic barriers affecting the national legal system. The principle of non-discrimination is not a mere and vague guideline underlying the CRPD, but is the keystone of the legal protection of other fundamental provisions, such as the right to respect for home and family life, health, education, work and employment, adequate living standards and social protection, and participation in political and public life.[66]

In light of this context, it is important to point out that the duty to provide reasonable accommodation illustrates the main non-discrimination obligation. According to the definition of Article 2 of the Convention, reasonable accommodation means 'necessary and appropriate modification and adjustments not imposing a disproportionate or undue burden, where needed in a particular case, to ensure persons with disabilities the enjoyment or exercise on an equal basis with others of all human rights and fundamental freedoms'. This provision has a 'peculiar bridging role' because its application affects all rights and promotes the indivisibility of human rights.[67] Thus, the recognition of the duty to guarantee reasonable accommodation within the general prohibition of non-discrimination implies the imposition of positive obligations to identify social barriers and take action to remove them.[68] The reasonable accommodation duty facilitates and accelerates the pragmatic application of the commitments embodied in the concept of substantive equality. This obligation entails the legal responsibility of different public and private actors including the state, employers, education and healthcare providers, providers of goods and services and private clubs.[69]

The only defence that allows a departure from the reasonable accommodation duty concerns the concept of 'disproportionate or undue burden' that should introduce a notion of progressive realisation into the non-discrimination

[66] Arts 23, 24, 25, 27, 28 and 29 of the UN Convention on the Rights of Persons with Disabilities expressly refer to the concept of non-discrimination.

[67] A Lawson, 'The UN Convention on the Rights of Persons with Disabilities and European Disability Law: A Catalyst for Cohesion?' in OM Arnardóttir and G Quinn (eds), *The United Nations Convention on the Rights of Persons with Disabilities: European and Scandinavian Perspectives* (Leiden, Martinus Nijhoff, 2009) 103.

[68] JE Lord and R Brown, 'The Role of Reasonable Accommodation in Securing Substantive Equality for Persons with Disabilities: The UN Convention on the Rights of Persons with Disabilities' in MH Rioux, LA Basser and M Jones (eds), *Critical Perspectives on Human Rights and Disability* Policy (The Hague, Martinus Nijhoff, 2011).

[69] ibid, 279.

analysis.[70] This clause has not been explicitly defined by the Convention, but it seems to reflect the approach of the Americans with Disabilities Act (ADA), in accordance with undue hardship as 'an action requiring significant difficulty or expense when considered in light of factors such as an employer's size, financial resources, and the nature and structure of its operation'.[71] However, specific proofs are required from the States Parties in order to demonstrate the existence of disproportionate or undue burdens and exclude consequently the application of the duty. For instance, in the case analysed above, the individual sought appropriate modifications and adjustments to allow the building of a hydrotherapy pool. The Committee noted that the State Party failed to explain the extent to which these adjustments would have required difficult expenses. It could therefore not conclude that the building of a hydrotherapy pool would have imposed a 'disproportionate or undue burden' on the State Party.[72]

The CRPD establishes a clear objective to accommodate persons with disabilities on an individual basis and confers the main responsibilities to provide reasonable accommodation to the State Party, which has the duty to adopt appropriate policies and measures including affirmative action programmes and incentives.

To conclude, it may be said that the legal framework of the Convention is characterised by a dynamic and transformative conception of equality and non-discrimination, which accommodates the multilayered disadvantages of persons with disabilities.[73] The CRPD not only abandons the formal approach towards equality, but also extends the substantive guarantees in favour of a vulnerable group of persons. It aims to promote an active and effective role for States Parties, which are under a positive duty to correct inequalities. The Convention stresses the increasing complexity of human rights law, which needs to be tailored to the specific experience of those persons who are prevented from the full enjoyment of their rights because of social and structural barriers.

F. Defining the Concept of Multiple and Intersectional Discrimination

The Convention embodies a concept of equality that takes into account both multiple and intersectional discrimination. Article 6 of the CRPD expressly mentions only 'multiple discrimination', but the UN Committee on the Rights of Persons with Disabilities clarified that this provision, like Article 7, must be

[70] Art 2(4) CRPD.

[71] Americans with Disabilities Act 1990 (ADA), as amended by the ADA Amendments Act 2008 (PL 110 325) Subchapter I – employment, s 12111.

[72] UN Committee on the Rights of Persons with Disabilities, *HM v Sweden* (n 60) 8.5.

[73] Arnardóttir (n 17) 60.

regarded as 'illustrative, rather than exhaustive, setting out obligations in respect of the two prominent examples of multiple and intersectional discrimination'.[74] The Committee emphasised that women and girls with disabilities are among those groups of persons with disabilities who most often experience multiple and intersectional discrimination.[75]

The CRPD recognises the difficult conditions faced by persons with disabilities who are subject to multiple or aggravated forms of discrimination on the basis of race, colour, sex, language, religion, political or other opinions, national, ethnic, indigenous or social origin, property, birth, age or other status.[76] The intersectional equality approach acknowledges the failure to classify a person on the basis of a single attribute because various characteristics of an individual or any combination of them may constitute grounds of discrimination.[77] The adoption of this model symbolises a significant improvement in the context of non-discrimination law, since it fills the gap between law and reality. This gap originates from the lack of legal instruments that address discrimination based on multiple grounds. The interaction between multiple identities and attributes increases the possibility to suffer from discrimination and accentuates the vulnerable conditions of disadvantaged groups.

The concept of multiple and intersectional discrimination comprises different types of situation. According to the UN Committee on the Rights of Persons with Disabilities, multiple discrimination is a 'situation where a person can experience discrimination on two or several grounds, in the sense that discrimination is compounded or aggravated'.[78] For instance, compound discrimination occurs when discrimination is based on two or more grounds and each ground increases the possibility to experience discrimination.[79] The famous UK case of *Perera v Civil Service* clearly illustrates this form of discrimination.[80] The applicant, who was born in Sri Lanka, claimed that his application for a job in the civil service had been rejected on several occasions on grounds of his colour or national origin. The requirements for the job such as age, experience in the UK, nationality and knowledge of the English language operated to exclude the claimant from successfully applying for the position. Thus, the lack of one factor did not prevent him from the possibility to obtain the job, but every discriminatory requirement contributed to decrease his chances to be selected for the position.

[74] UN Committee on the Rights of Persons with Disabilities, General Comment No 6 on equality and non-discrimination (n 54) para 36.

[75] ibid.

[76] Preamble. The States Parties to the present Convention, paragraph (p).

[77] P Uccellari, 'Multiple Discrimination: How Law can Reflect Reality' (2008) 1 *Equality Rights Review* 24.

[78] UN Committee on the Rights of Persons with Disabilities), General Comment No 6 on equality and non-discrimination (n 54) para 19.

[79] H Bielefeldt, *Tackling Multiple Discrimination Practices, Policies and Laws* (Luxembourg, Office for Official Publications of the European Communities, 2007).

[80] *Perera v Civil Service Commission (No 2)* [1983] ICR 428.

Intersectional discrimination is instead the category used to refer to a situation where two or more inseparable grounds interact with each other and constitute the basis of discrimination. For example, a woman with disabilities may experience discrimination for a job promotion, while at the same time non-disabled women or men with disabilities are not excluded from career advancement.

i. The Unsatisfactory One-Dimensional Approach to Discrimination

The first UN human rights treaties, as well as EU law and many national regulations, are informed by the 'single-ground approach', which conceptualises discrimination as separate illegal acts based on a single ground.[81] This model presents evident limitations that jeopardise the effective protection of persons with a multidimensional identity. For instance, if an individual has been discriminated against on different grounds, the person concerned can bring the complaint before the court in relation to a sole ground, choosing the most favourable grounds for obtaining a positive judgment. Otherwise, the claimant is obliged to claim alternative or cumulative grounds for introducing a judicial case.[82]

The famous case of *Bahl v the Law Society* exemplifies the limits of the one-dimensional approach to equality. In this case, an Asian woman claimed to have been subject to discriminatory treatment on grounds of race and gender.[83] The Employment Appeal Tribunal and the Court of Appeal ruled that it was not possible to consider both grounds in the same case, although the claimant experienced them as inevitably interconnected. It is worth noting that this legal model does not take into account the real discriminatory experience of the individual and the impact of the intersection between different characteristics.

As a result, the single-ground approach excludes situations from the protection of equality legislation where the claimant cannot demonstrate the existence of a comparator who has suffered the same treatment. For instance, a woman with disabilities, victim of intersectional discrimination, may not successfully bring a judicial case because of the presence of non-disabled women comparators in a claim relating to gender. At the same time, in a separate complaint relating to disability, the claimant would lose the lawsuit because of the existence of men with disabilities comparators. This flaw characterises several national legal systems that do not provide effective remedies to address the multiple nature of the discrimination.

The single-ground approach has been embodied in ICERD which prohibits race discrimination and does not allow for individual complaints based on both sex and racial grounds. The weaknesses of this approach have been recognised

[81] European Union Agency for Fundamental Rights (FRA), *Inequalities and multiple discrimination in access to and quality of healthcare* (Luxembourg, Publications Office of the European Union, 2013).

[82] Uccellari (n 77) 26. See also, *Bahl v The Law Society & Anor* [2004] EWCA Civ 1070.

[83] *Bahl v The Law Society and others* [2004] IRLR 799 CA.

by the monitoring Committee on the Elimination of Racial Discrimination that acknowledged the importance of condemning certain forms of racial discrimination towards women, specifically because of their gender.[84]

This development in the interpretation of the prohibition of discrimination has also been hailed by General Recommendation 18 of the Committee on the Elimination of Discrimination against Women. The Committee addressed the issue of discrimination against women, in particular those from the most disadvantaged sectors of society, such as women of African descent.[85] It was noted that the claimant had been subject to multiple discrimination not only on grounds of sex, but also because of her status as a woman of African descent and her socio-economic background.[86]

The last step of the legal evolution concerning the concept of multidimensional equality was the adoption of General Comment 20 of the Committee on Economic, Social and Cultural Rights (CESCR). According to the Comment:

> Some individuals or groups of individuals face discrimination on more than one of the prohibited grounds, for example women belonging to an ethnic or religious minority. Such cumulative discrimination has a unique and specific impact on individuals and merits particular consideration and remedying.[87]

The Committee pointed out the necessity to tackle intersectional and multiple discrimination. The jurisprudence of the international human rights bodies exhibited increasing interest towards multidimensional equality. In doing so, multiple and intersectional discrimination have been gradually recognised under international law. This changing attitude mirrors the complexity of the contents of human rights law and the multifaceted aspects informing the notion of substantive equality.

ii. Intersectional Equality under the CRPD: Women and Children with Disabilities

The Convention on the Rights of Persons with Disabilities could be said to be the first human rights treaty that expressly provides a comprehensive framework

[84] UN Committee on the Elimination of Racial Discrimination, General Recommendation No 25: Gender related dimensions of racial discrimination reprinted, UN Doc A/55/18, annex V, 152 (2000), reprinted in Compilation of General Comments and General Recommendations Adopted by Human Rights Treaty Bodies UN Doc HRI\GEN\1\Rev.6, 214 (2000).

[85] UN Committee on the Elimination of Discrimination against Women, General Recommendation No 18: Disabled Women, UN Doc A/46/38, 3 (1993), reprinted in Compilation of General Comments and General Recommendations Adopted by Human Rights Treaty Bodies, UN Doc. HRI/GEN/1/Rev.6, 243 (2003).

[86] FRA, *Inequalities and Multiple Discrimination in Access to and Quality of Healthcare* (n 81) 23.

[87] UN Committee on Economic, Social and Cultural Rights, General Comment No 20, Non-discrimination in Economic, Social and Cultural Rights (Art 2, para 2, of the International Covenant on Economic, Social and Cultural Rights), UN Doc E/C.12/GC/20 (2 July 2009).

for combating multiple and intersectional discrimination. Article 6 states that States Parties recognise that women and girls with disabilities are subject to multiple discrimination, and in this regard, shall take measures to ensure the full and equal enjoyment by them of all human rights and fundamental freedoms. In addition, States Parties are called on to take all appropriate measures to ensure the full development, advancement and empowerment of women, for the purpose of guaranteeing them the exercise and enjoyment of the human rights and fundamental freedoms set out in the Convention.[88] The CRPD legalises the idea according to which the combination of two inseparable grounds can bring about discrimination, taking into account the specific conditions of women and children with disabilities.[89] These groups of individuals are extremely susceptible to experiencing dual forms of discrimination within the family and society.[90] It is important to outline that unequal treatment due to gender is widespread in every region of the world and includes unlawful practices such as female genital mutilation, child marriage, the practice to compel women to become prostitutes and the ethnic tradition to deprive women of the freedom of choice in marriage. Moreover, women with disabilities are more disadvantaged in comparison to men with disabilities with regard to access to education, services, employment and social assistance. They are therefore less likely to be employed and will have lower wages than men.[91]

The intimate combination of both gender and disability status represents a 'double jeopardy' and increases the possibility of facing discrimination in the workplace.[92] The intersectional approach to equality acknowledged by the Convention marks a remarkable improvement in the protection of human rights at the international level because it contemplates the multilayered experience of discrimination. The prohibition of multiple and intersectional discrimination contributes to reinforcing a substantive model of equality that aims to break the cycle of disadvantage and remove social obstacles.[93] By contrast, the one-dimensional approach perpetuates the limits of the formal model of equality which does not accommodate those disadvantages of the individual's identity.

[88] Art 6 CRPD.

[89] AC Hendriks, 'UN Convention on the Rights of Persons with Disabilities' (2007) 14 *European Journal of Health Law* 273.

[90] Secretariat for the Convention on the Rights of Persons with Disabilities of the Department of Economic and Social Affairs; United Nations Population Fund; Wellesley Centers for Women, *Disability Rights, Gender, and Development: A Resource Tool for Action* (2008).

[91] T Emmett and E Alant, 'Women and disability: exploring the interface of multiple disadvantage' (2006) 23 *Development Southern Africa* 445.

[92] L Jans and S Stoppard, *Chartbook on Women and Disability in the United States. An InfoUse Report* (Washington, DC, US Department of Education, National Institute on Disability and Rehabilitation Research, 1999).

[93] S Fredman, *Discrimination Law*, 2nd edn (Oxford, Oxford University Press, 2011).

IV. The CRPD's Model of Disability: From a Social Construct Towards a Human Rights Approach

The CRPD introduces an ideal framework for tackling discrimination, and favours the true societal adaptation to the needs of persons with disabilities. The substantive equality paradigm is supported and reinforced by a social understanding of disability that emphasises the importance of eliminating external barriers that jeopardise the full enjoyment of human rights for persons with disabilities. The CRPD does not provide a strict legal definition of disability, but points out 'a soft threshold definition in the form of guidance which is open-ended and inclusive'.[94] The CRPD's Preamble recognises that disability 'is an evolving concept and that disability results from the interaction between persons with impairments and attitudinal and environmental barriers'. Moreover, Article 1 of the CRPD distinctly sets out a concept of disability that includes those individuals 'who have long-term physical, mental, intellectual or sensory impairments which in interaction with various barriers may hinder their full and effective participation in society on an equal basis with others'.

The CRPD enshrines a social construct of disability replacing the traditional 'medical view' which merely places the impairment within the individual.[95] The CRPD tries to overcome the limits of the medical model of disability, which locates the failure to meet the norm with the individual and regards disability as an impairment that needs to be cured. The medical approach recognises disability as the 'exclusive realm of helping and medical disciplines'[96] and prevents the application of the equality principle to persons with disabilities.[97] In doing so, this model reduces persons with disabilities to their impairments and does not acknowledge them as rights-holders. By contrast, the CRPD crystallises the concept according to which society contributes to disable persons with impairments.[98]

The social approach to disability has often been criticised because it does not consider the extent to which individual deficiencies concretely affect persons with disabilities.[99] In this regard, an accessible and inclusive society would not equalise persons with disabilities with non-disabled individuals.[100] However, it is worth

[94] G de Búrca, 'The EU in the Negotiation of the UN Disability Convention' (2010) 35 *European Law Review* 174.

[95] See, for instance: F Hasler, 'Developments in the Disabled People's Movement' in J Swain et al (eds), *Disabling Barriers, Enabling Environments* (London, Sage, 1993); M Oliver, *Understanding Disability: From Theory to Practice* (Basingstoke, Macmillan, 1996); S Wendell, *The Rejected Body: Feminist Philosophical Reflections on Disability* (New York, Routledge, 1996).

[96] T Degener, 'Disability in a Human Rights Context' (2016) 5 *Laws* 35.

[97] UN Committee on the Rights of Persons with Disabilities, General Comment No 6 on equality and non-discrimination (n 54).

[98] P Harpur, 'Embracing the New Disability Rights Paradigm: The Importance of the Convention on the Rights of Persons with Disabilities' (2012) 27 *Disability & Society* 1.

[99] T Shakespeare and N Watson, 'The Social Model of Disability: An Outdated Ideology?' (2002) 2 *Research in Social Science and Disability* 9.

[100] T Shakespeare, *Disability Rights and Wrongs* (Abingdon, Routledge, 2006) 51.

noting that the CPRD adopts a flexible and *evolving* concept of disability which takes into account the interplay between the individual impairment and the external barriers. By doing so, it aims to overcome the main limitations of a rigid model of disability and provides significant leeway to adapt the concept of disability to different socio-contextual circumstances.

It may be argued that the social model provides fertile ground to build and develop a new 'human rights' approach to disability in accordance with the individual impairment must be valued as part of human variation. The recent General Comment No 6 on equality and non-discrimination adopted by the UN Committee on the Rights of Persons with Disabilities expressly states that the

> [h]uman rights model of disability recognizes that disability is a social construct and impairments must not be taken as a legitimate ground for the denial or restriction of human rights. It acknowledges that disability is one of several layers of identity. Hence, disability laws and policies must take the diversity of persons with disabilities into account. It also recognizes that human rights are interdependent, interrelated and indivisible.[101]

The reasoning of the Committee embraces the new developments in academic literature concerning the human rights model of disability, which focuses on the inherent dignity of the human being and the inclusion of persons with disabilities in all decisions affecting their life. The social or contextual concept of disability embodied in the CPRD does not ignore the effects that impairments might have on individuals, but it seeks to promote a paradigm shift in the understanding of disability by focusing on those final results caused by the impairment in a given social context.

It may be said that the CPRD reshapes the social model of disability and recognises impairments as part of human diversity.[102] For instance, Article 3 of the CRPD explicitly lays down that 'respect for difference and acceptance of persons with disabilities' must be considered as part of human diversity and humanity. By doing so, it does not embrace 'a radical social constructionist view of disability, in which impairment has no underlying reality',[103] but rightfully rejects the idea of persons with disabilities as objects of charity, medical treatment and social assistance. The CRPD acknowledges that persons with disabilities are subjects of rights and active members of society. To this end, it requires the removal of those structural and external obstacles that obstruct the full enjoyment of their fundamental rights. The objective to ensure substantive equality is assisted by a social construction of disability that encourages the alteration of able-bodied norms and the adoption of reasonable adjustments to accommodate persons with disabilities.

[101] UN Committee on the Rights of Persons with Disabilities, General Comment No 6 on equality and non-discrimination (n 54).

[102] Degener (n 96); P Blanck and E Flynn, *Routledge Handbook of Disability Law and Human Rights* (London, Routledge, 2017).

[103] R Kayess and P French, 'Out of Darkness into Light? Introducing the Convention on the Rights of Persons with Disabilities' (2008) 8 *Human Rights Law Review* 1.

The CPRD provides the tools to drive a change in the judicial interpretation of the prohibition of discrimination on grounds of disability by expanding the analysis beyond those individual limitations caused by a medical condition.

V. Reconceptualising the Human Rights Dichotomy

International human rights law has traditionally been characterised by a distinction between civil and political rights on the one side and economic, social and cultural rights on the other.[104] Civil and political rights are generally regarded as rights of first generation, while socio-economic rights as second generation rights.[105] The third generation includes the right to development, the right to self-determination, minority rights and the right to a healthy environment. After the adoption of the 1948 Universal and Inter-American declarations of human rights which lay down a comprehensive catalogue of rights, the drafting of subsequent global treaties has reflected the classic division of rights into two categories. The content of the UDHR was codified into the two 1966 sister covenants: the ICESCR and the ICCPR.[106]

In this context, the traditional paradigm tends to distinguish between rights on the basis of their correspondent duties. Duties of restraint are associated with 'freedom-protecting civil and political rights', whereas positive duties are those relating to 'equality-promoting socio-economic rights'.[107] As a result, positive duties are immediately applicable; by contrast duties of restraint require to be realised progressively.[108] Moreover, civil and political rights are considered as justiciable and inexpensive, while social, economic and cultural rights as non-justiciable and costly. For instance, social rights have been traditionally viewed as not imbued of legal contents and inherently not-justiciable on the grounds that their implementation was a political matter, not a matter of law.[109]

[104] See generally, L Sohn, 'The New International Law: Protection of the Rights of Individuals rather than States' (1982) 32 *American University Law Review* 1. See also, P Alston, 'Conjuring up New Human Rights: A Proposal for Quality Control' (1984) 78 *American Journal of International Law* 607.

[105] T Meron, 'On a Hierarchy of International Human Rights' (1986) 80 *American Journal of International Law* 1.

[106] L Richardson, 'Economic, Social and Cultural Rights (and Beyond) in the UN Human Rights Council' (2015) 15 *Human Rights Law Review* 409. The International Covenant on Civil and Political Rights was adopted and opened for signature, ratification and accession by General Assembly Resolution 2200A (XXI) of 16 December 1966 and entered into force on 23 March 1976. The International Covenant on Economic, Social and Cultural Rights was adopted and opened for signature, ratification and accession by General Assembly Resolution 2200A (XXI) of 16 December 1966 and entered into force on 3 January 1976.

[107] Fredman, *Human Rights Transformed* (n 12).

[108] ibid, 69. See also Art 2.1 ICCPR and Art 2.1 ICESCR.

[109] See: EW Vierdag, 'The Legal Nature of the Rights Granted by the International Covenant on Economic, Social and Cultural Rights (ICESCR)' (1978) 9 *Netherlands Yearbook of International*

Nowadays, this dichotomy seems to be highly contested as the most recent international treaties adhere to a holistic and indivisible notion of human rights. For example, the EUCFR protects both civil and political and socio-economic rights. It has also been made legally binding by the Lisbon Treaty.[110] The Charter does not replicate traditional human rights documents, but aims to integrate civil and political rights with socio-economic rights, imposing positive and proactive duties on the state.[111] According to Gráinne de Búrca, the Charter does not distinguish between justiciability and non-justiciability. It is likely to 'function as a source of values and norms … to influence the interpretation of EU legislative and other measures and to feed into policy-making and into EU activities more generally.'[112]

In addition, the Declaration adopted during the Vienna World Conference on Human Rights explicitly emphasises that human rights are universal, indivisible and interdependent and interrelated.[113] The Vienna Declaration and Programme of Action underline the obligation of the international community to treat human rights globally in a fair and equal manner, on the same footing, and with the same emphasis. To this end, the duty of states, regardless of their political, economic and cultural systems, is to promote and protect all human rights and fundamental freedoms.[114] Despite that, the international protection of socio-economic rights continues to encounter legal difficulties and political obstacles as it demands positive and costly actions by states.[115] On the other hand, civil and political rights do not always trigger a positive duty on the state to provide all the necessary measures to guarantee the implementation of the right. This demonstrates that the demarcation between civil and political rights and socio-economic rights is still an interesting issue in the discourse of human rights law.[116]

Law 69; L Pech, 'France: Rethinking "Droits-Creances"' in M Langford (ed), *Socio-Economic Rights Jurisprudence: Emerging Trends in Comparative and International Law* (Cambridge, Cambridge University Press, 2007).

[110] See S Peers et al (eds), *The EU Charter of Fundamental Rights: A Commentary* (Oxford, Hart Publishing, 2009).

[111] S Fredman, 'Transformation or Dilution: Fundamental Rights in the EU Social Space' (2006) 12 *European Law Journal* 14.

[112] G de Búrca, 'Fundamental Rights and Citizenship' in B de Witte (ed), *Ten Reflections on the Constitutional Treaty for Europe* (Florence, European University Institute, 2003) 24.

[113] On 25 June 1993, representatives of 171 states adopted by consensus the Vienna Declaration and Programme of Action of the World Conference on Human Rights presenting to the international community a common plan for the strengthening of human rights work around the world.

[114] Vienna Declaration and Programme of Action, adopted by the World Conference on Human Rights in Vienna on 25 June 1993.

[115] Statement to the Vienna Conference by the UN Committee on Economic, Social and Cultural Rights, 1993: 'The shocking reality … is that states and the international community as a whole continue to tolerate all too often breaches of economic, social and cultural rights which, if they occurred in relation to civil and political rights, would provoke expressions of horror and outrage and would lead to concerted calls for immediate remedial action.'

[116] S Fredman, 'Human Rights Transformed: Positive Duties and Positive Rights' (2006) Legal Research Paper Series No 38/2006.

A. Disability Rights are Universal and Indivisible: Do Civil and Political Rights also Demand Economic Resources?

The CRPD overturns the stark dichotomy between civil and political rights and socio-economic rights. The Preamble specifies that a comprehensive and integral international convention is necessary to promote and protect the rights and dignity of persons with disabilities. The emergence of a new proactive model of rights seems crucial to redressing the profound social disadvantage of persons with disabilities and promoting their participation in civil, political, economic, social and cultural spheres with equal opportunities, in both developing and developed countries. In that regard, States Parties reaffirm the 'universality, indivisibility, interdependence and interrelatedness of all human rights and fundamental freedoms and the need for persons with disabilities to be guaranteed their full enjoyment without discrimination'.[117] This means that all rights require positive actions and affirmative programmes, including those civil and political rights which are merely associated with duties of restraint.

In order to guarantee the participation in political and public life of persons with disabilities, the UN Committee on the Rights of Persons with Disabilities pointed out the importance of enhancing the active participation of persons with disabilities in politics through affirmative action and ensuring the accessibility of all voting stations.[118] It took note of the difficult situation of persons with hearing impairments in accessing information due to lack of official recognition of the significance of sign language by Hong Kong, China. The Committee highlighted those fundamental obligations stemming from the freedom of expression and opinion, and access to information. It therefore urged Hong Kong, China, to enhance the training for and the services provided by sign language interpreters.[119] In this context, the proactive role of the state is central for assuring the effective enjoyment of civil and political rights in favour of persons with disabilities.

Even in relation to the freedom from exploitation, violence and abuse (Article 16), the Committee did not only recommend the state from abstaining to carry out those violations, but it was particularly concerned about the positive duties to investigate the incidents and prosecute the perpetrators. Finally, the Committee recognised the difficult conditions of women and girls with intellectual disabilities who may be subjected to sexual violence. Thus, it urged the state to guarantee sex education to children and adolescents with intellectual disabilities and appropriate training for law enforcement personnel on handling violence against women

[117] UN Convention on the Rights of Persons with Disabilities, UN Doc A/RES/61/106 (2007). Preamble, Recital c.

[118] UN Committee on the Rights of Persons with Disabilities, Concluding Observations on the Initial Report of China, Un Doc CRPD/C/CHN/CO/ (adopted by the Committee at its eighth session (17–28 September 2012).

[119] ibid, 71–72.

and girls with disabilities.[120] It may be argued that the full realisation of civil and political rights depends on the economic resources invested by the States Parties. All rights have budgetary implications and rights of persons with disabilities require supplementary funds.[121]

To give another example, in the observations on the initial report of Argentina, the Committee held that the Argentinian legal framework positively takes into account the principle of inclusive education for persons with disabilities. However, it concluded that the implementation of the right to education is limited, in practice,

> by a failure to tailor programmes and curricula to the needs of pupils with disabilities and by the prevalence of all sorts of barriers that prevent persons with disabilities from accessing the educational system without discrimination and on an equal footing with other students.[122]

Consequently, the Committee recommended the development of a comprehensive state education policy that assures the right to inclusive education and allocates sufficient budgetary resources. This example is one of many demonstrating the progressive emergence of a new substantive and demanding approach towards disability rights, in compliance with the commitments of the CRPD. This new legal approach is based on the indivisibilities of duties and a uniform level of protection that facilitates the interaction between the two different sets of rights.[123]

B. Disability Rights as (Quasi)-Justiciable Rights

Traditional theory separates civil and political rights from socio-economic rights also on grounds of justiciability, excluding the latter from the judicial arena. A right is generally considered 'justiciable' when it can be examined by a judge in a concrete set of circumstances and when this examination can imply a further determination of this right's significance.[124] Civil and political rights were seen as precise enough to be applied, while socio-economic provisions were thought of as vague and unenforceable. Positive duties associated with socio-economic rights were regarded as going beyond the institutional legitimacy of the courts as they entail a significant level of resource commitments.[125] They were deemed

[120] ibid, 66.

[121] IE Koch, 'From Invisibility to Indivisibility: The International Convention on the Rights of Persons with Disabilities' in O Arnardóttir and G Quinn (eds), *The United Nations Convention on the Rights of Persons with Disabilities: European and Scandinavian Perspectives* (Leiden, Martinus Nijhoff) 72.

[122] UN Committee on the Rights of Persons with Disabilities, Concluding observations (n 118) 38.

[123] See also Fredman, *Human Rights Transformed* (n 12) 67.

[124] K Arambulo, *Strengthening the Supervision of the International Covenant on Economic, Social and Cultural Rights: Theoretical and Procedural Aspects* (Antwerp, Intersentia, 1999) 55.

[125] See Fredman, *Human Rights Transformed* (n 12).

as excessively costly, requiring welfare measures by the state and therefore falling under the exclusive competence of political decision-makers. However, the CRPD has removed these conceptual boundaries between civil and political rights and socio-economic rights that inform the traditional human rights discourse. Currently, both categories of rights are justiciable before the UN Committee on the Rights of Persons with Disabilities. The Committee represents a quasi-justiciable body and has the competence to receive and consider communications from, or on behalf of, individuals or groups of individuals subject to its jurisdiction who claim to be victims of a violation by that State Party of the provisions of the Convention.[126] The treaty body has the competence to request that the State Party adopts interim measures as needed to avoid possible irreparable damage to the victim (Article 4). The Committee may also issue non-binding and quasi-judicial recommendations for eliminating violations and redressing any damage caused by them (Article 5).[127] The UN body may also promote an inquiry in case it receives reliable information indicating grave or systematic violations by a State Party of rights set forth in the Convention (Article 6). Interestingly, the decisions of the Committee explicitly reveal a resource-demanding approach that urges States Parties to provide welfare measures for implementing all disability rights. This approach entails the justiciability of those socio-economic rights that have usually been associated with non-justiciable duties.

i. The Right to Control One's Own Financial Affairs

In *Nyusti & Takacs v Hungary*, the Committee recognised the right to control one's own financial affairs in favour of persons with visual impairments.[128] The case originated from the compliant of two Hungarian citizens, who concluded a contract with the OTP Bank Zrt credit institution (OTP) in order to use banking cards. Despite that, the applicants were prevented from using the automatic teller machines (ATMs) because of the lack of assistance. The ATM keyboards were not marked with Braille, nor did the ATMs make audible instructions and voice assistance for banking card operations available. The applicants claimed that they were unable to use the services provided by the ATMs at the same level as non-disabled clients, although they paid annual fees for banking card services and transactions equal to the fees paid by other clients.[129]

[126] Art 1 of the Optional Protocol to the Convention on the Rights of Persons with Disabilities (A/RES/61/106).

[127] N Hart et al, 'Making Every Life Count: Ensuring Equality and Protection for Persons with Disabilities in Armed Conflicts' (2014) 40 *Monash University Law Review* 148.

[128] UN Committee on the Rights of Persons with Disabilities, Communication No 1/2010, UN Doc CRPD/C/9/D/1/2010 (Views adopted by the Committee at its ninth session, 15–19 April 2013).

[129] ibid, 2.1.

In light of this factual background, they claimed to be victims of direct discrimination in accessing the financial services provided by the ATMs compared with persons without disability. By contrast, the State Party underlined that the accessibility of banking services is a crucial issue which can only be achieved gradually, due to the related costs and technical viability, through the installation of new ATMs providing physical and info-communication accessibility. Therefore, the State Secretary recommended that OPT should adopt the appropriate machines in the future. At the same time, it found the compatibility of the Supreme Court's decision with the State Party's law, in accordance with OTP, is exempted from the obligation to assure equal treatment under the Equal Treatment Act because the applicants accepted the contractual terms for private current account services, including the facility of limited use.[130]

The Committee noticed that the State Party did not acknowledge the duty on private entities to provide accessibility of information, communications and other services for persons with visual impairments on an equal basis. The Committee instead emphasised that under Article 4, paragraph 1(e), of the Convention, States Parties have the general obligation 'to take all appropriate measures to eliminate discrimination on the basis of disability by any person, organization or private enterprise'. To this end, States Parties are required, pursuant to Article 9 of the Convention, 'to take appropriate measures to ensure to persons with disabilities access, on an equal basis with others, to, inter alia, information, communications and other services, including electronic services, by identifying and eliminating obstacles and barriers to accessibility'. In particular, the UN body recalled the specific duty of the State Party to guarantee that private actors provide accessible services to persons with disabilities. States Parties should take appropriate measures to develop, promulgate and monitor the implementation of minimum standards and guidelines for the accessibility of facilities and services open or provided to the public (Article 9, paragraph 2(a), of the Convention), and ensure that private entities that offer facilities and services which are open or provided to the public take into account all aspects of accessibility for persons with disabilities

[130] ibid, 2.16: 'The Supreme Court delivered its decision on 4 February 2009, rejecting both the request for judicial review by the authors and the request for judicial review by OTP. The Supreme Court shared the opinion of the Metropolitan Court of Appeal that the ATMs designed for sighted persons put blind or visually impaired persons in a disadvantageous situation, even though it seemed that they may use the ATMs under the same conditions as everybody else. The disadvantageous situation is induced by the fact that there is no Braille on the ATMs, and the owner of the banking card does not have voice assistance support when using the machines. The Supreme Court also agreed with the arguments of the second instance court with regard to OTP's exemption from the obligation to provide for equal treatment under the Equal Treatment Act. Furthermore, the Supreme Court asserted that the parties concluded a contract for private current account services, the content of which may be freely established by the parties. The Court stated that the authors took note of the contractual terms, including the facility of limited use, and by signing the contract, they agreed to their disadvantaged situation through implied conduct'.

(Article 9, paragraph 2(b)).[131] As a consequence, the Committee held that Hungary failed to fulfil the obligations embodied in Article 9, paragraph 2(b), of the Convention.

ii. Debunking the Argument of the 'Progressive Realisation of Socio-Economic Rights'

The case *Nyusti & Takacs v Hungary* exhibits interesting and innovative legal aspects in relation to the protection of socio-economic rights under international human rights law and the issue of accessibility. The State Party sought to advance the common justification of the 'progressive realization of economic, social and cultural rights' in order to deal with the accessibility of the ATMs and other banking services. In that regard, it argued that 'steps are to be taken to change the accessibility of the ATMs and other banking services, including accessibility not only for the blind, but also for persons with other disabilities' and 'the above target can only be achieved gradually'.[132] The notion of progressive realisation is often used by governments as an 'escape hatch' with the purpose to postpone or dodge the fulfilment of their human rights obligations.[133]

According to this argument, the lack of available resources constitutes a legitimate reason to avoid the immediate realisation of socio-economic rights. This justification introduces flexible elements in the application of human rights law and brings about a sort of uncertainty in relation to the content and extent of the legal obligations imposed by the UN treaties.[134] However, the CRPD sets out that with regard to economic, social and cultural rights, each State Party undertakes to take measures to the maximum of its available resources and, where needed, within the framework of international cooperation, with a view to achieving progressively the full realisation of these rights.[135] Despite the introduction of this controversial clause in the Convention's framework, the Committee did not hesitate to affirm the importance of an effective and successful implementation of disability rights at national level.

The Committee was not persuaded by the Hungarian government's assumption to gradually achieve accessibility due to costs involved. On contrary, the Committee observed that the measures adopted by OTP and other financial institutions have not ensured the accessibility of banking card services for the

[131] ibid, 9.5.

[132] ibid, 4.3.

[133] S Leckie, 'Another Step towards Indivisibility: Identifying the Key Features of Violations of Economic, Social and Cultural Rights' (1998) 20 *Human Rights Quarterly* 81.

[134] E Felne, 'Closing the "Escape Hatch": A Toolkit to Monitor the Progressive Realization of Economic, Social, and Cultural Rights' (2009) 1 *Journal of Human Rights Practice* 402.

[135] Art 4(2) CRPD.

applicants or other persons in a similar situation. The final decision clearly shows that the main objective of the Convention is to bring about a real change in society. The Committee required the adoption of 'a legislative framework with *concrete, enforceable and time-bound benchmarks* for monitoring and assessing the gradual modification and adjustment by private financial institutions of previously inaccessible banking services provided by them into accessible ones'.[136]

It may be said that the Committee plays a key role in monitoring the application of the Convention's provisions within the national systems and increasing the awareness of persons with disabilities with regard to their own rights. The aim of the Convention is to improve the legal protection of persons with disabilities. To this end, it promotes the justiciability and implementation of those socio-economic rights (such as the right to control one's own financial affairs) which can concretely enhance the protection of persons with disabilities, regardless of the amount of economic resources needed by States Parties.

iii. The Peculiar Case of Accessibility: A Bridge between Civil-Political and Socio-Economic Rights?

The above case confirms that the CRPD's goal is to ensure the justiciability of all human rights, in particular of those socio-economic rights that are often excluded from the political agenda of the States Parties. Notably, the issue of accessibility represents a critical point for the concrete empowerment of persons with disabilities. The concept of accessibility implies a profound adaptation of society, both in its public and in its private dimensions, to the specific needs of person with disabilities in order to enable all people to fully participate in all aspects of life.[137] Accessibility refers not only to the physical environment, but it also affects the participation of individuals in the political and economic sector.[138] It should be viewed as an essential instrument to pursue equality and non-discrimination. According to Article 9 of the CRPD, in order to enable persons with disabilities to live independently and participate fully in all aspects of life, States Parties have the obligation to introduce all appropriate measures to ensure that persons with disabilities have access to transportation, information and communications and other facilities and services open or provided to the public. Accessibility is a vital

[136] UN Committee on the Rights of Persons with Disabilities, Communication No 1/2010 (Views adopted by the Committee at its ninth session) (n 128) 10.1(a) (emphasis added).

[137] Office of the High Commissioner for Human Rights, Monitoring the Convention on the Rights of Persons with Disabilities Guidance for human rights monitors, Professional training series No 17, New York and Geneva, 2010.

[138] R Lang, 'The United Nations Convention on the right and dignities for persons with disability: A panacea for ending disability discrimination? La Convention des Nations Unies sur les droits des personnes handicapées: une solution pour mettre fin à la discrimination contre le handicap?' (2009) 3 *ALTER European Journal of Disability Research* 266.

precondition for the effective and equal enjoyment of different civil, political, economic, social and cultural rights by persons with disabilities.[139] The implementation of this provision is therefore crucial to ensure the full realisation of the rights of persons with disabilities.

[139] UN Committee on the Rights of Persons with Disabilities, General Comment No 2 on Article 9: Accessibility, UN Doc CRPD/C/GC/2 (eleventh session, 30 March–11 April 2014).

2

The New Role for Civil Society under the CRPD

This chapter gives an initial overview of the emergence of civil society groups in global governance and the role of disability advocacy organisations in the CRPD's negotiations and drafting. In particular, it will be shown that the Convention on the Rights of Persons with Disabilities (CRPD) encompasses a model of participatory democracy that requires the involvement of all relevant stakeholders in the entire policy chain, from conception to implementation, on the basis of an inclusive approach. The aim of this chapter is to assess to what extent non-governmental organisations (NGOs) can inform and improve the decision-making process at international level.

I. The Rise of Civil Society in Global Governance

The participation of NGOs in the CRPD's negotiations is a positive example of the relationship between society and international politics. Civil society can contribute to improving the quality of the decision-making process of international bodies and the functioning of global governance. According to Antonio Gramsci, civil society is 'a set of institutions through which society is organised and represented itself autonomously from the state'.[1] NGOs represent a fundamental and crucial segment of international civil society, which cannot be identified with the state or the market.[2] The concept of 'civil society' encompasses a broad range of social actors, such as voluntary associations, human rights promoters, educational institutions, environmental movements, organisations for development cooperation, academic forums and think tanks. On the other hand, global governance entails those laws, policies and institutions that define trans-border relations between states, citizens, intergovernmental and non-governmental organisations, and the market.[3]

[1] LR Kurtz, *Encyclopedia of Violence, Peace, & Conflict* (Amsterdam, Elsevier, 2008). See also, A Gramsci, *Quaderni dal Carcere, 1929–1935* (Roma, Istituto della Enciclopedia Italiana, 2017).

[2] H Cullen and K Morrow, 'International Civil Society in International Law: The Growth of NGO Participation' (2001) 1 *Non-State Actors & International Law* 7.

[3] TG Weiss, R Thakur and JG Ruggie, *Global Governance and the UN: An Unfinished Journey* (Bloomington, IND, Indiana University Press, 2010).

The realist idea according to which international relations are shaped exclusively by global power arrangements and state interests is outdated because it does not consider the emerging role of international civil society.[4] Global relations and contemporary governance are characterised by the interaction of transnational, regional and local actors that permanently operate in the international realm.[5] In this context, the multilayered identity of individuals is not adequately represented and protected by the interests of national governments. For this reason, the development of higher standards of protection for human rights at international level is the outcome of the decisive action of those multiple groups belonging to civil society.

The United Nations framework has often been criticised because its institutional structure marginalises the independent role of NGOs and individuals.[6] The UN Charter merely recognises the consultative role of NGOs in the formal process of deliberation of the Economic and Social Council (ECOSOC). Article 71 points out that

> the Economic and Social Council may make suitable arrangements for consultation with non-governmental organizations which are concerned with matters within its competence. Such arrangements may be made with international organisations and, where appropriate, with national organisations after consultation with the Member of the United Nations concerned.[7]

The United Nations (UN) has opened its doors to NGOs, but their participation is limited to the specific competences of the ECOSOC.[8]

Despite this state-centric approach, civil society has gradually carried out a 'quiet revolution' in the UN system.[9] For instance, it is noteworthy to stress the essential contribution of NGOs in the promotion of policy in favour of gender equality, child education, environmental protection and disability rights. NGOs have always boosted a bottom-up process for enhancing the international human rights framework. NGOs have carried out not only lobbying activities towards political institutions, but also campaigns to raise public awareness and understating of human rights issues and transnational law.[10] However, restricted access to the UN decision-making process has not thwarted NGOs in inspiring the international debate around significant issues.

[4] D Otto, 'Nongovernmental Organizations in the United Nations System: The Emerging Role of International Civil Society' (1996) 18 *Human Rights Quarterly* 107.

[5] JA Scholte, 'Civil Society and Democracy in Global Governance' (2001) Centre for the Study of Globalization and Regionalisation, CSGR Working Paper No 65/01.

[6] See TM Franck, 'The Emerging Right to Democratic Governance' (1992) 86 *American Journal of International Law* 46.

[7] Art 71 of the Charter of the United Nations (Chapter X: the Economic and Social Council), 26 June 1945.

[8] Otto (n 4) 127.

[9] T Mogami, 'The United Nations System as an Unfinished Revolution' (1990) 15 *Alternatives* 177.

[10] Scholte (n 5) 17.

The United Nations Conference on Environment and Development (UNCED) and the Fourth World Conference on Women (FWCW) are very recent examples of the outstanding involvement of international civil society in the global arena.[11] Since the UNCED in 1992, there has been a call for the broadest public participation in poverty eradication and sustainable development. Transnational civil society groups were key players in this process, complementing the work of state actors and intergovernmental organisations.[12] Thus, the CRPD's elaboration is the highest point of the increasing activity of NGOs in the UN system.

A. Participatory Democracy and Global Governance

Academic studies and political activists have often been concerned with making the global political system more democratic. Global governance is generally deemed as devoid of democratic legitimacy because of the lack of civil participation, transparency and accountability.[13] By contrast, a different school of thought tends to underline that the proper yardstick for the analysis of international institutions is not a national model of democracy.[14] International organisations are therefore intrinsically unable to encompass direct democratic deliberations. They lack those essential democratic mechanisms provided by national political systems for direct electoral or interest group accountability.[15]

In light of this backdrop, this book does not aim to equate national institutions and international bodies or argue that the latter will have to comply with the traditional model of representative democracy. However, the requirement of participatory democracy and the direct participation of civil society within international legal processes may have a positive impact on global governance.

B. Opening Up the Decision-Making Process

The increasing participation of NGOs can produce a remarkable impact on the functioning of global governance and constitute the starting point for opening up the international community's system to civil society's input and expertise.

[11] Otto (n 4) 136.

[12] Leadership Council, Sustainable Development Solutions Network, *An Action Agenda for Sustainable Development: Report for the UN Secretary-General* (6 June 2013).

[13] Scholte (n 5) 12.

[14] See, for instance: G Majone, *Regulating Europe* (London, Routledge, 1996); G Majone, 'Europe's Democratic Deficit' (1998) 4 *European Law Journal* 237; A Moravcsik, 'Is there a "Democratic Deficit" in World Politics? A Framework for Analysis' (2004) 39 *Government and Opposition* 336.

[15] R Dahl, 'Can International Organizations Be Democratic? A Skeptic's View' in I Shapiro and C Hacker-Cordon (eds), *Democracy's Edges* (Cambridge, Cambridge University Press, 1999).

International institutions such as the World Trade Organization (WTO) and the United Nations (UN) are pervaded by inadequate democratic standards.[16] This 'democratic deficit' implies the absence of identifiable and accountable decision-makers along with transparent and open decision-making processes. International governance regimes are permeated by the existence of intergovernmental networks and relations which may exclude the participation of citizens from the decision-making.[17] However, international organisations hold that they are not obliged to guarantee any democratic requirements because they are not elected by people and there is no collective transnational *demos* (in terms of supranational collective identity) to represent.[18]

The above scenario does not reflect the changing system of global governance, as much as the exponential increase in civil society and business groups that seek to participate in the decision-making process. The model of participatory democracy requires an institutional and political framework that creates the conditions for broader participation in and consultation with civil society at the international level.[19] Participation is at the heart of political practice. Participatory conditions constitute essential requisites of a deliberative decision-making process that includes stakeholders and promotes public participation. To this end, the process of deliberation should consider the preferences and interests of civil society.

Participatory democracy aims to strengthen the legitimacy of the entire global governance framework by opening up decisional procedures and involving more experts and organisations in shaping and delivering policy. The main contribution of civil society is represented by the possibility to guarantee visibility to stakeholders. In particular, NGOs are the voice of invisible groups of individuals who are not able to directly participate in social and political initiatives.[20] They can properly support stakeholders' concerns and provide specific information, expertise, analysis and reports to decision-makers. The active role of NGOs would enrich the international community's functioning and foster good governance.

C. Ensuring Transparent Procedures

NGO participation also represents a catalyst for enhancing the transparency of global governance. Transparency means openness of the policymaking and

[16] S Joseph, *Blame it on the WTO? A Human Rights Critique* (Oxford, Oxford Scholarship Online, 2011).

[17] P Nanz and J Steffek, 'Global Governance, Participation and the Public Sphere' (2004) 39 *Government and Opposition* 314.

[18] ibid, 317.

[19] The origins of the model of participatory democracy can be traced to the political debates of the late 1960s and 1970s. See for instance: C Pateman, *Participation and Democratic Theory* (Cambridge, Cambridge University Press, 1970); and CB Macpherson, *The Life and Times of Liberal Democracy* (Oxford, Oxford University Press, 1977).

[20] J Bebbington, J Unerman and B O'Dwyer, *Sustainability Accounting and Accountability* (London, Routledge, 2014).

rule-making processes by means of clear procedures and accessible decisions.[21] It implies control and public scrutiny to encourage the adequate accountability of decision-makers.[22] Transparency constitutes a fundamental principle to apply to the elaboration of international treaties because most of society is not always aware of the most important issues debated in the global arena. Civil society has appropriate instruments to involve citizens in sensitive topics of discussion and interact critically with policymakers. The role of civil society mitigates the 'democratic deficit' of global governance and brings human rights concerns into international law.

The increasing requests for more transparent global governance also pose significant dilemmas concerning the importance of countervailing competing legitimate interests, such as security, privacy and business secrets.[23] In this respect, it is worth noting that transparency should be considered as a legal presumption, as opposed to a strict and immovable rule. Accordingly, transparency entails the duty on international organisations to justify, based on clear and definite legal exceptions, the failure to provide public meetings and accessible documents. This obligation should be placed on institutions to ensure the proper fulfilment of the transparency requirement.

II. Mainstreaming Disability in the International Agenda

International organisations for the rights of persons with disabilities have performed a fundamental task in order to mainstream disability into global agendas, frameworks and processes. Mainstreaming is the process of assessing the implications for persons with disabilities of any planned action, including legislation, policies or programmes, in any area and at all levels.[24] It is part of a strategy for promoting disability rights in the design, implementation, monitoring and evaluation of policies and programmes in all political, economic and societal spheres. To this end, NGOs advance influential proposals, criticisms and perspectives for building an effective framework for the protection of persons with disabilities.

A crucial moment in the increasing activity of civil society was the World NGO Summit on Disability which took place in Beijing on 12 March 2001. During the summit, a Resolution concerning the importance of introducing an international convention on the rights of all disabled people was adopted.[25] The Resolution emphasised that

[21] DA Rondinelli and G Shabbir Cheema (eds), *Reinventing Government in the Twenty-First Century: State Capacity in a Globalizing Society* (West Hartford, CT, Kumarian Press, 2003).

[22] A Peters, 'The Transparency of Global Governance' in M Pazartzis et al (eds), *Reconceptualising the Rule of Law in Global Governance, Resources, Investment and Trade* (Oxford, Hart Publishing 2015).

[23] ibid, 4.

[24] Commission for Social Development (CSocD) (46th Session), 'Mainstreaming disability in the development agenda' (6–15 February 2008).

[25] G Quinn et al, *Human Rights and Disability: The current use and future potential of United Nations human rights instruments in the context of disability* (New York, United Nations Press, 2002).

the full inclusion of people with disabilities in society requires our solidarity in working towards an international convention that legally binds nations, to reinforce the moral authority of the United Nations Standard Rules on the Equalization of Opportunities for Persons with Disabilities.[26]

At a later stage, the involvement of NGOs in the drafting process of the CRPD has contributed to feeding into the policy discussion, in particular regarding the renewed concepts of disability, accessibility and multi-discrimination. It may be said that civil society has concrete tools to bring the interests of society into an international institutional system that facilitates participatory democracy.[27]

A. 'Nothing about us without us': A Commitment to Participatory Democracy

Article 4(3) of the CRPD lays down that

> in the development and implementation of legislation and policies to implement the present Convention, and in other decision-making processes concerning issues relating to persons with disabilities, States Parties shall closely consult with and actively involve persons with disabilities, including children with disabilities, through their representative organizations.

This provision shows that civil society has been expressly recognised as a fundamental actor in the international community.

The CRPD enshrines the motto 'nothing about us without us' that illustrates the importance of actively involving persons with disabilities in planning and implementing strategies and policies that affect their lives. The definition of policies requires the active involvement of persons with disabilities and their organisations, in particular the participation of NGOs in the negotiations of the Convention. This slogan has been used by most organisations for disabled people around the world in order to promote full participation and equalisation of opportunities for, by and with persons with disabilities. Persons with disabilities have fully participated in the process of mainstreaming disability in the international arena and developing a truly inclusive society in which all voices are heard.

i. The Participation of Persons with Disabilities in the Ad Hoc Committee

The elaboration and final adoption of the CRPD demonstrates how civil society can effectively contribute to shape and influence international law. In more practical

[26] Beijing Declaration on Disabled Persons in the New Millennium, World NGO Summit on Disability (12 March 2001).

[27] See P Herzog, 'Giving Shape to a European Civil Society and Opening Up the Institutional System' in O De Schutter, N Lebessis and J Paterson (eds), *Governance in the European Union* (Luxembourg, Office for Official Publications of the European Communities, 2001).

terms, one may refer to the work done by disability organisations which started their lobbying activities of Ad Hoc Committee before its first meeting in July 2002 in order to obtain access to sessions and meetings.[28] The Ad Hoc Committee was charged to take into account proposals and contributions for a disability rights treaty not only by states and relevant UN bodies, but by observers, entities and agencies, regional commissions and intergovernmental organisations, as well as civil society including NGOs, national disability and human rights institutions and independent experts.

The pressure exercised by disability organisations and advocates produced successful outcomes. To give an example, the UN General Assembly adopted a resolution concerning the participation of persons with disabilities in the Ad Hoc Committee on a comprehensive and integral international convention on protection and promotion of the rights and dignity of persons with disabilities.[29] The General Assembly recommended the Secretary General to facilitate the access and participation by persons with disabilities in the meetings and deliberations of the Ad Hoc Committee. To this end, the Assembly requested that UN meetings were organised in conference rooms well equipped to facilitate the participation of persons with mobility-related and other physical disabilities. Moreover, it demanded the adoption, to the extent necessary and possible, of measures to enable persons with hearing disabilities to participate in the deliberations of the Ad Hoc Committee.

The General Assembly expressly introduced the conditions for legitimate and active participation of NGOs in the discussions within the Ad Hoc Committee. The Assembly decided to allow access to all NGOs enjoying consultative status with the Economic and Social Council.[30] The UN body also extended the possibility to participate to those NGOs not accredited previously to the Ad Hoc Committee. The Assembly gave the opportunity to most non-accredited organisations to apply to the Secretariat for obtaining such accreditation, through the submission of all the information on the competence of the organisation and the relevance of its activities to the work of the Committee. The Ad Hoc Committee established certain and clear modalities for the NGOs' participation in the debate concerning the adoption of a comprehensive international instrument on the rights of persons with disabilities.[31] In doing so, NGOs had the opportunity to attend any public

[28] MA Stein and JE Lord, 'Participation in International Agreements as Transformative Social Change: The UN Convention on the Rights of Persons with Disabilities' in J Heymann (ed), *Making Rights Real* (Cambridge, Cambridge University Press, 2012).

[29] UN General Assembly, 'Participation of persons with disabilities in the Ad Hoc Committee on a Comprehensive and Integral International Convention on Protection and Promotion of the Rights and Dignity of Persons with Disabilities', UN Doc Dec 56/474 (23 July 2002).

[30] UN General Assembly, 'Accreditation and participation of non-governmental organizations in the Ad Hoc Committee on a Comprehensive and Integral International Convention on Protection and Promotion of the Rights and Dignity of Persons with Disabilities', UN Doc A/RES 56/510 (23 July 2002).

[31] UN General Assembly, 'Report of the Ad Hoc Committee Established by UNGA Res A/56/168', UN Doc A/RES/56/168 (19 December 2001) First Session (2002).

meeting and make statements. They were also allowed to receive copies of the official documents and make written or other presentations.

It may be argued that the drafting process within the Ad Hoc Committee represented a unique opportunity for civil society organisations (CSOs) to lobby and advocate for the rights of persons with disabilities.

ii. The Working Group on the Convention: Mixing State Delegates and Stakeholders

New Zealand's Ambassador Don McKay, Chairman of the Ad Hoc Committee, emphasised that the process of negotiating the CRPD 'truly enshrined the slogan of the international disability movement, "nothing about us without us"'.[32] The involvement of NGOs in the drafting process reached its peak after the second meeting of the Ad Hoc Committee convened in June 2003. Thus, during this meeting it was formally decided to set up a Working Group with the goal of preparing a draft text for the Convention, which would have provided the basis for future negotiations by Member States.[33] Non-governmental stakeholders, such as the European Disability Forum, Disabled Peoples' International (DPI) and Rehabilitation International made significant contributions to the Convention's elaboration.

The Working Group was composed of 12 NGOs, one representative from a human rights institution (the South African Human Rights Commission) and 27 representatives of national governments.[34] A fundamental role was performed by DPI, a human rights organisation engaged in the protection of disabled people's rights and the promotion of their full and equal participation in society. DPI had the ability to draw together the initiatives of several disability organisations in order to speak with a single voice during the negotiations. To this end, international disability organisations and NGOs decided to create the International Disability Caucus for shared scope to comment and influence the provisions' drafting. In doing so, DPI also favoured the participation of advocates from developing countries and arranged valuable workshops for enhancing the lobbying skills of the participants in UN meetings.[35]

[32] D McKay, 'The Convention on the Rights of Persons with Disabilities: A Benchmark for Action' (2007) 56 *International Rehabilitation Reviews* 2.

[33] The Working Group established by the Ad Hoc Committee met from 5 to 16 January 2004 to draft a text of an international convention on the rights of persons with disabilities. See also R Lang, 'Human Rights and Disability – New and Dynamic Perspective with the United Nations Convention on Disability' (2006) 17 *Asia Pacific Disability Rehabilitation Journal* 3.

[34] The Working Group was established by the Ad Hoc Committee in order to meet from 5 to 16 January 2004 to draft a text of an international convention on the rights of persons with disabilities.

[35] MA Stein and JE Lord 'Participation in International Agreements as Transformative Social Change: The UN Convention on the Rights of Persons with Disabilities' (2008) 83 *Washington Law Review* 449.

iii. Civil Society's Main Achievements

The participation of organisations of people with disabilities along with human rights institutions as full members of the Working Group ensured that the Convention effectively took into account disabled rights.[36]

It may be said that advocacy organisations successfully achieved global recognition of disability as a human rights issue. For instance, NGOs and National Human Rights Institutions (NHRIs) strongly advocated for the adoption of a definition of disability. To the same extent, they supported the adoption of a progressive 'social model' rather than the traditional and restrictive medical approach to disability.[37] By contrast, state delegations preferred to avoid the inclusion of a comprehensive definition of disability that would have been discordant with narrow national laws.[38] The final adoption of fundamental guidelines reflecting the 'social model' of disability symbolises a successful compromise obtained by virtue of the participation of non-governmental stakeholders in the drafting process.

To give another example, all German Disability Council associations, the European Women's Lobby and the International Disability Caucus promoted the acknowledgement of multi-discrimination against women with disabilities in the CRPD's framework.[39] A twin-track approach based on both gender and disability grounds found the opposition of several States Parties because of the existing protection guaranteed by the Convention on the Elimination of All Forms of Discrimination Against Women.[40] Nonetheless, disabilities organisations achieved the specific recognition of the vulnerability of women with disabilities within a separate and independent provision dealing exclusively with women's issues (Article 6 CRPD).

The unprecedented level of participation and lobbying activities of civil society groups brought about notable changes in the drafting of the Convention. The negotiations of the CRPD show an innovative and fascinating framework with regard to the adoption of international legal instruments because the participation of civil society has actively informed the process for making international human rights law.

[36] A Dhanda, 'Constructing a New Human Rights Lexicon: Convention on the Rights of Persons with Disabilities' (2008) 5 *SUR International Journal of Human Rights* 42.

[37] G de Búrca, 'The EU in the Negotiation of the UN Disability Convention' (2010) 35 *European Law Review* 174.

[38] H Woodburn, 'Nothing about us without Civil Society: The Role of Civil Society Actors in the Formation of the UN Convention on the Rights of Persons with Disabilities' (2013) 7 *Political Perspectives* 75.

[39] S Arnade and S Haefner, *Standard Interpretation of the UN Convention on the Rights of Persons with Disabilities (CRPD) from a Female Perspective, Position and Reference Paper on the Significance of References to Women and Gender in the Convention on the Rights of Persons with Disabilities* (Berlin, Netzwerk Artikel, 2011).

[40] Woodburn (n 38) 88.

III. Civil Society's Role in Implementing the CRPD at National Level

The significant contribution of NGOs to the development of a new participatory governance at the international and national levels also emerges from the framework for monitoring the implementation of the CRPD. It calls for the full participation of civil society, in particular persons with disabilities and their representative organisations in the monitoring process. In other words, civil society is called to exercise effective influence on the implementation of the law and the application of disability rights in practice. To this end, the Convention points out a fundamental institutional change in order to accelerate the concrete implementation of the rights of persons with disabilities.[41] Article 33(2) of the CRPD sets forth that:

> States Parties shall, in accordance with their legal and administrative systems, maintain, strengthen, designate or establish within the State Party, a framework, including one or more independent mechanisms, as appropriate, to promote, protect and monitor implementation of the present Convention. When designating or establishing such a mechanism, States Parties shall take into account the principles relating to the status and functioning of national institutions for protection and promotion of human rights.

The idea of creating independent mechanisms to promote, protect and monitor human rights in line with the Paris Principles is not completely new under international law.[42] The first treaty introducing these independent mechanisms was the 2006 Optional Protocol to the Convention against Torture and other Cruel, Inhuman or Degrading Treatment or Punishment, which lays down the obligation to set up national mechanisms for the prevention of torture at the domestic level.[43] The establishment of independent national mechanisms represents an opportunity to strengthen human rights protection. International institutions cannot guarantee an appropriate level of respect for human rights without effective national systems that operate to achieve the same outcome. For this reason, the CRPD created a legal bridge between the international and national levels in order to facilitate structural changes and concretely improve the life of persons with disabilities. The Convention expressly refers to the Paris Principles for the creation of such mechanisms, as they constitute a set of international standards which frame the functioning of NHRIs. These guidelines were adopted during the

[41] G De Beco, 'Article 33(2) of the Convention on the Rights of Persons with Disabilities: Another Role for National Human Rights Institutions?' (2011) 29 *Netherlands Quarterly of Human Rights* 84.

[42] ibid. See UN General Assembly, 'Principles relating to the Status of National Institutions' adopted by General Assembly resolution 48/134 of 20 December 1993', UN Doc A/RES/48/134 (20 December 1993) (Paris Principles).

[43] Optional Protocol to the Convention against Torture and other Cruel, Inhuman or Degrading Treatment or Punishment (adopted on 18 December 2002, entered into force on 22 June 2006).

1993 World Conference on Human Rights in Vienna and aim to guarantee the independent work of NHRIs for implementing human rights.[44]

A. Institutionalising Civil Society

NHRIs have important responsibilities such as the submission of opinions, recommendations, proposal and reports on any matters concerning the promotion and protection of human rights to government, parliament and any other competent body.[45] Moreover, they perform the main task of fostering and ensuring harmonisation of national legislation, regulations and practices with the international human rights instruments to which the state is a party, and their effective implementation.[46] NHRIs should also 'publicize human rights and efforts to combat all forms of discrimination by increasing public awareness, especially through information and education and by making use of all press organs'.[47] NHRIs are dynamic and pluralistic hubs which incorporate state and non-state actors in compliance with the Paris Principles.[48]

The involvement of civil society groups is expressly mentioned by the provisions regarding the composition of such national mechanisms. According to the Paris Principles, the composition of national institutions and the appointment of its members 'shall be established in accordance with a procedure which affords all necessary guarantees to ensure the pluralist representation of the social forces (of civilian society) involved in the protection and promotion of human rights'. In particular, NHRIs' structure should include specific categories such as

> non-governmental organizations responsible for human rights and efforts to combat racial discrimination, trade unions, concerned social and professional organizations, for example, associations of lawyers, doctors, journalists and eminent scientists; trends in philosophical or religious thought; universities and qualified experts; Parliament and Government departments.[49]

This backdrop highlights the importance of involving of NGOs in the delicate process of reinforcing the rule of law and implementing human rights. National independent mechanisms can rely on the collaboration of NGOs that have awareness and expertise in issues concerning marginalised individuals. Article 33(2) of the CRPD represents fertile ground for the active inclusion of civil society in the complex challenge of bringing rights home.

[44] Paris Principles (n 42).
[45] ibid, 3(A).
[46] ibid, 3(B).
[47] ibid, 3(G).
[48] De Beco (n 41) 91.
[49] Paris Principles, Principle 2, 'Composition and guarantees of independence and pluralism'.

At the national level, the direct participation of persons with disabilities emerges both from the composition of independent national institutions and their formal relationship with civil society. For instance, the British Equality and Human Rights Commission requires that at least one member of the 15 commissioners is a person with a disability.[50] The Scottish Human Rights Commission requires that it should be composed of commissioners with NGO or academic backgrounds.[51] A broad representation of civil society can also be found in the composition of the Board of Trustees of the German Institute for Human Rights which encompasses human rights NGOs, media and academic exponents.[52] In particular, in accordance with Article 33(2) of the Convention, in May 2009 the German government founded the National CRPD Monitoring Body at the German Institute for Human Rights. Italy has also established a national Observatory concerning persons with disabilities that includes several members of NGOs and civic associations.[53]

In addition to the formal involvement of civil society representatives in the independent national bodies mentioned above, NGOs generate an influential impact in the monitoring process through positive actions and systematic engagements. A good practice is represented by the National CRPD Monitoring Body in Germany which has the duty to assess the situation of persons with disabilities within the country through regular meetings with disability advocacy organisations, the inspection of care facilities and consultations with experts. To this end, it can release statements and recommendations in relation to political, administrative and judicial decisions.[54] This shows that the Monitoring Body works closely with civil society organisations; in fact it hosts the Civil Society Consultations in Berlin three times each year. Consultations take place in inclusive and accessible environments and promote the open exchange of experiences between the National CRPD Monitoring Body and civil society disability advocacy organisations. Moreover, the Civil Society Consultations also focus on the importance of planning shared strategies for the implementation of the rights of persons with disabilities. Currently, more than 60 organisations are regularly invited to participate in these events. According to the rules of the German institution, consultations are theoretically open to all civic associations and NGOs that are interested in issues concerning the CRPD's application, but only those organisations formally invited by the Monitoring Body have the right to participate. However, it may be said that Germany assimilated the fundamental objectives of Article 33(2) of the CRPD by means of the creation of a national institution tailored to the participatory requirements emphasised by the CRPD.

[50] UK Equality Act 2006.

[51] European Union Agency for Fundamental Rights (FRA), *Strong and effective national human rights institutions challenges, promising practices and opportunities* (Luxembourg, Publications Office of the European Union, 2020).

[52] The German Institute for Human Rights was established in March 2001 on the recommendation of the German Federal Parliament.

[53] Act No 18/2009 of 3 March 2009, pursuant to inter-Ministerial decree no 16 of 6 July 2010.

[54] Information on how the National CRPD Monitoring Body works is available at: www.institut-fuer-menschenrechte.de/en/monitoring-body/.

Undoubtedly, cooperation with civil society is an essential element of the system outlined by the Convention in order to enrich the implementation process of the law. The designation of independent and pluralistic mechanisms composed by NGOs and persons with disabilities fosters the implementation of the CRPD's provisions. The Convention recognises those obstacles that prevent States Parties guaranteeing the protection of all vulnerable individuals and provides a flexible framework which promotes a partnership between state and non-state actors. It is submitted here that it is necessary to maintain a sort of continuity between the contribution of disability rights advocacy groups to the CRPD's drafting and the following implementation process. In doing so, transformative changes are more likely to occur by virtue of civil society's permanent participation throughout the entire policy chain. In the EU context, several countries are acting in compliance with the principle of participatory democracy embodied in the innovative treaty's scenario. Different actors such as NHRIs, NGOs, human rights organisations and civic associations along with governments are fully involved at all levels for realising the ambitious goal of an inclusive society. Traditional legal tools, new bottom-up strategies and participatory conditions must be combined to transpose international obligations into the national realm.

B. Awareness-Raising: A Synergetic Action between States Parties and NGOs

Public campaigns and activities are also fundamental instruments for increasing citizens' awareness of transnational issues and improving social attitudes towards persons with disabilities.[55] Public awareness and civic education can contribute to consolidate the legal framework for the protection of persons with disabilities. The concept of 'awareness-raising' is expressly embodied in the CRPD and refers to the duty of States Parties to raise awareness throughout society, including at the family level, regarding persons with disabilities, and to foster respect for the rights and dignity of persons with disabilities.[56] States Parties have the positive obligation to introduce effective measures for combating stereotypes, prejudices and harmful practices relating to persons with disabilities, including those based on sex and age. Moreover, they are called upon to promote awareness of the capabilities and contributions of persons with disabilities.

Hence, the Convention recognises States Parties as duty-holders in the crucial process of the awareness-raising of disabilities rights in society and indicates specific measures for pursuing this objective. The measures required by Article 8(2) of the CRPD seek to change social attitudes towards persons with disabilities. To this end, they promote the improvement of the education system, the support

[55] Scholte (n 5) 17.

[56] Art 8 CRPD (Awareness-raising).

of the media and the adoption of awareness-training programmes regarding persons with disabilities. The Convention provides the opportunity to implement human rights through 'non-legislative methods' thus moving beyond the classical structures of previous international human rights treaties.[57]

Civic awareness of disability rights depends considerably on the efforts of those NGOs that are key players in raising awareness of such issues throughout society. The lack of participation of civil society at international or national level would jeopardise achieving this crucial objective. Thereby, States Parties cannot underestimate the fundamental contribution of NGOs for carrying out social education activities and attracting the attention of the media. The Convention confers an unprecedented duty on States Parties to raise awareness of disability issues and requires the vital involvement of representative organisations of persons with disabilities in order to effectively bring change at the national level. The synergetic action of States Parties and NGOs constitutes an essential partnership to engage the public community in a dynamic dialogue on disability rights, cultural and social values.

IV. Participatory Democracy in the EU: From the White Paper to the Lisbon Treaty

The striking involvement of NGOs in drafting, monitoring and implementing the CRPD raises challenging issues with regard to the role of civil society in the EU system. The CRPD's adoption encourages the development of good governance at the international level and highlights the beneficial outcomes of civil society's consultation. As mentioned above, Article 4(3) lays down the crucial concept of 'nothing about us without us' in order to promote a permanent and productive consultation between governments and persons with disabilities.

Participatory rights are not incompatible with the traditional model of representative democracy, but rather constitute a fundamental tool to legitimate democracy and reinforce the idea of European citizenship.[58] European institutions have a long history of informal consultations with the voluntary sector. This form of cooperation was expressly acknowledged for the first time by Declaration 23 of the Treaty on European Union,[59] which stresses 'the importance, in pursuing the objectives of Article 117 of the Treaty establishing the European Community, of cooperation between the latter and charitable associations and foundations

[57] M Stein and P Stein, 'Beyond Disability Rights' (2007) 58 *Hastings Law Journal* 1203. See also, P Harpur, 'Embracing the New Disability Rights Paradigm: The Importance of the Convention on the Rights of Persons with Disabilities' (2012) 27 *Disability & Society* 1.

[58] L Pech, 'La solution au "déficit démocratique": une nouvelle gouvernance pour l'Union Européenne?' (2003) 2 *Journal of European Integration* 131.

[59] Treaty on European Union [1992] OJ C 191/1.

as institutions responsible for welfare establishments and services'. Civil society can therefore perform a complementary role in the decision-making process and ensure that policymakers at the EU level systematically consider the perspectives and grassroots experiences of citizens to provide effective policies. In addition, voluntary associations can disseminate information from the European level down to the local level to increase citizens' awareness and promote a common European identity.

Against this background, the EU Commission proposed not jeopardising creativity and free expression of civil society through over-bureaucratised and institutionalised procedures of consultation.[60] To this end, it recommended the introduction of flexible but systematic relations between the voluntary sector and the European institutions without compromising the principle of subsidiarity and the specificities of each Member State.

The necessity to update the EU political system has also been reaffirmed in the White Paper of the Commission on European Governance.[61] Political leaders admitted the existence of an increasing mistrust of EU institutions and a deep lack of confidence in a complex and undefinable system such as the European Union. As a result, the EU Commission put emphasis on the commitment to renew the EU political framework by means of a less top-down model and on complementing its policies with non-legislative tools.[62]

The White Paper basically reflects those fundamental values underlying the idea of participatory democracy and outlines five principles of good governance: openness, participation, accountability, effectiveness and coherence. The concept of openness affects the functioning of the EU institutions which should operate in a more open manner. They should constantly release communications concerning their actions and decisions in an accessible and understandable language for the general public. Participation influences the quality of EU policies and implies the involvement of civil society in the entire 'policy chain, from conception to implementation' on the basis of an 'inclusive approach'.[63] Accountability requires a clarification of roles in the legislative and executive procedures with the purpose of assessing the political and legal responsibilities of EU institutions. Effectiveness concerns the adequate impact of policies at the national level and the proportional implementation of law, which have to respond to clear and shared objectives. Coherence is an essential element of future EU policies for solving urgent issues relating to climate and demographic changes, diversity and European enlargement. For this purpose, the White Paper calls for strong political leadership and institutional responsibility to advance a cohesive approach within the EU multilayered

[60] European Commission, 'Promoting the role of voluntary organisations and foundations in Europe', COM(97) 241 final, [1998] OJ C 95.

[61] European Commission, 'European Governance – A White Paper', COM 428 final ([2001] OJ C 287/1).

[62] ibid.

[63] ibid, II. Principles of good governance.

system. These strategic commitments launched by the Commission remain decisive and impelling matters in the current EU agenda.

The Treaty of Lisbon also emphasises the importance of strengthening the participation of civil society in the EU political debate. Thus, according to Article 15 of the Treaty on the Functioning of the European Union (TFEU):[64]

> In order to promote good governance and ensure the participation of civil society, the Union's institutions, bodies, offices and agencies shall conduct their work as openly as possible. The European Parliament shall meet in public, as shall the Council when considering and voting on a draft legislative act. Any citizen of the Union, and any natural or legal person residing or having its registered office in a Member State, shall have a right of access to documents of the Union's institutions, bodies, offices and agencies, whatever their medium, subject to the principles and the conditions to be defined in accordance with this paragraph.

The TFEU tends to move towards a broader participatory democracy for citizens in European affairs and recognises that political institutions have to build democratic connections with people to launch more effective and relevant policies.[65] However, despite these efforts the EU continues to denote significant democratic shortcomings,[66] in particular with regard to the lack of procedural or 'input legitimacy',[67] which requires the inclusion of those who are affected by a regulation in the decisional procedure.[68]

The concept of participatory democracy entails a decision-making process which involves all stakeholders and is based on 'the action of interest groups and citizens' initiatives'.[69] It is different from the idea of representative democracy that relies on a peculiar form of legitimacy by input in accordance with which citizens are represented at Union level by voting at European and national elections.[70]

A. The Inclusive Process of the EUCFR's Adoption: The 'Convention' Method

Participatory democracy has not been fully realised in the EU system, but significant developments are under way. For instance, the EU Charter of Fundamental Rights (EUCFR) was adopted on the basis of an unusually transparent and inclusive

[64] Consolidated version of the Treaty on the Functioning of the European Union [2008] OJ C115/471.

[65] European Commission, 'European Governance – A White Paper' (n 61).

[66] See also, D Ferri, 'European Citizens … Mind the Gap! Some Reflections on Participatory Democracy in the EU' (2013) 5 *Perspectives on Federalism* 56.

[67] F Scharpf, *Governing in Europe* (Oxford, Oxford University Press, 1999).

[68] D Ferri, 'Participation in EU Governance: A "Multi-Level" Perspective and a "Multifold" Approach' in C Fraenkel-Haeberle et al (eds), *Citizen Participation in Multi-Level Democracies* (Leiden, Brill–Nijhoff, 2015).

[69] European Economic and Social Committee, 'The Role and contribution of civil society organisations in the building of Europe', CES 851/99 (22 September 1999) point 5.2.

[70] O De Schutter, 'Europe in Search of its Civil Society' (2002) 8 *European Law Journal* 198.

process.[71] During the drafting of the Charter there was wide and plural participation of different actors such as jurists, human rights experts in the EU legal order, NGOs and civic associations. The Charter's elaboration has seen the coexistence of legal technicians and political advocacy groups. According to Olivier De Schutter, the total openness of the decisional procedure encourages the legitimacy of the process, but requires a 'structured' participation of civil society.[72]

The scholar underlined the side effects provoked by open and broad participation without definite rules and guidelines. During the Charter's drafting, this openness shifted the power from its 62 members to the Secretariat of the Convention engaged with the evaluation of several amendments presented to reshape the final document. Moreover, the collective decision on the Charter brought about a fragmentation of responsibilities because none of the actors claimed paternity of the deliberation. The lack of certain rules concerning the requirements to participate in the drafting process downgraded the right to 'be consulted' to a simple right to 'freedom of expression'. In light of these deficiencies, De Schutter suggested opening up intergovernmental conferences to those organisations that represent common concerns at the EU level by adopting formal procedures to select those interest groups that can effectively inform the deliberative process.

In the first place, CSOs have to represent the interests of European society and be permanently based in the EU. The criteria of 'representativeness' must be the first requirement to be assessed in order to allow these organisations to take part in the decision-making process. The Economic and Social Committee also states that 'the assessment of the degree of representativeness of NGOs must under no circumstances be based solely on quantitative criteria, it must also involve qualitative criteria'.[73] The Committee holds that representativeness of civic organisations should be measured not only in relation to the number of members they represent, but that the 'judgement must take account of the ability of such bodies to put forward constructive proposals and to bring specialist knowledge to the process of democratic opinion-forming and decision-making'.[74] Therefore, NGOs have to guarantee an adequate level of expertise to flesh out the political arena and establish a real dialogue with the EU institutions. Civil organisations would not merely have the right to be heard, but they would be entitled to receive feedback concerning the impact of their proposals on the decision-making process.

The 'Convention' method has also been applied during the elaboration of the EU Constitutional Treaty, which attracted the attention of CSOs and participatory democracy advocates.[75] However, the drafting of the EUCFR still symbolises the

[71] ibid.

[72] ibid, 208.

[73] European Economic and Social Committee, 'The Commission and non-governmental organisations: building a stronger partnership', CES 811/2000 (13 July 2000) 4, point 2.2.5.

[74] ibid, 4.

[75] B Finke, 'Civil Society Participation in EU Governance' (2007) 2 *Living Reviews in European Governance* 4.

most relevant experiment in good governance at EU level, but at the same time reveals shortcomings and weaknesses of an incomplete model of participatory democracy. The concept of participatory governance is a crucial point of reference for the EU's future and requires an output-oriented paradigm of citizen involvement. This governance approach intended 'as a process and a state whereby public and private actors engage in the international regulation of societal relationships and conflicts'[76] is a necessary condition for the development of the EU system.

B. How to Improve EU Participatory Democracy? The Good Practice of the CRPD

The CRPD's adoption constitutes a good exercise in participatory democracy, which offers some guidelines to structure the participation of civil society in the political arena. A focal point regards the accreditation and participation of NGOs in the decision-making process.

The drafting of the EU Charter of Fundamental Rights has been characterised by a total and 'random' openness. This means that the participation of NGOs in the decision-making process has not been informed by clear guidelines to assess the 'representativeness' of civil society groups.

By contrast, the involvement of NGOs in the UN Ad Hoc Committee's work of the CRPD has been regulated by precise and formal rules. The accreditation of NGOs has been granted to all NGOs enjoying consultative status with the Economic and Social Council.[77] In addition, participation has also been broadened to those NGOs that could demonstrate they can carry out relevant activities in respect to the work of the Committee. The application to be accredited to the Ad Hoc Committee was also based on clear requirements and accurate conditions. NGOs had to submit an application package containing specific information such as

> the purpose of the organization, the programs and activities of the organisations in areas relevant to the Ad Hoc Committee, confirmation of the activities of the organization at the national, regional or international level, copies of the annual or other reports of the organization with financial statements, a description of the membership of the organizations and a copy of the constitution and by-laws of the organization.[78]

[76] B Kohler-Koch and B Rittenberger, 'Review Article: The Governance Turn in EU Studies' (2006) 3 *Journal of Common Market Studies* 205.

[77] UN General Assembly, 'Accreditation and participation of non-governmental organizations in the Ad Hoc Committee on a Comprehensive and Integral International Convention on Protection and Promotion of the Rights and Dignity of Persons with Disabilities' (n 30).

[78] UN General Assembly, 'Report of the Ad Hoc Committee Established by UNGA Res A/56/168' (n 31) Seventh Session (2006).

In this way, participation of civil society groups in the decision-making process has been well structured and formalised.

It may be also argued that the establishment of precise rules concerning the participation of civil society is easier when the treaty being drafted focuses on a very specific issue (disability rights) rather than a whole set of human rights. This statement may be debunked by underlining the legal complexity of an international human rights treaty such as the CRPD that addresses several aspects of human rights law including accessibility, gender equality, legal capacity, health and development, work, education, situations of risks and humanitarian emergencies. The involvement of NGOs with different backgrounds and objectives has contributed to improving the quality of the protection ensured by the CRPD.

Those NGOs involved in the CRPD's elaboration properly represented the main interests of civil society and met the qualitative criteria established by the Economic and Social Committee. The lack of appropriate 'representativeness' that reduced the quality of democratic participation in the Charter's drafting has been successfully overcome in the UN Convention's framework. The model of participatory democracy embodied in the CRPD may offer important solutions in respect of the problem of 'representativeness' which undermines the functioning of global and EU governance.

Civil society groups may not reflect all the interests for which they purport to act and increase inequalities relating to class, gender, nationality, race and religion in case they depict a disproportional representation of society.[79] To avoid 'fake' inclusiveness, the involvement of CSOs in deliberative procedures should be based on a strict control of their representative capacity. This assessment should be mainly focused on qualitative criteria, such as the capacity of NGOs to represent common interests and carry out effective advocacy activities. In the CRPD's context, necessary prerequisites have been clarified ex ante in order to prove the high quality of the NGOs' activities for promoting disability rights at the international level and obtain accreditation to the Ad hoc Committee. A structured participation also contributes to consolidate NGOs' efforts that would 'receive appropriate feedback on how their contributions and opinions have affected the eventual policy decision, thereby making the relationship a real dialogue'.[80] To conclude, the imposition of certain requirements for authorising the participation of civic organisations in the institutional system constitutes an essential condition to enhance the effectiveness of civil dialogue. Such a structuration would not hamper the autonomy of CSOs; on the contrary it promotes the participation of 'representative' groups that can advance constructive proposals and bring relevant expertise to the decision-making process.

[79] Scholte (n 5) 20.

[80] European Commission, 'The Commission and Non-Governmental Organisations: building a stronger partnership', presented by President Prodi and Vice-President Kinnock (18 January 2000).

In light of these observations, civil dialogue stands out for its beneficial effects in the political and legal background of the CRPD. Participatory rights are actively emerging both from the new international human rights instruments and from the increasing demand of good governance at the EU level. The institutional architecture of the European Union now opens the doors to civil society. Article 15 of the TFEU is a key provision to further enhance 'input legitimacy'.

In particular, the European Union should 'learn the lesson' from the CRPD and promote a structured participation of civil society in the decision-making process. The legal challenges stemming from the EU's ratification of the CRPD are an unmissable opportunity to start a new participatory democratic course which gives a voice to invisible groups of people and produces effective equality norms.

3

Ten Years after EU Accession to the CRPD: From Theory to Reality

This chapter will look at how the principles of equality and non-discrimination are conceptualised and implemented in the EU legal system. A wide focus will be given to the analysis of the main judgments of the Court of Justice of the European Union (CJEU) concerning the interpretation and application of the framework. This chapter will assess how the prohibition of discrimination on grounds of disability is understood in the case law of the CJEU and will examine whether the CJEU's interpretation of EU law is in line with the Convention on the Rights of Persons with Disabilities (CRPD).

I. An Overview of the Prohibition of Discrimination under EU Law

The concepts of equality and non-discrimination are deeply rooted in the EU legal framework. Article 2 of the Treaty on European Union (TEU) for instance establishes that:

> [T]he Union is founded on the values of respect for human dignity, freedom, democracy, equality, the rule of law and respect for human rights, including the rights of persons belonging to minorities. These values are common to the Member States in a society in which pluralism, non-discrimination, tolerance, justice, solidarity and equality between women and men prevail.

Moreover, Article 3(3) of the TEU points out that the Union 'shall combat social exclusion and discrimination, and shall promote social justice and protection, equality between women and men, solidarity between generations and protection of the rights of the child'. Currently, the Treaty of Lisbon has helped consolidate the principles of equality and non-discrimination as fundamental values of the Union by imposing a mainstreaming duty to prohibit discrimination within EU institutions. Article 10 of the Treaty on the Functioning of the European Union (TFEU), as amended by the Treaty of Lisbon, lays down that 'in defining and implementing its policies and activities, the Union shall aim to combat discrimination based on sex, racial or ethnic origin, religion or belief, disability, age or sexual orientation'. Actions to address discrimination require the 'consent procedure', and the consent of the European Parliament is needed to adopt a Directive. Article 19 of the TFEU sets out that:

> Without prejudice to the other provisions of the Treaties and within the limits of the powers conferred by them upon the Union, the Council, acting unanimously in accordance with a special legislative procedure and after obtaining the consent of the European Parliament, may take appropriate action to combat discrimination based on sex, racial or ethnic origin, religion or belief, disability, age or sexual orientation.

According to the latter provisions, EU secondary law has to promote equality and ensure the protection against discrimination in the EU legal context. The importance of the prohibition of discrimination has also been confirmed by the CJEU in the famous case of *Mangold v Helm*,[1] where the Court declared non-discrimination on grounds of age to be a general principle of Community law.[2]

A. The EU Charter of Fundamental Rights

The right to equality and non-discrimination also plays a significant role in the EU Charter of Fundamental Rights (EUCFR), which acquired a legally binding status after the entry into force of the Treaty of Lisbon.[3] The Charter now binds both the EU institutions and Member States when they act within the scope of EU law[4] Article 21 of the Charter states that:

> 1. Any discrimination based on any ground such as sex, race, colour, ethnic or social origin, genetic features, language, religion or belief, political or any other opinion, membership of a national minority, property, birth, disability, age or sexual orientation shall be prohibited.
> 2. Within the scope of application of the Treaty establishing the European Community and of the Treaty on European Union, and without prejudice to the special provisions of those Treaties, any discrimination on grounds of nationality shall be prohibited.

The Charter provides a wider list of possible grounds of discrimination in comparison with the European Treaties as amended by the Lisbon Treaty, but at the same time it does not introduce any new rights in the area of EU anti-discrimination law. The Charter 'addresses discrimination by the institutions and bodies of the Union themselves, when exercising powers conferred under the Treaties, and by Member States only when they are implementing Union law'.[5]

[1] Case C-144/04 *Werner Mangold v Rüdiger Helm* [2005] ECR I-9981, ECLI:EU:C:2005:709.

[2] L Pech, 'Between Judicial Minimalism and Avoidance: The Court of Justice's Sidestepping of Fundamental Constitutional Issues in *Römer and Dominguez*' (2012) 49 *Common Market Law Review* 1841.

[3] Charter of Fundamental Rights of the European Union [2000] OJ C 364/01.

[4] G de Búrca, 'After the EU Charter of Fundamental Rights: The Court of Justice as a Human Rights Adjudicator?' (2013) 20 *Maastricht Journal of European and Comparative Law* 168.

[5] Explanations (1) relating to the Charter of Fundamental Rights (2007/C 303/02) [2007] OJ C303/17, Explanation on Article 21 Non-discrimination.

The Charter however represents an essential instrument for the interpretation of provisions of EU law, which contributes to improve the protection of fundamental human rights within the European Union. Article 47 of the EU Charter sets out the right to an effective remedy to everyone whose rights and freedoms guaranteed by the law of the Union might have been violated by executive power. As a result, the CJEU has been placed at the heart of the new EU architecture on fundamental rights and symbolises the key guarantor of the Charter.[6] The Court's legal reasoning has often made reference to the Charter's content since it became a legally binding instrument of EU law.[7] According to the Commission's report, EU courts have increasingly referred to the Charter in their judgments.[8] The number of decisions quoting the Charter grew from 43 in 2011 to 87 in 2012. In 2013, this number amounted to 113 and exponentially increased to 356 in 2018,[9] when the CJEU also referred to the Charter in a number of cases concerning non-discrimination.[10]

B. The Convention for the Protection of Human Rights and Fundamental Freedoms

Ultimately, it is worth noting that disability is not expressly included in the list of prohibited grounds in the European Convention on Human Rights (ECHR). Article 14 of the ECHR merely states that 'the enjoyment of the rights and freedoms … shall be secured without discrimination on any ground such as sex, race, colour, language, religion, political or other opinion, national or social origin, association with a national minority, property, birth or other status'. Despite that, the European Court of Human Rights (ECtHR), in the case of *Glor v Switzerland*, reiterated that Article 14 contains a non-exhaustive list of prohibited grounds, which also includes discrimination based on disability.[11]

Interestingly, the accession of the EU to the Convention became a legal obligation under the Treaty of Lisbon. Article 6(2) of the TEU, as amended by the Lisbon Treaty, provides that the European Union 'shall accede' to the Convention.

[6] S Carrera, M De Somer and B Petkova, 'The Court of Justice of the European Union as a Fundamental Rights Tribunal: Challenges for the Effective Delivery of Fundamental Rights in the Area of Freedom, Security and Justice' (2012) 49 CEPS Justice and Home Affairs Liberty and Security in Europe Papers.

[7] de Búrca (n 4) 169.

[8] EU Commission, *2014 Report on the application of the EU Charter of Fundamental Rights* (Luxembourg, Publications Office of the European Union, 2015).

[9] EU Commission, *2018 Report on the application of the EU Charter of Fundamental Rights* (Luxembourg, Publications Office of the European Union, 2019).

[10] Case C-414/16 *Egenberger v Evangelisches Werk für Diakonie und Entwicklung eV*, ECLI:EU:C:2018:257; and Case C-68/17 *IR v JQ*, ECLI:EU:C:2018:696; Case C-673/16, *Relu Adrian Coman and Others v Inspectoratul General pentru Imigrări and Ministerul Afacerilor Interne*, ECLI:EU:C:2018:385.

[11] *Glor v Switzerland*, App No 13444/04 (ECtHR, judgment 30 April 2009).

The EU's accession to the ECHR would bring about a comprehensive and coherent legal framework for protecting human rights across the continent. EU law would be subject to external control to ensure the observance of the rights and freedoms of the ECHR. However, accession to the Convention may create several issues in relation to the autonomy of the EU's legal order, the EU competences and the CJEU's position as the ultimate guardian of EU law.[12] In April 2013, following almost three years of technical discussions, a revised draft agreement was finalised from the 47 Council of Europe countries and the Commission to regulate EU accession to the ECHR.[13] In July 2013, the European Commission asked the CJEU for an opinion concerning the compatibility of the draft agreement with the EU Treaties. The Court concluded that the draft agreement was not compatible with EU law and provided a checklist of amendments to ensure its compatibility with the EU Treaties.[14]This context shows that the EU accession under the current draft agreement has become highly complicated. It is hoped therefore that the ECHR and EU authorities will find durable solutions to harmonise the judicial work of the ECtHR and the CJEU, enhancing the protection of fundamental fights in the Union system.

II. Disability Rights in the EU

Disability policy has always been regarded as part of the European social agenda.[15] EU social policy was consolidated by the introduction of the Treaty of Amsterdam on 1 May 1999. A remarkable aspect of the Treaty establishing the European Community, as amended by the Treaty of Amsterdam, was the adoption of a new anti-discrimination provision.[16] According to Article 13 of the EC Treaty:

> [W]ithout prejudice to the other provisions of this Treaty, and within the limits of the powers conferred by it upon the Community, the Council, acting unanimously on a proposal from the Commission, and after consulting the European Parliament, may take appropriate action to combat discrimination based on sex, racial or ethnic origin, religion or belief, disability, age or sexual orientation.

[12] X Groussot, T Lock and L Pech, 'EU Accession to the European Convention on Human Rights: A Legal Assessment of the Draft Accession Agreement of 14th October 2011' (2011) Foundation Robert Schuman, Policy Paper European Issues no 218.

[13] Fifth negotiation meeting between the Steering Committee for Human Rights (CDDH) ad hoc negotiation group and the European Commission on the accession of the European Union to the European Convention on Human Rights, Final report to the CDDH (Strasbourg, 10 June 2013).

[14] Opinion of the Court (Full Court) of 18 December 2014. Opinion pursuant to Article 218(11), ECLI:EU:C:2014:2454.

[15] A Waldschmidt, 'Disability Policy of the European Union: The Supranational Level' (2009) 4 *ALTER European Journal of Disability Research* 8.

[16] I Bryan, 'Equality and Freedom from Discrimination: Article 13 EU Treaty' (2002) 24 *Journal of Social Welfare and Family Law* 223.

The inclusion of this Article brought about a ground-breaking change at EU level, to the extent that it laid down the competence of the Community to launch legal measures to counteract discrimination on grounds of disability for the first time.[17] European disability policy has since been characterised by a rights-based approach which enshrines civil and social rights.[18] The key idea of this approach is that societal factors operate to exclude persons with disabilities from fully participating in society. As a consequence, such disabling barriers should be tackled by laws and policies to guarantee equal opportunity to persons with disabilities.[19]

In more practical terms, this led the Commission to enact a Community action programme (HELIOS I) to promote vocational training and rehabilitation, economic integration, social integration and an independent way of life for disabled people.[20] It also adopted a second programme to improve social integration and employment for persons with disabilities.[21] Moreover, a third disability programme (HELIOS II) was introduced to foster equal opportunities for and the integration of disabled people. This programme stressed the importance of the political mobilisation of persons with disabilities and established the European Disability Forum (EDF).[22] Finally, the 1993 Social Policy Green Paper introduced the fundamental concept of 'mainstreaming' intended as 'acceptance of people as full members of society, with opportunities for integrated education, training and employment, and to lead their lives independently'.[23] This new approach aimed at accelerating the integration of persons with disabilities into ordinary schools and their effective inclusion in the open labour market.

In line with these important changes, at the end of November 2000, the Council of Ministers adopted an 'anti-discrimination package' comprising two fundamental legal instruments: the Race Directive[24] and the Equality Framework Directive.[25]

[17] E Howard, 'The EU Race Directive: Time for Change?' (2007) 8 *International Journal of Discrimination and the Law* 237. See also on Disability Law and Policy in the EU, A Broderick and D Ferri, *International and European Disability Law and Policy: Text, Cases and Materials* (Cambridge, Cambridge University Press, 2019).

[18] D Mabbett, 'The Development of Rights-based Social Policy in the European Union: The Example of Disability Rights' (2005) 43 *Journal of Common Market Studies* 97.

[19] A Lawson, 'The EU Rights Based Approach to Disability: Strategies for Shaping an Inclusive Society' (2005) 6 *International Journal of Discrimination and the Law* 4269.

[20] HELIOS I (Second) Community Social Action Programme for Disabled People [1988] OJ L104/38.

[21] Memorandum of the Commission to the Council concerning the employment of disabled people in the European Community (COM 86(9) of 24 January 1986).

[22] HELIOS II (Third) Community Action Programme to Assist Disabled People [1993] OJ L56/30. See also, Mabbett (n 18) 108.

[23] European Commission, 'Green Paper European Social Policy: Options for the Union' COM(93) 551 final, 48.

[24] Directive 2000/43/EC of the Council of 29 June 2000 implementing the principle of equal treatment between persons irrespective of racial or ethnic origin [2000] OJ L180/22.

[25] Directive 2000/78/EC of the Council of 27 November 2000 establishing a general framework for equal treatment in employment and occupation [2000] OJ L303/16.

III. The EU Anti-Discrimination Framework: Directive 2000/78/EC

The Equality Framework Directive (Directive 2000/78/EC; the Equality Framework Directive) lays down a general framework for combating discrimination on grounds of religion or belief, disability, age or sexual orientation with regard to employment and occupation. The material scope of the Directive is confined to the area of employment and occupation.[26] By contrast, the Racial Equality Directive also covers access to and supply of goods and services, housing, education, transport, healthcare, social security and social assistance.[27]

The objective of the Equality Framework Directive is to ensure that persons with disabilities do not suffer discrimination and enjoy equal treatment in the workplace. To this end, Article 2 of the Directive establishes that 'the principle of equal treatment shall mean that there shall be no direct or indirect discrimination whatsoever on any of the grounds referred to in Article 1'. The Directive also considers harassment (Article 2.3) and instruction to discriminate (Article 2.4) as different forms of prohibited discrimination.

A. Exploring the Meaning of Direct Discrimination

According to Article 2(2)(a) of the Equality Framework Directive, direct discrimination on grounds of disability occurs 'where one person is treated less favourably than another is, has been or would be treated in a comparable situation'. The assessment of the less favourable treatment should be based on a comparative exercise. To this end, the comparator must not have the same characteristics as the claimant and must enjoy better treatment.[28]

Moreover, in the situation where it is not possible to identify the comparator, the Equality Framework Directive allows a comparison with a *previous* or *hypothetical* comparator by referring to another person who '*has been*' or '*would be*' treated more favourably.[29] By doing so, the Directive aims to enlarge the protection of persons with disabilities and permits the comparison with an individual

[26] R Whittle, 'The Framework Directive for Equal Treatment in Employment and Occupation: An Analysis from a Disability Rights Perspective' (2002) 27 *European Law Review* 303.

[27] L Waddington and A Lawson, *Disability and non-discrimination law in the European Union: An analysis of disability discrimination law within and beyond the employment field* (Luxembourg, Publications Office of the European Union, 2009).

[28] L Waddington, 'Fine-tuning Non-discrimination Law: Exceptions and Justifications Allowing for Different Treatment on the Ground of Disability' (2014) 15 *International Journal of Discrimination and Law* 1.

[29] R Whittle, 'The concept of disability discrimination and its legal construction in *Discrimination and affirmative action on the labour market – legal perspectives* (in preparation of the Swedish Presidency of the European Union) (National Institute for Working Life, Sweden, 6–7 November 2001).

who receives better treatment in a similar situation without sharing the same characteristics of the person discriminated against.

The Equality Framework Directive does not merely allow the possibility to compare a disabled person with a non-disabled individual, but it offers the additional opportunity to draw a comparator by referring to a person with different disabilities. The term '*another*' used by the Directive constitutes an open clause for identifying the comparator.[30] The Directive's approach seeks to overcome the legal shortcomings of national legislation that only take into account comparisons between a person who has a disability and another who has not.

B. Introducing the Concept of Indirect Discrimination

Article 2(2)(b) of the Equality Framework Directive lays down a comprehensive definition of indirect discrimination according to which

> indirect discrimination shall be taken to occur where an apparently neutral provision, criterion or practice would put persons having a particular religion or belief, a particular disability, a particular age, or a particular sexual orientation at a particular disadvantage compared with other persons unless:
>
> I. that provision, criterion or practice is objectively justified by a legitimate aim and the means of achieving that aim are appropriate and necessary, or
>
> II. as regards persons with a particular disability, the employer or any person or organisation to whom this Directive applies, is obliged, under national legislation, to take appropriate measures in line with the principles contained in Article 5 in order to eliminate disadvantages entailed by such provision, criterion or practice.[31]

This prohibition constitutes a fundamental tool for achieving substantive equality and reinforcing the protection of vulnerable groups of individuals. In the case of *Coleman v Attridge Law*, Advocate General Poiares Maduro of the CJEU stated that indirect discrimination should be intended as an inclusionary mechanism 'by obliging employers to take into account and accommodate the needs of individuals with certain characteristics'.[32] Indirect discrimination may occur where an employer's neutral policy or practice puts an employee in a disadvantaged position in comparison to other employees.[33] For instance, a job recruitment process that requires presentation skills may indirectly discriminate against an applicant who suffers from a stammer, and in particular where the presentation skills are not relevant to the job. This neutral practice is likely to be regarded as indirect

[30] ibid, 5.

[31] Art 2(2)(b) of Directive 2000/78/EC.

[32] Opinion of AG Poiares Maduro in Case C-303/06 *Coleman v Attridge Law* [2008] ECR I-05603, ECLI:EU:C:208:61.

[33] I Chopin and C Germaine-Sahl, *European Anti-Discrimination Law Review* (Luxembourg, Publications Office of the European Union, 2014).

discrimination in accordance with EU law. The Directive places great emphasis on this prohibition as it represents a significant percentage of disability discrimination and considerably enlarges the protection for persons with disabilities.[34]

C. Reasonable Accommodation: The Paramount Obligation

The main duty imposed on employers by the Equality Framework Directive relates to the introduction of necessary adaptations to the workplace in order to accommodate the special needs of persons with disabilities. Article 5 of the Directive lays down that:

> In order to guarantee compliance with the principle of equal treatment in relation to persons with disabilities, reasonable accommodation shall be provided. This means that employers shall take appropriate measures, where needed in a particular case, to enable a person with a disability to have access to, participate in, or advance in employment, or to undergo training, unless such measures would impose a disproportionate burden on the employer. This burden shall not be disproportionate when it is sufficiently remedied by measures existing within the framework of the disability policy of the Member State concerned.

The obligation to provide reasonable accommodation is the cornerstone of the Directive because it seeks to enable persons with disabilities to have access to, participate in, or advance in employment. The assessment of the proper accommodation must be based on a specific analysis of the individual situation and the employment at issue.[35]

The Equality Framework Directive determines the appropriate measures to adapt the workplace to the disability, such as the adaptation of premises and equipment, patterns of working time, the distribution of tasks or the provision of training or integration resources.[36] Reasonable accommodation must not impose an excessive inconvenience or cost to the employer. Recital 21 of the Preamble sets out the 'disproportionate burden' limit that should take into account the financial cost of the measures entailed, the scale and financial resources of the organisation and the possibility of obtaining public funding.

It may be said that the EU provision imposes a crucial binding obligation on employers to remove environmental barriers and promote substantive equality for persons with disabilities.[37] The Equality Framework Directive however fails

[34] Whittle, 'The Framework Directive for Equal Treatment in Employment and Occupation' (n 26) 5.

[35] Waddington and Lawson (n 27).

[36] Recital 20 of the Preamble to the Equality Framework Directive 2000/78/EC.

[37] JE Lord and R Brown, 'The Role of Reasonable Accommodation in Securing Substantive Equality for Persons with Disabilities: The UN Convention on the Rights of Persons with Disabilities' in MH Rioux, LA Basser and M Jones (eds), *Critical Perspectives on Human Rights and Disability Policy* (The Hague, Martinus Nijhoff, 2011).

to define the failure to make reasonable accommodation as a specific 'form of discrimination' as set out under the CRPD.[38] Lisa Waddington emphasises the importance of this classification because it may increase 'awareness of the rights-based nature of the duty to accommodate' and 'the seriousness of a failure to comply with this duty'.[39]

IV. Filling in the Gap: The Evolving Concept of Disability

In order to apply the legal guarantees enshrined in the Equality Framework Directive, the first fundamental step is to identify the conditions for a person to be classed as having disabilities. The Directive does not provide for a definition of disability or general guidelines on the personal scope of the legislation.[40] Therefore, national courts have faced serious obstacles in regard to the interpretation of the prohibition of discrimination on grounds of disability in the absence of any assistance from the CJEU. This is why the debate surrounding the legal category of disability quickly became a crucial issue for the Court to address.[41]

A. The EU Approach to Disability

The first important case referred to the CJEU with the purpose of clarifying the provision of the Equality Framework Directive that prohibits disability discrimination was *Chacón Navas v Eurest Colectividades SA*.[42] In this case, the national court asked whether a worker who had been dismissed solely because of her sickness could fall under the protection of the Directive. In addition, the national court referred another question in relation to the possibility of adding 'sickness' to the list of protected grounds covered by the Directive.

The preliminary ruling before the CJEU originated from national proceedings between Ms Chacón Navas and Eurest Colectividades SA (Eurest) concerning her dismissal while she was on leave of absence from her employment on grounds of sickness. Sonia Chacón Navas was employed by Eurest, a company

[38] L Waddington and A Broderick, *Realising equality: A comparison of the UN Convention on the Rights of Persons with Disabilities and EU equality and non-discrimination law* (Luxembourg, Publications Office of the European Union, 2018).

[39] L Waddington, 'Equal to the Task: Re-Examining EU Equality Law in Light of the United Nations Convention on the Rights of Persons with Disabilities' (2013) 4 *European Yearbook of Disability Law* 169, 190.

[40] Waddington and Lawson (n 27) 14.

[41] M Bell, 'The Implementation of European Anti-Discrimination Directives: Converging towards a Common Model?' (2008) 79 *Political Quarterly* 36.

[42] Case C-13/05 *Chacón Navas v Eurest Colectividades SA* [2006] ECR 1-6467, ECLI:EU:C:2006:456.

specialising in catering, and she was certified as unable to work on grounds of sickness. She was considered by the Public Health Service to not be in a position to return to work in the short term. The applicant was forced to stay at home for eight months due to her illness after which, on 28 May 2004, she received written notice of her dismissal. However, the notification letter did not lay down any specific reasons for the dismissal, while acknowledging that it was unlawful and offering her compensation. In the action before the Spanish court, Navas sought a declaratory judgment that her dismissal was void on the grounds of the unequal treatment and discrimination to which she had been subject. As a consequence, she sought reinstatement to the position in which she had previously been working.

The national court acknowledged that she was fired merely on account of her sickness. At the same time, it found that Spanish law did not recognise illness as protected grounds along with age, disability, gender, or race to void a dismissal.[43] The referring court observed that, according to Spanish case law, there are precedents to the effect that this type of dismissal is classified as unlawful rather than void because 'illness' and 'disability' are separate concepts.[44] It is worth noting that under Spanish law, dismissals are regarded as void in cases where they occur in violation of the employee's fundamental rights, such as the right not to be discriminated against on those grounds prohibited by the Constitution or by law.[45] Accordingly, an employee would obtain the right to be reinstated to their previous position. By contrast, dismissals are unlawful when they breach statutory requirements and the employer only has the obligation to compensate the former employee.[46] The Spanish court recognised the necessity to protect the worker in a timely manner under the prohibition of discrimination on grounds of disability because sickness is often capable of causing an irreversible disability.[47] It correctly argued that 'the protection intended by the legislature would, in large measure, be nullified because it would thus be possible to implement uncontrolled discriminatory practices'.[48] In light of this complex background, the Madrid court decided to refer two questions to the CJEU in order to get out of the impasse and in doing so, displayed a degree of sympathy for Ms Chacón Navas' situation.[49]

[43] V Perju, 'Impairment, Discrimination, and the Legal Construction of Disability in the European Union and the United States' (2011) 44 *Cornell International Law Journal* 280.

[44] *Chacón Navas v Eurest Colectividades SA* (n 42) para 21.

[45] Legislative Royal Decree No 1/1995 of 24 March 1995 approving the amended text of the Workers' Statute (Estatuto de los Trabajadores, BOE No 75 of 29 March 1995) 9654; 'the Workers' Statute') distinguishes between unlawful dismissal and void dismissal.

[46] ibid, Art 56(1) and (2) of the Workers' Statute.

[47] *Chacón Navas v Eurest Colectividades SA* (n 42) para 23.

[48] ibid.

[49] L Waddington, 'Case C-13/05, Chacón Navas v Eurest Colectividades SA, Judgment of the Grand Chamber of 11 July 2006' (2007) 44 *Common Market Law Review* 487.

i. *A First Controversial Approach of the CJEU*

In 2005, the CJEU made a pronounced influential judgment on the definition of disability under Directive 2000/78/EC. According to the Court, 'the concept of disability must be understood as referring to a limitation which results in particular from physical, mental or psychological impairments and which hinders the participation of the person concerned in professional life'.[50] In order for the limitation to fall under the category of disability, 'it must therefore be probable that it will last for a long time'.[51] Thus, the Court set out a distinction between temporary sickness and long-term disability.

The definition elaborated by the EU judges is quite controversial, as it is based on an obsolete and charitable model of disability.[52] The ruling placed strong emphasis on the personal impairments, which would hinder the full participation of persons with disabilities in professional life, rather than on discriminatory treatment. This approach moves away from the socio-political model that stresses the need to remove environmental barriers and encourages the inclusion of persons with disabilities within society.[53] The definition adopted by the CJEU did not take into account the guidance of the major EU institutions, which have all highlighted the importance of eliminating the social barriers that persons with disabilities face.[54] For instance, the Council affirmed its commitment to equal opportunities for people with disabilities and to the principle of avoiding or abolishing all forms of negative discrimination based solely on disability.[55] The Commission also emphasised that:

> Historically, the response to disability has been mainly one of social compensation through charity and the development of specialist caring services outside the mainstream of society. However necessary and well intentioned they might be, such responses have compounded the problem of exclusion and under-participation. The traditional approaches are slowly giving way to a stronger emphasis on identifying and removing the various barriers to equal opportunities and full participation in all aspects of life.[56]

The CJEU, first, failed to comply with the commitments and guidelines of the EU institutions which require accommodating the legitimate demands for equal rights of persons with disabilities who are no longer passive recipients of

[50] *Chacón Navas v Eurest Colectividades SA* (n 42) para 43.

[51] ibid, para 45.

[52] S Favalli and D Ferri, 'Defining Disability in the EU Non-Discrimination Legislation: Judicial Activism and Legislative Restraints' (2016) 22 *European Public Law* 541.

[53] E Flynn, *From Rhetoric to Action: Implementing the UN Convention on the Rights of Persons with Disabilities* (Cambridge, Cambridge University Press, 2011).

[54] Waddington and Lawson (n 27) 17.

[55] Council and Representatives of the Governments of the Member States, 'Equality of opportunity for people with disabilities' [1997] OJ C 12/1.

[56] Commission, 'A New European Community Disability Strategy' (Communication) COM(96) 406.

compensation.[57] This decision may be due to poor legal research carried out by the CJEU which did not take into account the emerging disability strategy embraced by the EU.

Second, the Court held that workers are not protected by the prohibition of discrimination on grounds of disability as soon as they develop any type of sickness. The CJEU overlooked the possibility that sickness is often the main cause of irreversible disability and that workers must be protected in a timely manner under the prohibition of discrimination on grounds of disability. The judges refused the arguments of the Advocate General who advised regarding those persons who suffer from long-term or permanent diseases as disabled.[58] This decision seems extremely vague. It did not distinguish between illnesses that have long-lasting effects and conditions that are not durable.[59] For instance, the UK Equality Act 2010 states that, for the purpose of deciding whether a person is disabled, a long-term effect of the impairment is one which has lasted at least 12 months.[60] It is worth noting that sickness was not regarded by analogy as additional grounds to those in relation to which Directive 2000/78/EC prohibits discrimination. By doing so, the Court confirmed a closed list of prohibited grounds of discrimination. However, the CJEU recently identified the legal circumstances under which a worker, who is temporarily unable to work, may be considered to have a disability. In the case of *Daouidi*, the CJEU overcame the main gaps of *Chacón Navas* and positively provided specific guidelines to determine the extent to which a long-term limitation amounts to disability.[61]

Finally, the CJEU gave an important interpretation of Article 5 of the Equality Framework Directive on the duty to provide reasonable accommodation and held that 'dismissal on grounds of disability is not justified by the fact that the person concerned is not competent, capable and available to perform the essential functions of his post'.[62] This interpretation is very significant because it reinforces the obligation of the employer to take appropriate measures in order to enable a person with a disability to have access to, participate in, or advance in employment. Hence, this obligation implies that employers cannot dismiss workers where they could perform their duties if reasonable accommodation is provided.

ii. Chacón Navas: *A Missed Opportunity*

The case of *Chacón Navas* represents the first decision of the CJEU dealing with the definition of disability under the Equality Framework Directive. The Court

[57] Commission, 'Equal opportunities for people with disabilities: A European Action Plan' (Communication) COM/2003/0650.

[58] *Chacón Navas v Eurest Colectividades SA* (n 42) Opinion of AG Geelhoed, para 85.

[59] Waddington, 'Case C-13/05, Chacón Navas v Eurest Colectividades SA' (n 49) 493.

[60] UK Equality Act 2010, Schedule 1, para 2.

[61] Case C-395/15 *Daouidi v Bootes Plus SL and Others*, ECLI:EU:C:2016:917.

[62] *Chacón Navas v Eurest Colectividades SA* (n 42) para 52.

was called upon to define the personal scope of the Directive and interpret the disability provisions concerning reasonable accommodation. The Court's approach raises several issues as it highlights a controversial 'medical model' of disability in conflict with the developments which had occurred at EU and international level.[63] It focuses on the individual's impairments, and not on the failure of society to consider such limitations. The main shortcoming of the judgment is that sickness itself is not enough to trigger protection under the prohibition of discrimination on grounds of disability. The Court did not consider the possibility of including those illnesses which are characterised by long-term or permanent limitation within the Directive's scope.

By contrast, the CJEU was correct in interpreting the duty to provide reasonable accommodation in compliance with the Equality Framework Directive and therefore in precluding dismissals on grounds of disability. In light of the above, one may argue that the Court established a narrow definition of disability and missed the opportunity to enhance the legal protection of the Directive.

B. An Intriguing Evolution: The Case of *Ring and Skouboe Werge*

The ratification of the CRPD by the EU in 2010 started to positively influence the judicial application and interpretation of EU equality law.[64] In *Ring and Skouboe Werge*, the CJEU adopted a revolutionary judgment according to which:

> [T]he concept of disability must be interpreted as including a condition caused by an illness medically diagnosed as curable or incurable where that illness entails a limitation which results in particular from physical, mental or psychological impairments which in interaction with various barriers may hinder the full and effective participation of the person concerned in professional life on an equal basis with other workers, and the limitation is a long-term one.[65]

The understanding symbolises a turning point in EU anti-discrimination law because it expressly embraces the innovative contents of the CRPD and extends the concept of disability. Moreover, the CJEU stressed that the 'primacy of international agreements concluded by the European Union over instruments of secondary law means that those instruments must as far as possible be interpreted in a manner that is consistent with those agreements'.[66] In doing so, the Court

[63] D Estrada-Tanck, 'Human rights of persons with disabilities in international and EU law' (2016) Working Paper EUI AEL, 2016/01.

[64] On 23 December 2010, the European Union (EU) ratified the United Nations Convention on the Rights of Persons with Disabilities (CRPD).

[65] Joined Cases C-335/11 and C-337/11 *HK Danmark, acting on behalf of Jette Ring v Dansk almennyttigt Boligselskab* (C-335/11); *HK Danmark, acting on behalf of Lone Skouboe Werge v Dansk Arbejdsgiverforening, acting on behalf of Pro Display A/S* (C-337/11), ECLI:EU:C:2013:222, para 47.

[66] ibid, para 29.

rightly acknowledged the EU's commitment to adopt and implement a cohesive policy in line with the international provisions of the CRPD.

i. *Facts and Questions*

This preliminary ruling case took place after an action was brought by two applicants, Ms Ring and Ms Werge, before a Danish court. The issue regarded a national law permitting the dismissal of employees with only one month's notice in cases where they had been on sick leave for a period of 120 days over a 12-month period (paragraph 5(2) of the Law on the legal relationship between employers and salaried employees, hereafter FL).[67] The applicants claimed that they had a disability and they had been subject to unlawful discriminatory treatment. Ms Ring was employed by DAB and was absent from work on several occasions from 6 June 2005 to 24 November 2005. The medical certificates stated that she was suffering from constant lumbar pain, but it did not predict the return date to full-time employment.[68] On 24 November 2005, she received a dismissal letter. Similarly, Ms Skouboe Werge, an employee of Pro Display, was the victim of a road accident on 19 December 2003 and started to suffer from whiplash injuries. From that moment, she went first on part-time sick leave for four weeks and then on full-time sick leave. The Danish National Office for Accidents at Work and Occupational Diseases quantified Ms Skouboe Werge's degree of invalidity at 10 per cent and her loss of working capacity at 65 per cent. She was also dismissed with only one month's notice.

The trade union HK, acting on behalf of the two applicants, brought proceedings against their employers in the Maritime and Commercial Court (Sø-og Handelsret), seeking compensation on the basis of the Anti-Discrimination Law. HK claimed that both employees were suffering from a disability and that their employers had the duty to offer them reduced working hours, by virtue of the obligation to provide accommodation pursuant to Article 5 of Directive 2000/78/EC.[69] HK also argued that paragraph 5(2) of the FL could not apply to those two applicants because their absences were caused by their disability. The employers however submitted that the applicants' state of health was not covered by the concept of 'disability' within the definition of Directive 2000/78/EC because the

[67] Para 5(2) of the Law on the legal relationship between employers and salaried employees (Lov om retsforholdet mellem arbejdsgivere og funktionærer, the FL) provides: 'However, it may be stipulated by written agreement in the individual employment relationship that the employee may be dismissed with one month's notice to expire at the end of a month, if the employee has received his salary during periods of illness for a total period of 120 days during any period of 12 consecutive months. The validity of the notice shall be dependent on it being given immediately on the expiry of the 120 days of illness and while the employee is still ill, but its validity shall not be affected by the employee's return to work after the notice of dismissal has been given'. See also, Waddington, 'Fine-tuning Non-discrimination Law' (n 28) 11.

[68] *Ring and Skouboe Werge* (n 65) para 15.

[69] ibid, para 23.

illness affected only their full-time working capacity. According to this stance, the applicants could not fall within the definition of disability elaborated during the *Chacón Navas* case because they were able to work part-time and consequently they were not completely excluded from professional life.[70] In addition, the employers held that, in cases of absence on grounds of illness caused by a disability, the dismissal of a worker with a disability pursuant to paragraph 5(2) of the FL does not constitute discrimination, and is therefore not contrary to the Equality Framework Directive. Against this controversial background, the Danish court referred several questions to the CJEU in order to obtain clarification of the concept of disability. The national court also asked whether a reduction in working hours can amount to a measure covered by Article 5 of Directive 2000/78/EC. Finally, the Court was called upon to decide if the Directive precluded the application of a provision of national law under which an employer is entitled to dismiss an employee with a shortened notice period, where 'the absence is caused by the disability' or where 'the absence is due to the fact that the employer has not implemented the measures appropriate in the specific situation to enable a person with a disability to perform his work'.[71]

ii. Defining Disability and the Personal Scope of the Directive

The first relevant point of this judgment affects the definition of disability under EU law. Interestingly, for the first time the CJEU strongly adhered to the concept of disability enshrined in the CRPD, focusing on those barriers that may hinder the full and effective participation of the person concerned in professional life on an equal basis with other workers. The CRPD rejects the medical model and lays down that 'disability is an evolving concept that results from the interaction between persons with impairments and attitudinal and environmental barriers that hinders their full and effective participation in society on an equal basis with others'.[72] As noted above, the ruling of the CJEU also acknowledged the legal supremacy of the CRPD over European law. As a preliminary point, the Court emphasised Article 216(2) of the TFEU[73] and observed that international agreements concluded by the EU are binding on its institutions, and consequently prevail over acts of the EU.[74]

[70] P McTigue, 'From Navas to Kaltoft: The European Court of Justice's Evolving Definition of Disability and the Implications for HIV-Positive Individuals' (2015) 15 *International Journal of Discrimination and the Law* 1.

[71] *Ring and Skouboe Werge* (n 65) para 26(4).

[72] Preamble to the Convention on the Rights of Persons with Disabilities (adopted by the General Assembly, 24 January 2007) A/RES/61/106.

[73] TFEU, Art 216, para 2: 'The Union may conclude an agreement with one or more third countries or international organisations where the Treaties so provide or where the conclusion of an agreement is necessary in order to achieve, within the framework of the Union's policies, one of the objectives referred to in the Treaties, or is provided for in a legally binding Union act or is likely to affect common rules or alter their scope'.

[74] *Ring and Skouboe Werge* (n 65) para 28.

The Court therefore interpreted the 'missing' concept of disability under the Directive in compliance with the international standards of the CRPD.

Moreover, the CJEU stated that disability does not require complete impossibility to work, but does imply a hindrance to the exercise of a professional activity. The Court refused the argument of the employers according to which disability necessarily implies complete exclusion from work because it would be incompatible with the purpose of Directive 2000/78/EC, which aims to enable a person with a disability to have access to or participate in employment. It may be argued that the Court embraced a 'flexible' concept of disability that results from the combination of individual impairments and social barriers. In doing so, the Court correctly interpreted and enlarged the personal scope of Directive 2000/78/EC by covering not only disabilities that are congenital or derive from accidents, but also those disabilities caused by curable or incurable illness.

iii. Reasonable Accommodation as Adaptation of Working Hours?

The second crucial issue of the preliminary ruling regards the possibility of including 'a reduction in working hours' within the accommodation measures required by the Directive. The courts noted that neither Article 5 of Directive 2000/78/EC nor recital 20 in its Preamble mention reduced working hours. The recital only mentions the concept of 'patterns of working time'. The employers argued that the latter category only refers to such matters as the organisation of the patterns and rhythms of work in connection with the production process.

The Court extended the concept of 'patterns of working time' to such adaptations of working hours that accommodate the peculiar needs of persons with a disability who are not capable, or no longer capable, of working full-time to work part-time. The duty to provide reasonable accommodation envisages not only material but also organisational measures. The term 'pattern' of working time therefore may include the rhythm or speed at which the work is done. The CJEU did not find any relevant fact to justify the exclusion of Ms Ring from occupying a part-time post. After her dismissal, Ms Ring started a new part-time job as a receptionist with another company. The Court underlined that Danish law promotes public assistance to undertake accommodation measures whose purpose is to facilitate the access to the labour market of persons with disabilities, including initiatives aimed at encouraging employers to recruit and maintain persons with disabilities in employment. In light of the foregoing, the Court held that a reduction in working hours may constitute one of the accommodation measures under Article 5 of Directive 2000/78/EC.

This part of the judgment is remarkable as it clarifies the legal content of the duty to take appropriate measures according to the provision of reasonable accommodation. The definition of appropriate measures under recital 20 of the Directive is not exhaustive and leaves a wide margin of appreciation to Member States in determining the appropriateness of such measures. Recital 20 generically states that 'appropriate measures should be provided, ie effective and practical measures to adapt the workplace to the disability, for example adapting premises and equipment, patterns of working time, the distribution of tasks or the provision of training or integration resources'. The conclusions of the Court contributed to enlarging the protection afforded by the Directive and strengthen the rights of persons with disabilities in the workplace. The CJEU expressly interpreted recital 20 and Article 5 of Directive 2000/78/EC in line with the second paragraph of Article 2 of the CRPD which defines the duty to provide reasonable accommodation. The Court should therefore be commended for clarifying the concept of reasonable accommodation under EU law and highlighting that it 'must be understood as referring to the elimination of the various barriers that hinder the full and effective participation of persons with disabilities in professional life on an equal basis with other workers'.[75]

iv. Addressing Indirect Discrimination: Legitimate Aim, Necessity and Proportionality

The CJEU was also called upon to decide the compatibility of national legislation with EU law where an employer is allowed to terminate an employment contract with a reduced period of notice if the disabled worker has been absent because of illness for 120 days during the previous 12 months, where those absences are the consequence of the employer's failure to take the appropriate measures. In this regard, the CJEU set out that where the absence of workers is attributable to the employer's failure to adopt appropriate accommodation measures, such national legislation should be in conflict with Directive 2000/78/EC.[76]

In addition, the referring court asked if the Directive precludes national legislation under which an employer can terminate the employment contract with a reduced period of notice if the disabled worker has been absent because of illness, where the absence is caused by his disability. The Court noted that paragraph 5(2) of the FL, which relates to absences on grounds of illness, applies in the same way to disabled and non-disabled persons who have been absent for more than 120 days on those grounds. As a consequence, this provision does not bring about difference of treatment based *directly* on disability, within the meaning of Article 1 in conjunction with Article 2(2)(a) of the Directive. The Court correctly argued that a person with a disability 'is more exposed to the risk of application of the shortened notice period laid down in Paragraph 5(2) of the FL than a worker without a disability'.[77] The CJEU explicitly referred to the observations of the Advocate General, according to which a worker with a disability runs the additional risk of an illness connected with his disability. This circumstance implies

[75] ibid, para 54.
[76] ibid, paras 66 and 67.
[77] ibid, para 76.

that the worker is more exposed to the risk of accumulating days of absence on grounds of illness, and therefore of reaching the 120-day limit. It may be said that the 120-day rule is more likely to place workers with disabilities at a disadvantage than workers without disabilities. Thus, it establishes a difference of treatment indirectly based on disability under the meaning of Article 2(2)(b) of Directive 2000/78/EC.

In this case, the CJEU examined whether that difference of treatment is objectively justified by a legitimate aim and whether the means of achieving that aim are appropriate and necessary. The Danish government submitted that paragraph 5(2) of the FL aims to encourage employers to recruit and maintain workers who often are absent because of illness. The latter measure would allow employers to dismiss workers with a shortened period of notice, where the absences are too long. At the same time, those workers can retain their employment during the period of illness. The Danish government argued that the provision is adopted in the interests both of employers and employees. The government underscored the general regulation and functioning of the Danish labour market which promotes not only the flexibility and freedom of contracts, but also the protection of workers. In line with the government's considerations, DAB and Pro Display observed that the 120-day rule is intended to protect those workers who are sick for long periods of time because employers who agree to apply it are inclined to wait longer before dismissing a worker. The CJEU remarked that the promotion of recruitment represents a legitimate aim of the social or employment policy of the Member States. Theoretically speaking, such aims may be regarded as objectively justifying a difference in treatment on grounds of disability. Nonetheless, the Court clarified that it is for the referring court to assess whether the means used by the Danish employers to realise those aims can be considered as appropriate and necessary. In this respect, such assessment must take into account the additional risks faced by disabled persons, who generally encounter several obstacles in re-entering the labour market compared with persons without disabilities. The Court placed great emphasis on the importance of accommodating the specific needs of persons with disabilities. By doing so, it laid down that Directive 2000/78/EC precludes

> national legislation under which an employer can terminate the employment contract with a reduced period of notice … where those absences are the consequence of his disability, unless that legislation, as well as pursuing a legitimate aim, does not go beyond what is necessary to achieve that aim, that being for the referring court to assess.[78]

In addressing crucial issues such as legitimate aim, necessity and proportionality, the Court had to counterweight delicate and competing (private and public) interests: the legitimate aim of the Danish government to promote recruitment in

[78] ibid para 92.

the labour market and the opposing interest of workers with disabilities not to be discriminated against. In this respect, the CJEU established a fundamental criterion to assess whether a provision goes beyond what is necessary to achieve the aims pursued. The provision must be 'placed in its context and the adverse effects it is liable to cause for the persons concerned must be considered'.[79] This approach seems highly valuable as it takes into account the relevant factors that hamper the professional life of persons with disabilities. To the same extent, it leaves a wide margin of appreciation to national courts in determining the concrete risks run by disabled persons in re-entering the labour market.

v. A Significant, but Incomplete, Development for EU Equality Law

The judgment in *Ring and Skouboe Werge* can be viewed as one of the most important steps forward in the protection of persons with disabilities in the EU legal framework. This case is the first disability discrimination-related preliminary reference following the conclusion of the CRPD by the EU. It represents a unique opportunity for mainstreaming disability rights, as it places the CRPD at the centre of EU law. The Court not only pointed out that the CRPD forms 'an integral part of the European Union legal order', but also that the Equality Framework Directive must be interpreted in a manner consistent with such international instrument. This decision may accelerate the process of revising and updating EU equality legislation by expressly referring to the primacy of international agreements over instruments of EU secondary law. The CRPD's ratification implies that the EU has the legal obligation to adopt all appropriate legislative, administrative and other measures for the implementation of the rights of persons with disabilities.

This judgment addresses different complex issues such as (1) the personal scope of the Equality Framework Directive; (2) the meaning of indirect discrimination; and (3) the legal content of the duty to provide reasonable accommodation in the workplace.

First, the Court applied a 'socio-contextual' model of disability which focuses on those external barriers which may hinder the full and effective participation of the person concerned in professional life on an equal basis with other workers.[80] The CJEU overcame those shortcomings that characterise the medical definition of disability developed in the case of *Chacón Navas*. In particular, the Court clarified the status of persons who are sick under Directive 2000/78/EC. In doing so, it filled the legal gap left by the *Chacón Navas* judgment which merely held that sickness could not be added to the list of grounds covered by the Directive. The Court adopted a broader approach according to which individuals

[79] ibid, para 89.
[80] Waddington and Broderick (n 38).

can be protected as long as their condition led to the required degree of impairment. The impairment must be on a 'long-term' basis as established by Article 1 of the CRPD. In addition, the Court enlarged the Directive's personal scope by stressing that a disability does 'not necessarily imply complete exclusion from work or professional life'. This interpretation properly pursues the Directive's objective to foster a labour market favourable to social integration that aims at combating discrimination against groups such as persons with disabilities. Employment and occupation are key elements in guaranteeing equal opportunities for all and contribute strongly towards the full participation of citizens in economic, cultural and social life and to realising their potential.[81] The 'hindrance' to exercise professional life does not require the full 'impossibility' to carry out professional activities. Such interpretation positively allows persons with disabilities who are only able to work part-time to fall under the protection of the Directive. In other words, the Court definitively abandoned the medical paradigm of disability and laid the foundations on which to build a new comprehensive legal framework in compliance with international law. However, this judgment raises some concerns for those cases where an individual is limited by external obstacles and not by a specific individual impairment.[82] Lisa Waddington and Andrea Broderick argue that this interpretation of disability fails to cover individuals who are disabled only because of false assumptions and prejudices about their specific ability. In this regard, the Court's definition does not fully apply the 'human rights' model of disability of the CRPD.[83]

Second, the Court considered the compatibility with Directive 2000/78/EC of Danish legislation allowing for a shortened period of notice. It observed that such law applies to the same extent to disabled and non-disabled persons who have been absent for more than 120 days on the grounds of illness. The Court acknowledged the existence of indirect discrimination because a neutral provision puts persons having a disability at a particular disadvantage compared with other persons without a disability. The prohibition of indirect discrimination has been rightly applied to cover workers with disabilities who are more likely to accumulate days of absence on grounds of illness. In more general terms, this provision has the effect of protecting those individuals who face greater difficulties and barriers in the workplace. The recognition of indirect discrimination as a form of discrimination reflects a more substantive approach to the concept of equality and enhances the protection of vulnerable categories of individuals.[84] It should be observed that the Court applied the justification test to examine whether the difference of treatment was justified by a legitimate aim. To this end, it sought to balance public and

[81] Preamble to Directive 2000/78/EC.

[82] Waddington and Broderick (n 38) 57.

[83] ibid.

[84] L Waddington and A Hendriks, 'The Expanding Concept of Employment Discrimination in Europe: From Direct and Indirect Discrimination to Reasonable Accommodation Discrimination' (2002) 18 *International Journal of Comparative Labour Law and Industrial Relations* 403.

private interests. It held that the 120-day rule 'must be placed in its context and the adverse effects it is liable to cause for the persons concerned must be considered'. The CJEU's reasoning significantly considered the relevant factors that affect the professional life of workers with disabilities. On the contrary, it overlooked the impact of such an interpretation on the freedom of the Danish government to regulate its labour market. In this respect, the Danish 'flexicurity' model combines flexibility and security. It is based on flexible hiring and firing rules, a considerable social safety net and active labour market policies.[85] The Court's interpretation may therefore constitute a burdensome obligation for Member States adopting flexible labour market regulations.[86] The CJEU instructed the Danish court to 'take account of relevant factors relating in particular to workers with disabilities' (paragraph 90), noting that such workers often find it difficult to re-enter the workforce following dismissal and have 'specific needs in connection with the protection their condition requires' (paragraph 91).[87] This additional protection requirement may narrow the freedom of employers to organise and manage their workforce.

Third, the last interesting question faced by the Court concerned the interpretation of Article 5 of Directive 2000/78/EC that creates the obligation for employers to provide reasonable accommodation. As noted in the first chapter, this duty constitutes the main non-discrimination obligation in the CRPD's context. The duty to provide reasonable accommodation contributes to an effective achievement of substantive equality in the workplace through the imposition of positive obligations on employers. It entails the responsibility of public and private actors to ensure persons with disabilities the enjoyment or exercise of all human rights on an equal basis with others.[88] In this case, the CJEU explicitly stated that the CRPD's provision prescribes a broad definition of 'reasonable accommodation' and found that the adaptation of working hours accommodates the specific needs of persons with disabilities who are not capable, or no longer capable, of working full-time. This understanding may be considered as highly relevant because it takes into account those organisational measures that do not constitute a disproportionate burden on employers. Moreover, when the failure of the employer to provide reasonable accommodation is the main cause of the employee's absence from work, the national legislation under which an employer can terminate the employment contract with a reduced period of notice breaches the purpose of the Directive. The link between the employer's failure to act and

[85] JD Schmidt and J Hersh, 'The Past has No Future: Revisiting Danish Flexicurity' in PK Chopra (ed), *Globalisation and Labour Market Dynamics* (Leeds, Wisdom House Publications, 2016).

[86] M Ventegodt Liisberg, 'Flexicurity and Employment of Persons with Disability in Europe in a Contemporary Disability Human Rights Perspective' in L Waddington et al (eds), *European Yearbook of Disability Law Vol 4* (Cambridge, Intersentia, 2013).

[87] I Chopin and C Germaine-Sahl, *European Anti-Discrimination Law Review* (Luxembourg, Publications Office of the European Union, 2013).

[88] Lord and Brown (n 37).

the employee's absence from work is a necessary condition to prove the violation of the obligation to provide reasonable accommodation. Even if the CJEU's conclusions seem to represent an important development for EU equality law, the Court left to the national court the final decision on whether a reduction in working hours is a disproportionate burden on employers. Moreover, as pointed out by Waddington and Broderick, the CJEU missed the opportunity to define the failure to make reasonable accommodation as a form of discrimination in line with the CRPD.[89]

C. Obesity and Disability: The Case of *Kaltoft v Municipality of Billund*

The recent case of *Fag og arbejde (FOA) v Kommunernes landsforening (Kl)*[90] represents a crucial and controversial step in the process concerning the jurisprudential interpretation of the Equality Framework Directive's personal scope.

The main dispute regards Mr Kaltoft, hired as a childminder by the Municipality of Billund, one of the Danish public administrative authorities. During his work period, he was obese according to the definition of the World Health Organisation. Kaltoft attempted to lose weight with the support of the health programme provided by the Municipality of Billund. After a leave of one year, due to family reasons, he resumed his work as a childminder. Thereafter, he started to receive several unexpected visits from the head of the childminders with the purpose of monitoring his weight loss. During those visits, the head of the childminders pointed out that Mr Kaltoft's weight had remained unchanged.[91] The education inspectors of the Municipality of Billund were asked to dismiss a childminder and the head of the childminders decided to nominate Mr Kaltoft. The Municipality of Billund formally notified Mr Kaltoft of its intention to dismiss him 'following a specific assessment on the basis of a decline in the number of children, thus that of the workload, having severe financial implications on the childminding service and on its organization'.[92] However, he claimed to be the only childminder dismissed because of the alleged decline in workload and expressed the opinion that his dismissal was induced by his obesity.

The workers' union Fag og Arbejde (FOA), acting on behalf of Mr Kaltoft, brought an action before the District Court of Kolding claiming that Mr Kaltoft had been discriminated against on grounds of obesity. In this context, the Danish court referred a question for a preliminary ruling to the CJEU with the purpose of asking whether obesity can be deemed a disability covered by

[89] Waddington and Broderick (n 38) 71.
[90] Case C-354/13 *Fag og arbejde (FOA) v Kommunernes landsforening (KL)*, ECLI:EU:C:2014:2463.
[91] ibid, para 20.
[92] ibid, para 25.

Directive 2000/78/EC. Moreover, it asked which criteria would be decisive in assessing whether a person's obesity falls under the protection of the prohibition of discrimination. The CJEU was also asked to decide if discrimination on grounds of obesity in the labour market is contrary to EU law, as expressed in Article 6 TEU concerning fundamental rights.

i. The Prohibition of Discrimination on Grounds of Obesity

The CJEU properly highlighted that EU law does not provide for any prohibition on grounds of obesity as such. In particular, neither Article 10 of the TFEU nor Article 19 of the TFEU make any reference to obesity. At the same time, neither EU secondary legislation nor Directive 2000/78/EC set out a general principle of non-discrimination on grounds of obesity with regard to employment and occupation. The Court pointed out that only the general principle of non-discrimination, which is also enshrined in the EU Charter of Fundamental Rights, is binding for Member States where the national situation at issue falls under the scope of EU law. The principle of non-discrimination represents one of the fundamental rights which form an integral part of the general principles of EU law. In light of these considerations, the CJEU decided not to operate any extension by analogy of the Directive's scope beyond the listed grounds. It held that EU law must be interpreted as not laying down a general principle of non-discrimination on grounds of obesity as such with regard to employment and occupation.[93] This interpretation seems to rely on the fact that only Article 21 of the Charter includes an open-ended prohibition of discrimination which could potentially cover obesity as a stand-alone ground. Thus, Article 6(1) of the TEU precludes recourse to the Charter to extend '*in any way*' the competences of the European Union as defined in the Treaties. Similarly, Article 51(2) of the Charter states that it 'does not extend the field of application of Union law beyond the powers of the Union or establish any new power or task for the Union, or modify powers and tasks as defined in the Treaties'. These provisions, according to Advocate General Jääskinen, lay down an outer-boundary of EU fundamental rights law that is pertinent to the present case.[94]

ii. The Prohibition of Discrimination in the Labour Market: The CJEU's Minimalist Approach

The *Kaltoft* judgment is particularly silent with respect to the nature of the principle of non-discrimination in the labour market. The Court concluded that

[93] ibid, para 40.

[94] Case C-354/13 *FOA, acting on behalf of Karsten Kaltoft v Kommunernes Landsforening (KL), acting on behalf of the Municipality of Billund* [2014] Opinion of AG Jääskinen, para 19, ECLI:EU:C:2014:2106.

the situation, in so far as it relates to a dismissal purportedly based on obesity, does not fall within the scope of EU law. The provisions of the EUCFR are likewise inapplicable in such a situation. The Court implicitly embraced the Advocate General's arguments according to which the general principle of EU law precluding discrimination on grounds of age, which is reflected in Article 21(1) of the EU Charter, and which can, in some circumstances, have horizontal direct effects on two private parties, could not be applied in this case. He argued that 'there is nothing in the relevant age-discrimination rulings pointing toward the existence of a general principle of law precluding discrimination in the labour market generally'. Nor can constitutional provisions common to a handful of Member States, or a protocol to the ECHR, such as Protocol 12, establish a general principle of law which would oblige Member States to combat discrimination on grounds which, unlike age, are not spelled out in the Treaties or in EU legislation.[95] The Advocate General recalled Article 51(1) of the EU Charter that only binds the Member States when they are 'implementing' EU law. He considered the fact that discrimination occurred in a substantive field such as the labour market 'as an insufficient foundation for concluding that a Member State is implementing EU law'.[96] In a case where the objective of the main proceedings is not related to the interpretation or application of a rule of EU law, the requisite link should be regarded as insufficient. The CJEU avoided deciding whether the principle of non-discrimination in the labour market, as either a Charter right or a general principle as expressed by Directive 2000/78/EC, may be invoked in proceedings between private parties. Moreover, the CJEU did not clarify the criteria to assess the 'link' between a provision of Member State law and the substantive scope of an equally specific provision of EU law. By contrast, the Court purely handed down that dismissals based on obesity fall outside the scope of EU law and therefore the provisions of the Charter are inapplicable in such a context. In doing so, the Court confirmed the emergence of 'judicial minimalism' in preliminary references cases.[97] This approach does not help identify the nature and horizontal effects of the Charter's provisions in national civil proceedings between private parties, in particular with regard to the prohibition of discrimination.

iii. Is Obesity a Disability under the Equality Framework Directive?

The CJEU first dealt with the issue of admissibility. The Danish government observed that the referring question concerning the possibility to consider the obesity of a worker as a 'disability' was inadmissible. It argued that the facts did not exhibit the inability of Mr Kaltoft to carry out his functions during the period

[95] ibid, para 26

[96] ibid, para 20.

[97] Pech (n 2).

in which the Municipality of Billund employed him. In addition, the government held that the answer could be clearly deduced from the existing case law of the CJEU and the referring court could itself give a ruling in the main proceedings on the definition of 'disability' within the meaning of Directive 2000/78/EC.[98] The Court regarded the question as admissible because, according to Article 267 of the TFEU, it is solely for the national court before which the dispute has been brought, to determine both the need for a preliminary ruling and the relevance of the questions which it submits to the Court under Article 267 of the TFEU.

The Court then turned to examine the matter of the preliminary reference. Its analysis began with the explanation of the concept of 'disability' which includes not only the impossibility of exercising a professional activity, but also the hindrance to exercise such an activity. The Court clarified that the complete inability of the worker to carry out his professional tasks does not constitute a compulsory condition to apply the Directive's provisions. On the contrary, it is sufficient to assess the hindrance to the exercise of a professional activity to trigger the protection of EU law. The main purpose of the Directive 2000/78/EC is to enable a person with a disability to have access to or participate in employment. Interestingly, the Court also asserted that the concept 'does not depend on the extent to which the person may or may not have contributed to the onset of his disability'.[99] The Court mentioned the legal contents of the CRPD outlining the definition of disability previously adopted in the case of *Ring and Skouboe Werge*. It concluded that obesity may be a disability if it entails a limitation resulting from an impairment which hinders equal participation in the workplace. It is worth noting that the CJEU identified three main criteria which fell under the Directive's protection: the existence of a personal and long-term limitation; the interaction between a person with impairments and the environmental barriers; and the hindrance to fully exercise professional life. In accordance with the above considerations, the Court stated that:

> [I]n the event that, under given circumstances, the obesity of the worker concerned entails a limitation which results in particular from physical, mental or psychological impairments that in interaction with various barriers may hinder the full and effective participation of that person in professional life on an equal basis with other workers, and the limitation is a long-term one, obesity can be covered by the concept of 'disability' within the meaning of Directive 2000/78/EC.[100]

At first glance, this understanding of the concept of disability may be considered as a proper implementation of the human rights model adopted by the CPRD. However, the judgment tends to emphasise the physical constraints of the claimant as a 'test' to assess whether he fell within the Directive's personal

[98] *Fag og arbejde (FOA) v Kommunernes landsforening (KL)* (n 90) para 44.
[99] ibid, para 56.
[100] ibid, para 59.

scope. Paragraph 60 of the judgment stated that disability falls under the meaning of Directive 2000/78/EC

> if the obesity of the worker hindered his full and effective participation in professional life on an equal basis with other workers *on account of reduced mobility or the onset, in that person, of medical conditions* preventing him from carrying out his work or causing discomfort when carrying out his professional activity (emphasis added).

It is unclear from the judgment whether attitudinal and external barriers would have been sufficient to establish the existence of disability in this case. The Court also failed to clarify if the various barriers hindering the person's professional life include those discriminatory treatments based on false assumptions and prejudices of an individual's ability.[101] As a result, *Kaltoft* does not make a true break with the medical model of disability as it excessively focuses the analysis on those physical impairments of the individual.

iv. Should Obesity be Considered a Disability?

In *Kaltoft*, the Court did not consider obesity per se as a disability, unless it results in a limitation that hinders equal participation in employment. This judgment refused the 'fat rights' claim according to which obesity should be regarded per se a prohibited ground of discrimination or should be expressly included under the concept of disability.[102] The Court's approach has been considered 'cautious' because it left the national court to decide whether obesity constituted a disability.[103] The Court's reluctance to expressly define obesity as a disability has also been ascribed to the consequences that could have affected the labour market and the costs imposed on Member States.[104] It may be said that the inclusion of obesity per se under the concept of disability is not required by Directive 2000/78/EC or the CRPD's provisions. There is no evidence in the Directive to suggest that workers are protected by the prohibition of discrimination on grounds of disability as soon as they develop any type of sickness. The case law establishes that only when a 'curable or incurable illness' entails a 'long-term' limitation, can it be covered by the concept of 'disability' within the meaning of Directive 2000/78/EC. However, Waddington and Broderick point out that the human rights model of disability under the CRPD does not require that 'the relevant impairment actually leads to a limitation' in order to assess discriminatory treatment. The CRPD also covers those individuals who are disabled only because of socially created barriers, such as false assumptions and prejudices, who do not experience a limitation relating to a specific impairment. The CRPD sets out that disability is an 'evolving'

[101] Waddington and Broderick (n 38) 58.

[102] DL Hosking, 'Fat Rights Claim Rebuffed: *Kaltoft v Municipality of Billund*' (2015) 44 *Industrial Law Journal* 460.

[103] Favalli and Ferri (n 52); M Butler, 'Obesity As A Disability: The Implications or Non-Implications Of *Kaltoft*' (2014) 20(3) *Web Journal of Current Legal Issues*.

[104] Butler, ibid.

concept that demands the coexistence of a long-term physical, mental, intellectual or sensory impairment with the hindrance to fully participate in society. It seems that the Convention adopts a flexible and dynamic concept of disability which demands a case-by-case assessment of those situations falling under this wide notion. The CJEU's legal reasoning still highlights some aspects of an outdated medical model of disability that merely identifies disability as a medical condition located within the individual.

D. The Case of *Daouidi:* Clarifying the Long-Term Nature of the Impairment

Daouidi illustrates the CJEU's judicial interpretation of the personal scope of the Equality Framework Directive and the necessary requirements to assess the 'long-term' nature of the impairment.[105]

Mr Daouidi worked as a kitchen assistant and dislocated his left elbow after slipping on the kitchen floor of the restaurant in which he worked. As a result, he initiated the procedure to have his temporary incapacity for work recognised. He could not return to work immediately and while he was still temporarily unable to work, Mr Daouidi received a notice of disciplinary dismissal. He submitted that the dismissal was discriminatory and that, in particular, he was covered by the concept of 'disability', within the meaning of Directive 2000/78/EC. The Spanish court was therefore called on to decide whether his impairment could be classified as 'long-term' in order to apply the disability legislation. However, the Spanish court referred the case to the CJEU and asked whether Mr Daouidi would fall under the concept of disability in the Equality Framework Directive, given the uncertain duration of his injury.

The CJEU positively recognised that the CRPD may be relied on to interpret Directive 2000/78/EC, which must, as far as possible, be interpreted in a consistent manner with the UN Convention's provisions. The Court clarified that the Equality Framework Directive also covers those disabilities caused by an accident. Therefore, if an accident entails a limitation resulting in particular from long-term physical, mental or psychological impairments which, in interaction with various barriers, may hinder the full and effective participation of the person concerned in professional life on an equal basis with other workers, and if that limitation is long-term, it may come within the concept of 'disability' within the meaning of Directive 2000/78/EC.[106] The CPRD instead does not define 'long-term' with regard to a physical, mental, intellectual or sensory impairment. To the same extent, Directive 2000/78/EC does not identify the concept of a 'long-term' limitation of a person's capacity for the purposes of the concept of disability.

[105] *Daouidi v Bootes Plus SL and Others* (n 61).
[106] ibid, para 45.

The CJEU provided specific guidelines to assess the long-term nature of the impairment which have to be taken into account by the national court to assess the concept of disability under the Equality Framework Directive. It pointed out that the long-term nature of the limitation must be assessed in relation to the condition of incapacity of the individual concerned at the time of the alleged discriminatory act adopted against him or her. The evidence of a long-term limitation should include the fact that the incapacity of the person does not 'display a clearly defined prognosis as regards short-term progress' or the fact that it 'is likely to be significantly prolonged before that person has recovered'.[107] Moreover, national courts have to consider all the 'objective evidence' relating to that person's condition, in particular documents and certificates, 'established on the basis of current medical and scientific knowledge and data'.[108] In a case where the capacity of the person concerned is recognised as long-term, it is necessary to demonstrate that unfavourable treatment on grounds of disability represents discrimination under the meaning of Article 2(1) of Directive 2000/78/EC.

This judgment, on one side, may be considered as highly relevant because it helps to better define the concept of disability under EU equality law by providing precise guidelines to assess the long-term nature of the individual impairment. The Court emphasises the need to ensure a uniform application of EU law and the principle of equality in light of the objective pursued by the legislation in question. This approach seems to overcome the flaws of the *Chacón Navas* judgment where the Court did not explain the conditions under which a long-term limitation amounts to disability. In *Chacón Navas*, the Court stated that 'sickness' and 'disability' are different concepts. It defined disability as a 'limitation which results in particular from physical, mental or psychological impairments and which hinders the participation of the person concerned in professional life'.[109] But, it did not adopt any specific guidance to verify when a limitation falls within the concept of disability. The Court merely concluded that it must be probable that the impairment will last for a long time. In addition, the Court excluded that 'workers are protected by the prohibition of discrimination on grounds of disability as soon as they develop any type of sickness'.[110] By doing so, it disregarded the possibility of considering, as falling under the concept of disability, a sickness which caused long-term or permanent limitations.

On the other side, in the case of *Daouidi*, the CJEU's interpretation concerning the concept of disability still retains a major focus on the (long-term) nature of the medical impairment rather than its interaction with external barriers. The CJEU indeed emphasises the importance of medical evidence, such as documents and certificates relating to the person's condition, to identify the duration of the

[107] ibid, para 56.
[108] ibid, para 59.
[109] *Chacón Navas v Eurest Colectividades SA* (n 42) para 43.
[110] ibid, para 44.

individual's limitation.[111] Such assessment may be problematic for persons with psychosocial disabilities, given the medical difficulties in diagnosing the precise nature of psychological or mental health impairments.

Nevertheless, the CJEU offers significant guidance to legally identify the long-term nature of the impairment and include under the protection of the Equality Framework Directive a wider category of limitations that, in interaction with various barriers, may hinder the full and effective participation of persons with disabilities in professional life.

E. Absence from Work on Grounds of Sickness: The Case of *Ruiz Conejero*

Ruiz Conejero is one of the most recent judgments in the field of disability discrimination of the CJEU, which was called on to decide whether Directive 2000/78/EC precludes the application of a provision of national law under which an employer is entitled to dismiss an employee on objective grounds for intermittent absences from work, when his absence from work was caused by his disability.[112]

i. Factual Background and CJEU Key Findings

In this case the claimant, Mr Ruiz Conejero, was a cleaning agent in a hospital in Cuenca (Spain) who was recognised by the Public Health Medical Services as having a disability due to degenerative joint disease and polyarthrosis, aggravated by obesity. He was dismissed under Article 52(d) of the Workers' Statute on the ground that the cumulative duration of his absences, albeit justified, had exceeded the limits laid down in that provision.[113] He sought the annulment of his dismissal on the ground that it constituted discrimination based on disability.

The CJEU first underlined that the

> concept of disability within the meaning of Directive 2000/78 has to be understood as referring to a limitation of capacity which results in particular from long-term physical, mental or psychological impairments which, in interaction with various barriers, may hinder the full and effective participation of the person concerned in professional life on an equal basis with other workers.[114]

By doing so, it recalled the previous CJEU case law on the definition of disability that is not yet fully in compliance with the CRPD because of its limited reference

[111] Waddington and Broderick (n 38) 60.
[112] Case C-270/16 *Carlos Enrique Ruiz Conejero v Ferroser Servicios Auxiliares SA and Ministerio Fiscal*, ECLI:EU:C:2018:17.
[113] ibid, para 18.
[114] ibid.

to professional life, and not to society in general.[115] The Court emphasised that if the obesity of the worker, on account of reduced mobility or the onset of medical conditions, prevents his work or causes discomfort during his professional activity, such a state is covered by the concept of 'disability' within the meaning of Directive 2000/78/EC, as also established in *Kaltoft*.[116]

The Court then clarified that Article 52(d) of the Workers' Statute applies in the same way to persons with disabilities as to persons without disabilities who have been absent from work because it uses a criterion that is not inseparably linked to disability. On the other side, the Court assessed that Article 52(d) of the Workers' Statute is liable to entail 'indirect discrimination' on grounds of disability, since a worker with a disability is more likely to be dismissed than a worker without a disability, having a greater risk of accumulating days of absence because of illness, and consequently of reaching the limits laid down in the Workers' Statute.[117]

Finally, the Court ascertained whether the measures have a 'legitimate aim' and do not exceed what is 'necessary' in order to attain that aim. It set out that the national court has to examine whether the measures under Article 52(d) of the Workers' Statute are designed to meet the aim of combating absenteeism from work, without affecting occasional and sporadic absences. To this end, the factors to be taken into account include 'the direct and indirect costs that must be borne by companies as a result of absenteeism from the workplace'.[118] Moreover, the proportionality test should consider the greater risks run by persons with disabilities who have specific needs and generally face several obstacles in re-entering the labour market.

ii. Drawing the Line between Illness and Disability

This judgment raises some concerns in relation to the distinction between absences on grounds of 'illness' and 'disability'. Broderick argues that this distinction would require employers to carefully assess periods of absence to determine when these absences are strictly related to an employee's disability.[119] The CJEU pointed out that only 'long-term' illnesses are covered by the concept of disability,[120] while the UN Committee on the Rights of Persons with Disabilities clarified that 'a health impairment which initially is conceived of as illness can develop into an

[115] A Broderick, '*Ruiz Conejero*: (Re-)Conceptualizing Disability-based Discrimination and Sickness Absence at Work' (2019) 5 *International Labor Rights Case Law* 1, 86.

[116] *Carlos Enrique Ruiz Conejero v Ferroser Servicios Auxiliares SA and Ministerio Fiscal* (n 112) para 30.

[117] ibid, para 39.

[118] ibid, para 47.

[119] Broderick (n 115) 90.

[120] A Broderick and P Watson, 'Disability in EU Non-discrimination Law' in D Ferri and A Broderick (eds), *Research Handbook on EU Disability Law* (Cheltenham, Edward Elgar Publishing, 2020).

impairment in the context of disability as a consequence of its duration or its chronicity'.[121]

This judgment instead marks an important development with regard to the interpretation of indirect discrimination. The CJEU correctly found that Article 2(2)(b)(i) of Directive 2000/78/EC precludes the dismissal of a worker on the grounds of his intermittent absences from work, in a situation where those absences are the consequence of sickness attributable to a disability. It also provided specific guidelines to carry out the 'proportionality test' in order to balance the rights of persons with disabilities and the legitimate aim of employees to tackle absenteeism.[122]

F. Defining Disability beyond the Labour Market: The Case of *Glatzel*

The CJEU's interpretation of the concept of disability also went beyond the legal borders of the prohibition of discrimination in the workplace.

Wolfgang Glatzel v Freistaat Bayern concerns the application of Directive 2006/126/EC on driving licences[123] and the definition of disability beyond the employment area in relation to Article 21 of the EU Charter of Fundamental Rights according to which any discrimination based on any grounds such as disability shall be prohibited.[124]

Mr Glatzel lost his driving licence on the ground that he had driven under the influence of alcohol. His application for a new driving licence for categories C1 and C1E (heavy goods vehicles) was refused on the ground that he suffered from unilateral amblyopia, involving a substantial functional loss of vision in one eye. He did not meet the requirements of Directive 2006/126/EC which sets out that drivers of heavy vehicles must have visual capacity of at least 0.1. Following an unsuccessful objection against that decision, Mr Glatzel brought an action before the Verwaltungsgericht Regensburg (Administrative Court, Regensburg). As that court dismissed his action, Mr Glatzel brought an action before the Bayerischer Verwaltungsgerichtshof. The Court observed that

> there is no ground on which to prohibit persons who have a visual acuity of less than 0,1 in one eye from driving a motor vehicle where, first, they have binocular vision, second, their field of binocular vision satisfies the requirements laid down in point 6.4 of Annex III to Directive 2006/126 and, third, they have learned fully to compensate for their lack of spatial vision.[125]

[121] UN Committee on the Rights of Persons with Disabilities, *SC v Brazil*, Communication No 10/2013 UN Doc CRPD/C/12/D/10/2013, para 6.3.

[122] Broderick and Watson (n 120) 137.

[123] Directive 2006/126/EC of the European Parliament and of the Council of 20 December 2006 on driving licences [2006] OJ L403/18.

[124] Favalli and Ferri (n 52).

[125] Case C-356/12 *Wolfgang Glatzel v Freistaat Bayer* [2014] ECR, para 31, ECLI:EU:C:2014:350.

The Court therefore referred to the CJEU for a preliminary ruling concerning the validity of the strict requirements established by Directive 2006/126/EC in light of Articles 20, 21(1) and 26 of the Charter concerning equality before the law, non-discrimination on grounds of disability, and the integration of persons with disabilities.

i. The Problematic CJEU Assessment

Even if this case does not fall under the scope of the Equality Framework Directive, it is highly relevant as it addresses several important issues such as the legal understanding of disability and the legal value of the CPRD and the EU Charter of Fundamental Rights.

It is worth noting that the CJEU correctly recalled the notion of disability developed in the case of *Ring and Skouboe Werge* expressly mentioning Article 1(2) of the UN Convention.[126] However, the Court concluded that it 'did not have sufficient information to ascertain whether such impairment constitutes a disability within the meaning of Article 21(1) of the Charter'. The Court mainly focused its analysis on the nature of the individual impairment and those medical standards required by EU law.[127] In doing so, the external barriers hindering the participation of the person concerned in professional life have been completely overlooked. This approach reflects the obsolete medical paradigm of disability that has been rejected by the recent developments of international human rights law.

The Court incorrectly disregarded the opinion of the Advocate General who underlined that

> from the definition given by the Court and from that given by the United Nations, disability must not be understood according to the *degree of the deficiency at issue*, but must be determined having regard to the *end result occasioned by* that deficiency in a given social context or environment.[128]

Accordingly, to assess a disability the analysis should focus on the final consequences of the deficiency and not on the impairment itself. A person should be considered as having a disability, whether the interplay between the deficiency and the external environment brings about a restriction of the activity of the person concerned, who is prevented from participating in professional life on an equal basis with others. The Advocate General's Opinion reflects an appropriate understanding of disability and proposes an adequate solution of the case at issue. In *Glatzel*, the interaction between the individual impairment (the amblyopia which affected the vision in his right eye) and those high standards required by

[126] D Ferri, 'Disability in the EU Charter of Fundamental Rights' in D Ferri and A Broderick (eds), *Research Handbook on EU Disability Law* (Cheltenham, Edward Elgar Publishing, 2020).

[127] C O'Brien, 'Driving Down Disability Equality?' (2014) 21 *Maastricht Journal of European and Comparative Law* 723.

[128] *Wolfgang Glatzel v Freistaat Bayer* (n 125) Opinion of AG Bot, para 35 (emphasis added).

Directive 2006/126/EC to release a category C1 or category C1E driving licence, prevents the claimant from fully participating in professional life. This reasoning should have been upheld by the CJEU which instead confirmed a reluctant approach towards the human rights model of disability of the CRPD.

In this case, the CJEU was called to on identify the interaction between the personal deficiency and the disabling rules of the social context. Moreover, it should have found a balance between the individual interest to not be discriminated against on grounds of disability and the collective considerations of safety. The Court merely concentrated its analysis on the claimant's visual impairment and resorted in a simplistic way to the overriding considerations of road safety as an objective justification.

This judgment illustrates how the Court is progressively departing from the rights-centred approach enshrined in the CPRD and lowering the protection of persons with disability under EU law.

ii. The Role of the CRPD: A Confusing Approach

The Court adopted an inconsistent position with regard to the legal value of the CRPD within the EU legal framework. The CJEU stated that the CRPD is an integral part of the EU legal order, but it specified that the CRPD's provisions are subject, in their implementation or their effects, to the adoption of subsequent acts of the contracting parties. The provisions therefore do not constitute, from the point of view of their content, unconditional and sufficiently precise conditions which allow a review of the validity of the measure of EU law.[129]

This judgment exemplifies the controversial and undefined relation between the CPRD and EU law. The Court denied the possibility to challenge provisions of EU law in light of the CRPD's obligations and therefore restricted the sphere of application of Article 216(2) TFEU, according to which international agreements concluded by the EU are binding on the institutions and on its Member States. This approach seems highly contradictory as it acknowledges that the CPRD is part of the EU legal order but in a *partial* and *limited* way. This means that the CRPD does not produce any legal effects per se in the EU system as it requires implementing measures by the Member States.[130] Only those implementing measures should be consistent with the CPRD's provisions, which however do not offer unconditional and sufficiently precise conditions to produce direct effect.[131]

This reasoning confirms the negative trend in the CJEU's jurisprudence to protect EU norms from the interference of international human rights law.

[129] *Wolfgang Glatzel v Freistaat Bayer* (n 125) para 69.

[130] O'Brien, 'Driving Down Disability Equality?' (n 127) 729.

[131] M Chamon, 'Negotiation, Ratification and Implementation of the CRPD and its Status in the EU Legal Order' in D Ferri and A Broderick (eds), *Research Handbook on EU Disability Law* (Cheltenham, Edward Elgar Publishing, 2020) 68.

The same approach has been adopted in the case of *Z v A Government Department and the Board of Management of a Community School*, that will be further analysed in chapter four in order to illustrate and criticise the judicial approach of the CJEU in relation to the CRPD.[132]

iii. The EU Charter of Fundamental Rights: A Narrow Interpretation

Article 26 of the Charter is a fundamental provision for the protection of persons with disabilities according to which 'the Union recognises and respects the right of persons with disabilities to benefit from measures designed to ensure their independence, social and occupational integration and participation in the life of the community'. In *Glatzel*, the CJEU embraced a narrow interpretation of Article 26 of the Charter and merely labelled it as a principle.[133] The Court stated that Directive 2006/126/EC implements the principle contained in Article 26 of the Charter and recognised the applicability of the latter provision to the case in the main proceedings.[134] The CJEU also concluded that the principle enshrined in Article 26 does not require the EU legislature to adopt any specific measure and it must be given more specific expression in EU or national law in order to produce legal effects. Accordingly, Article 26 'cannot by itself confer on individuals a subjective right which they may invoke as such'.[135]

The Court clearly reduced the sphere of application of Article 26 by classifying it as a 'principle' that cannot confer a subjective right on individuals. This interpretation may be problematic when identifying the conditions which 'would give rise to an Article 26 case'.[136] This Article is indeed considered as a non-interference provision binding only the EU. Moreover, it generates minimal effects as it merely aims at *recognising* and *respecting* the rights of persons with disabilities. This approach reflects the general and vague wording of Article 26 that does not specify the nature of those obligations and measures that Member States should fulfil and enact to integrate persons with disabilities.

The CJEU's reasoning is disputable because it refuses to acknowledge the human rights approach underlying Article 26 of the EU Charter and the importance of those positive rights required to promote the integration of persons with

[132] Case C-363/12 *Z v A Government Department and the Board of Management of a Community School*, [2013] EUECJ C 363/12.

[133] O'Brien, 'Driving Down Disability Equality?' (n 127) 730; *Wolfgang Glatzel v Freistaat Bayern* (n 125) Judgment, para 74, '[T]he court is allowed for the interpretation and review of the legality of legislative acts of the European Union which implement the *principle* laid down in that article, namely the integration of persons with disabilities'.

[134] ibid, para 75.

[135] ibid, para 78.

[136] C O' Brien, 'Article 26 – Integration of Persons with Disabilities' in S Peers et al (eds), *The EU Charter of Fundamental Rights: A Commentary* (Oxford, Hart Publishing, 2014) 735.

disabilities. This provision should help the CJEU in aligning the judicial interpretation of EU norms with the human rights model of disability and identifying the obligations of the EU in the area of social and occupation inclusion. The case of *Glatzel* shows that the CJEU is still uncomfortable in recognising the full legal effect of the Charter provisions, and the potential of the Charter is therefore far from being fully exploited to foster disability rights under EU law.

G. Is the CJEU Still a Real Promoter of Disability Rights?

Ten years after the ratification of the CRPD by the EU, the judgments of the CJEU still present some gaps in relation to the practical interpretation and implementation of the human rights model of disability embodied in the CRPD.[137]

The case of *Kaltoft v Municipality of Billund* symbolises a contradictory approach of the CJEU with regard to the personal scope of the Equality Framework Directive. EU law does not consider obesity as a self-standing ground of discrimination and the CJEU therefore concluded that the existence of discrimination on grounds of obesity must be assessed on a case-by-case basis. The main flaw in the CJEU reasoning is the reference to a concept of disability which excessively focuses on physical limitations and retains some elements of an outdated medical approach. This is a negative development in comparison to the interpretation adopted in *Ring and Skouboe Werge*, when the CJEU started to align the EU concept of disability with the new paradigm embraced by the CRPD. It appears that the CJEU's initial 'judicial activism' is gradually converting into a sort of 'judicial prudence' when addressing sensitive issues that may significantly impact the labour market. The uncertain position in relation to the prohibition of discrimination in the labour market and the return to a medical model of disability reveal the CJEU's cautious approach that restricts the substantive content of EU equality law and avoids clarifying the legal (and economic) implications for Member States.

By contrast, the CJEU closely interpreted the prohibition of indirect discrimination and the duty to provide reasonable accommodation with the CRPD. The CJEU stated that apparently neutral provisions may place workers with disabilities at a particular disadvantage compared with workers without disabilities. These provisions may therefore bring about indirect discrimination under the meaning of Article 2(2)(b) of Directive 2000/78/EC. This interpretation seems to be consistent with the UN Convention which has strongly influenced the judicial interpretation of EU secondary law and consolidated the rights of persons with disabilities in EU case law. Similarly, in *Ring and Skouboe Werge*, the notion of reasonable accommodation has been correctly interpreted as including adaptions in working hours. The Court drew attention to the importance of eliminating the barriers that

[137] L Waddington, 'Saying All the Right Things and Still Getting It Wrong: The Court of Justice's Definition of Disability and Non-Discrimination Law' (2015) 22 *Maastricht Journal of European and Comparative Law* 576.

hamper the effective participation of persons with disabilities in professional life on an equal basis with other workers. Despite this positive development, the Court interpreted the 'reasonableness' of an accommodation according to its financial implications, in contrast to the criteria of 'relevance, appropriateness and effectiveness' adopted by the UN Committee on the Rights of Persons with Disabilities.[138] In addition, the Court failed to assess that the denial of reasonable accommodation is a form of discrimination, as set out in the CRPD.

Against this background, it may be said that the CJEU has certainly performed a crucial role in better protecting the rights of persons with disabilities in the EU legal framework. More generally speaking, the last rulings of the CJEU show the meaningful and favourable effects of the Equality Framework Directive on tackling discrimination in the workplace against persons with disabilities. However, a more coherent judicial approach is required in relation to the legal understanding of the concept of disability. A clear understanding of disability would also be needed under EU law that takes into account the CRPD's legal standards and clarifies the ambiguous CJEU jurisprudence. To do so, the EU should put in place a comprehensive legal framework to reinforce the human rights model of disability and the prohibition of discrimination in the labour market.

[138] Broderick and Watson (n 120) 129.

4

The EU Legal Framework: Associative and Intersectional Discrimination

To have a complete overview of the prohibition of discrimination grounds of disability, this chapter will explore the phenomenon of associative, multiple and intersectional discrimination from a legal perspective. The aim is to identify how the EU legal framework tackles associative, multiple and intersectional discrimination and to what extent these issues may be addressed in light of the CRPD's rules.

I. Discrimination by Association on Grounds of Disability

The Court of Justice of the European Union (CJEU), for the first time, introduced the concept of discrimination by association in EU law in the *Coleman* case.[1] This case clarifies whether the Directive prohibits discrimination against an individual by virtue of his or her association with someone who is a disabled person.[2] As will be shown below, this case represents an important development for EU anti-discrimination law as it extends the personal scope of Directive 2000/78/EC (Directive 2000/78/EC; Equality Framework Directive) to those individuals who do not personally possess the protected characteristics.[3]

A. The *Coleman* Case: Factual Background

The claimant, Sharon Coleman, was a legal secretary and mother of a disabled child. She alleged that she was discriminated against and harassed at work after

[1] Case C-303/06 *Coleman v Attridge Law and Steve Law* (2008) ECLI:EU:C:208:61. See also, I Chopin and C Germaine-Sahl, *European Anti-Discrimination Law Review* (Luxembourg Publications Office of the European Union, 2009).

[2] L Waddington and A Lawson, *Disability and non-discrimination law in the European Union* (Luxembourg Publications Office of the European Union, 2009) 17.

[3] Directive 2000/78/EC of the Council of 27 November 2000 establishing a general framework for equal treatment in employment and occupation [2000] OJ L303/16.

the birth of her child. Her son's condition required specialised and particular care, but her former employer refused to allow her the same flexibility with regard to her working hours and the same working conditions as those of her colleagues who were parents of non-disabled children. Ms Coleman was described as 'lazy' when she requested time off to care for her child, whereas parents of non-disabled children were allowed time off.[4] She received insulting comments about both her and her child and was threatened with dismissal after having occasionally arrived late at the office because of problems related to her son's condition. She submitted that such threats were not made to employees with non-disabled children who were late for similar reasons.

Ultimately, Coleman accepted voluntary redundancy and started a procedure before an employment tribunal claiming that she had been unfairly dismissed and had been subject to discrimination because she was the mother of a disabled child. Her claim was based on the Disability Discrimination Act 1995 and Directive 2000/78/EC. The claimant argued that the Directive prohibits discrimination not only against disabled persons themselves, but also against individuals who are victims of discrimination because they are associated with a disabled person. The employment tribunal found that the case raised questions of interpretation of EU law and decided to refer some questions to the CJEU for a preliminary ruling. The Court was called upon to decide whether the prohibition of discrimination on grounds of disability only protects from direct discrimination and harassment persons who are themselves disabled, or also protects employees because of their association with a person who has a disability.

B. The Advocate General's Opinion

The Opinion of the Advocate General represents a landmark legal reasoning because it underlines that equality constitutes a fundamental principle of Community. Advocate General Poiares Maduro pointed out that Article 13 EC, now Article 19(1) of the Treaty on the Functioning of the European Union (TFEU), is an expression of the commitment of the Community legal order to the principle of equal treatment and non-discrimination.[5] He contributed to clarify the aim of Article 13 EC and of Directive 2000/78/EC which is the protection of the dignity and autonomy of persons belonging to those suspect classifications.[6] A person's dignity and autonomy may be affected when an individual is directly targeted because they have a suspect characteristic. At the same time, he recognised that discrimination can occur in different ways, not only targeting a person who has a particular characteristic. By contrast, another 'way of undermining the dignity

[4] *Coleman v Attridge Law and Steve Law* (n 1) para 26.

[5] Opinion of AG Poiares Maduro in Case C-303/06, *Coleman v Attridge Law and Steve Law* [2008] ECR I-5603, ECLI:EU:C:208:61.

[6] ibid, para 10.

and autonomy of people who belong to a certain group is to target not them, but third persons who are closely associated with them and do not themselves belong to the group'.[7] The Advocate General emphasised that a substantive approach towards equality should also address these subtler forms of discrimination because they concretely affect vulnerable people belonging to suspect classifications. He convincingly argued that this form of discrimination jeopardises the ability of persons who have a suspect characteristic to exercise their autonomy. In light of this conceptual background, Advocate General Poiares Maduro turned his attention to the Directive and found that the Coleman case raised an issue of direct discrimination. According to his conclusion, Directive 2000/78/EC must be interpreted as establishing a general framework for equal treatment in employment and occupation that 'protects people who, although not disabled themselves, suffer direct discrimination and/or harassment in the field of employment and occupation because they are associated with a disabled person'.[8]

Advocate General Poiares Maduro released a meaningful Opinion with regard to the general principles underlying EU equality law and the scope of Directive 2000/78/EC. He emphasised that human dignity and personal autonomy are fundamental values of equality law which are protected by Article 13 EC, now Article 19 of the TFEU. He considered that directly targeting a person who has a particular characteristic does not constitute the only way of discriminating against him or her, but there are also 'more subtle and less obvious ways of doing so'.[9] In this respect, he correctly stressed a robust conception of equality that entails other, subtler forms of discrimination. For instance, one way of undermining the dignity and autonomy of people who share a certain characteristic is to target not them, but a third person who is closely associated with them.

Furthermore, the Advocate General offered a detailed analysis of the functioning of Directive 2000/78/EC. He clarified that the Directive performs an *exclusionary* function.[10] This understanding means that religious belief, age, disability and sexual orientation are excluded from the set of legitimate grounds an employer may rely on to treat one employee less favourably than another. According to this approach, the prohibition of direct discrimination is based on an exclusionary mechanism that prevents an employer from relying on certain grounds to treat employees differently. By contrast, the prohibition of indirect discrimination encompasses an *inclusionary* mechanism that obliges employers to take into account and accommodate the needs of individuals who belong to certain groups. In doing so, he coherently included discrimination by association in the scope of the prohibition of direct discrimination as a natural consequence of the exclusionary mechanism through which the prohibition of direct discrimination operates. Discrimination on grounds of religion, age, disability and sexual

[7] ibid, para 12.
[8] ibid, para 25.
[9] ibid, para 12.
[10] ibid, para 18.

orientation represents unfair treatment breaching the dignity and autonomy of individuals. As a result, the fact that an employee who is the object of discrimination does not possess a certain characteristic is irrelevant. The Directive operates at the *level of grounds of discrimination* and requires that an individual has been mistreated on account of 'disability', not on account of '*her* or *his* disability'. This reasoning shifts the emphasis from the person who is discriminated against to the grounds of discrimination covered by Directive 2000/78/EC. It may significantly reinforce EU equality law by triggering the Directive's protection not merely when the claimant is disabled herself or himself, but every time there is an instance of less favourable treatment because of disability.

C. Analysis of the Judgment: Who Falls under the Protection of Discrimination by Association?

The CJEU held that the Equality Framework Directive does not limit the principle of equal treatment to people who themselves have a disability within the meaning of the Directive.[11] On the contrary, the purpose of the Directive, with regard to employment and occupation, is to combat all forms of discrimination on grounds of disability. The analysis of the CJEU focused on the principle of equal treatment enshrined in the Directive, which does not apply to a particular category of person, but to the grounds mentioned in Article 1. In order to support this interpretation, the Court recalled the wording of Article 13 EC, which constitutes the legal basis of Directive 2000/78/EC and confers on the Community the competence to take appropriate action to combat discrimination based, inter alia, on disability.

The CJEU also acknowledged that Directive 2000/78/EC includes a number of provisions which apply only to disabled people. For instance, Article 5 sets out the duty to provide reasonable accommodation and implies that employers must take appropriate measures, where needed in a particular case, to enable a person with a disability to have access to, participate in, or advance in employment. Similarly, Article 7(2) also lays down that, with regard to disabled persons, Member States have the right to maintain or adopt provisions on the protection of health and safety at work or to measures aimed at creating or maintaining provisions or facilities for safeguarding or promoting their integration into the working environment. Interestingly, the Court found that disability-specific measures do not exclude from the Directive's scope individuals who do not have a disability themselves.[12] In light of the foregoing considerations, the Court stated that:

> Where an employer treats an employee who is not himself disabled less favourably than another employee is, has been or would be treated in a comparable situation, and it is

[11] L Waddington, 'Case C-303/06, S Coleman v Attridge Law and Steve Law, Judgment of the Grand Chamber of the Court of Justice of 17 July 2008' (2009) 46 *Common Market Law Review* 665.

[12] ibid, 670.

> established that the less favourable treatment of that employee is based on the disability of his child, whose care is provided primarily by that employee, such treatment is contrary to the prohibition of direct discrimination laid down by Article 2(2)(a).

Moreover, the Court applied the same conclusions with regard to the prohibition of harassment and found that it is not limited only to people who are disabled. Accordingly, where it is established that the harassment is suffered by an employee who is not himself disabled but is related to the disability of his child, such conduct is contrary to the prohibition of harassment laid down in Article 2(3).[13]

The wide approach of the Court prevents depriving the Directive 2000/78/EC of an important element of its effectiveness and reinforces the protection which it is intended to guarantee. However, the Court seems to underline some important requirements to trigger the legal protection under the category of discrimination by association. The CJEU indeed stressed not only the importance of the relationship between Ms Coleman and her son, but also noted that the employee primarily needed to take care of her disabled child.[14] In doing so, the Court acknowledged that two determinant elements are required to assess discrimination by association: (i) the existence of a profound legacy; and (ii) an apparent level of dependency between the two individuals. This interpretation is likely to extend the protection to those relatives who have the main caring duties with regard to family members with a disability. The decision of the Court provides clear guidance in interpreting the prohibition of discrimination and ensuring protection against direct discrimination and harassment based on the association with a disabled person.[15]

D. The Controversial Nature of Reasonable Accommodation

As noted above, an interesting matter addressed by the CJEU relates to the application of the duty to provide reasonable accommodation according to Articles 5 and 7(2) of Directive 2000/78/EC. In relation to the latter obligations, the Court adopted a different interpretation of the Directive's provisions and placed great emphasis on the personal nature of these measures. Thus, the Court clarified that they are specifically related to disabled persons as they only concern

[13] *Coleman v Attridge Law and Steve Law* (n 1) para 63.

[14] D Schiek and A Lawson, *European Union Non-Discrimination Law and Intersectionality Investigating the Triangle of Racial, Gender and Disability Discrimination* (Farnham, Ashgate Publishing, 2011) 42.

[15] Waddington and Lawson, *Disability and non-discrimination law in the European Union* (n 2) 18. See also, L Waddington and A Broderick, *Realising equality: A comparison of the UN Convention on the Rights of Persons with Disabilities and EU equality and non-discrimination law* (Luxembourg, Publications Office of the European Union, 2018) 75; A Broderick and P Watson, 'Disability in EU Non-discrimination Law' in D Ferri and A Broderick (eds), *Research Handbook on EU Disability Law* (Cheltenham, Edward Elgar Publishing, 2020) 126.

positive discrimination measures in favour of persons with disabilities. Moreover, they are specific measures which 'would be rendered meaningless or could prove to be disproportionate if they were not limited to disabled persons only'.[16] In this way, the Court evaluated reasonable accommodation as 'positive discrimination measures' in favour of only disabled persons.

Lisa Waddington and Andrea Broderick argue that the Court's reasoning implies that a non-disabled person cannot enjoy the right to reasonable accommodation because of their association with a disabled person.[17] The CJEU's stance is not compatible with the provisions of the Convention on the Rights of Persons with Disabilities (CRPD) that implicitly enshrine such a duty in order to protect those persons who associate with a person with a disability and are discriminated against by harassment or an unjustified denial of reasonable accommodation.[18]

In addition, the Court did not define a denial of reasonable accommodation as a form of discrimination as specified by the CRPD. On this occasion, the Court's interpretation missed the opportunity to improve the Directive's framework and include the failure to adopt reasonable accommodation within the prohibition of discrimination on grounds of disability. The inclusion of reasonable accommodation into the formal prohibition of non-discrimination would facilitate the realisation of the rights of persons with disabilities and would be desirable under EU law.

E. Concluding Remarks: A Shift Towards Substantive Equality

The judgment delivered in the *Coleman* case constitutes an important improvement in EU non-discrimination law as it sets out the conditions needed to apply the legal protection against discrimination by association under Directive 2000/78/EC. For the first time, the Court introduced the concept of discrimination by association, which occurs when an individual is discriminated against because of his or her association with someone who possesses a disability or on another protected ground. The CJEU significantly extended the fundamental guarantees to those persons who do not have the protected characteristics. The ratio of the judgment is to protect individuals who primarily take care of persons with disabilities and who may encounter several environmental obstacles in the workplace. The approach of the Court contributes to empowering a vulnerable category of people through a wide interpretation of the personal scope of Directive 2000/78/EC. The CJEU's ruling instead raises some concerns in relation

[16] *Coleman v Attridge Law and Steve Law* (n 1) para 42.
[17] Waddington and Broderick (n 15) 76.
[18] ibid, 73.

to the duty to provide reasonable accommodation. Now, the CRPD implicitly also protects those individuals who associate with a person with a disability and are discriminated against by a denial of reasonable accommodation, and under Article 2 of the TFEU recognises the failure to adopt reasonable accommodation as an unlawful form of discrimination.

It must be said that this judgment was handed down before the ratification of the CRPD by the European Union, but it exhibits crucial developments in relation to the personal scope of Directive 2000/78/EC marking an important shift towards substantive equality. The Court rightly focused its analysis not on the individual impairment of the claimant, but on the fact that disability was the ground of the less favourable treatment which she claimed to have suffered. The CJEU shifted the attention from the personal characteristics of the individual to the external barriers hindering her professional life. In doing so, the CJEU anticipated the implementation of some fundamental aspects of the social-contextual model of disability introduced by the CRPD. As noted above, this approach has not been fully endorsed in the recent judgments of *Kaltoft* and *Glatzel*, where the Court showed a sort of judicial reluctance to developing a clear and coherent position in relation to the personal scope of the Directive and the legal definition of disability.

II. Why Does Multiple and Intersectional Discrimination Matter?

To complete the discussion concerning the prohibition of discrimination on grounds of disability, this chapter will now explore the phenomenon of multiple and intersectional discrimination from a legal perspective. The aim is to identify how the EU legal framework tackles multiple and intersectional discrimination and to what extent this phenomenon may be addressed in light of the CRPD's rules. As noted in the chapter one, the UN Committee on the Rights of Persons with Disabilities held that the Convention covers both multiple and intersectional discrimination. 'Multiple discrimination' is based on multiple characteristics and includes a situation where a person can experience discrimination on two or several grounds. 'Intersectional discrimination' instead 'refers to a situation where several grounds operate and interact with each other at the same time in such a way that they are inseparable and thereby expose relevant individuals to unique types of disadvantage and discrimination'.[19] EU anti-discrimination law is only single-ground oriented. It lacks a comprehensive approach towards

[19] UN Committee on the Rights of Persons with Disabilities, General Comment No 6 on equality and non-discrimination, UN Doc CRPD/C/GC/6 (adopted by the Committee at its nineteenth session (14 February–9 March 2018) para 19.

discrimination and does not provide a specific instrument to address multiple and intersectional discrimination. Directive 2000/78/EC vaguely refers to multiple discrimination against women in the Preamble, but it contains no precise reference to this form of discrimination in the binding norms.[20] Directive 2000/43/EC (Race Equality Directive) does not mention disabled women or disability as a ground of multiple or intersectional discrimination.[21] Directive 2006/54/EC does not prohibit discrimination against women with disabilities or any other form of multiple and intersectional discrimination.[22] At EU level, the main effort to tackle this issue was made during the European Year of Equal Opportunities for All 2007.[23] The major objective of the European Year was to raise awareness of the right to equality and non-discrimination and of the problem of multiple discrimination. It sought to address multiple discrimination based on two or more of the grounds listed in Article 19 of the TFEU and to promote a balanced treatment of all these grounds.

From the perspective of international human rights law, only the CRPD mentions the concept of multiple and intersectional discrimination and lays down a specific Article that prohibits discrimination against women and children with disabilities. Multiple discrimination is also addressed in the Action Plan 2006–2015 of the Council of Europe, which acknowledges that persons with disabilities face specific barriers and experience two-fold discrimination.[24] It takes into account not only the situation of women and children with disabilities, but also the particular conditions of ageing persons with disabilities and people with disabilities from minorities such as refugees, migrants and Roma. The Plan requires the adoption of relevant policies and implementation measures to remove the barriers and challenges faced by each of these groups in order to ensure that individuals can reach their full potential alongside other citizens.

In this framework, the adoption of equality law based on an intersectional approach is crucial because the fragmentation in discrimination legislation may lead to several legal problems as it brings about hierarchies of equality grounds and different levels of protection.[25] Diverse equality provisions imply different definitions of the same key concepts and different approaches in terms

[20] Recital 3 of the Preamble.

[21] Directive 2000/43/EC of the Council of 29 June 2000 implementing the principle of equal treatment between persons irrespective of racial or ethnic origin [2000] OJ L180/22.

[22] Directive 2006/54/EC of the European Parliament and of the Council of 5 July 2006 on the implementation of the principle of equal opportunities and equal treatment of men and women in matters of employment and occupation (recast) [2006] OJ L204/23.

[23] Decision No 771/2006/EC of the European Parliament and of the Council of 17 May 2006 establishing the European Year of Equal Opportunities for All (2007) towards a just society [2006] OJ L146/1.

[24] Council of Europe, 'Action Plan to promote the rights and full participation of people with disabilities in society: improving the quality of life of people with disabilities in Europe 2006–2015, Rec(2006)5.

[25] Schiek and Lawson (n 14) 31.

of protection.[26] In that regard, the protection afforded by EU disability equality law is weaker compared with race and gender anti-discrimination law. The Race Equality Directive has a broader application than the Equality Framework Directive. The former prohibits discrimination in a wide range of activities such as employment and occupation, education, housing, and goods and services. On the contrary, the scope of the Framework Equality Directive is confined to employment and occupation. As a consequence, a disabled woman of colour may be merely protected with regard to a limited range of areas or may need recourse to different pieces of legislation to obtain legal protection. The discrepancies in the protection afforded to different grounds and the single approach to equality reduce the guarantees in favour of those individuals who are subject to multiple and intersectional discrimination. Moreover, the absence of proactive duties to deal with intersectional disadvantages in both directives jeopardises the effective eradication of multiple and intersectional discrimination.[27]

III. The *Odar* Case: Disability and Age Discrimination

Odar exhibits how the CJEU's interpretation of the Equality Framework Directive tends to consider the different grounds of discrimination as 'separate harms'.[28] In the *Odar* case, the Court considered both disability and age discrimination, but found that there was only indirect discrimination on grounds of disability.[29] The Court held that the special calculation method adopted to determine compensation for employees over the age of 54 was discriminatory for those disabled employees who would be entitled to an early disability pension.[30]

Dr Odar worked for Baxter Deutschland Gmbh which operated a redundancy scheme based on age, length of service and gross monthly pay. Dr Odar was over 54 and suffered from severe disabilities. According to the German state pension scheme, the claimant was entitled to an ordinary old age pension at 65

[26] L Waddington and M Bell, 'More Equal than Others: Distinguishing European Union Equality Directives' (2001) 38 *Common Market Law Review* 587. See also generally, R Xenidis, 'Multiple Discrimination in EU Anti-Discrimination Law: Towards Redressing Complex Inequality?' in U Belavusau and K Henrard (eds), *EU Anti-Discrimination Law Beyond Gender* (Oxford, Hart Publishing, 2018).

[27] S Fredman, 'Positive Rights and Positive Duties: Addressing Intersectionality' in D Schieck and V Chege (eds), *European Union Non-Discrimination Law: Comparative Perspectives on Multidimensional Equality Law* (Abingdon, Routledge-Cavendish, 2009).

[28] A Numhauser-Henning, *Elder Law: Evolving European Perspectives* (Cheltenham Edward Elgar Publishing, 2017).

[29] Case C-152/11 *Odar v Baxter Deutschland*, EU:C:2012:772.

[30] G de Búrca, 'The Decline of EU Anti-Discrimination Law? (2016) Note for the Colloquium on Comparative and Global Public Law (NYU).

and an additional pension for severely disabled people at 60. When the claimant ended his employment contract, he received a gross redundancy payment of €303,253.31. However, by applying the standard formula, if he was not aged over 54, Dr Odar would have received €616,506.63. The claimant therefore claimed both direct age discrimination and indirect disability discrimination due to the calculation criteria of his redundancy payment. In this case, a special formula was applied to workers aged over 54 which had the effect of reducing compensation. As observed by Advocate General Sharpston in her Opinion, the 'special formula calculation … will always be lower for a severely disabled worker than for a non-disabled worker of the same age'.[31] The fact that the calculation is neutrally based on the pensionable age means that disabled workers will receive less compensation on termination of employment because of their serious disability.

Against this background, the CJEU held that the special formula that applies to workers aged over 54 represents differential treatment on the grounds of age. However, the Court found that that the age-based criteria was justified under Article 6(1) of the TEU as a proportional means to distribute on a fair basis limited financial resources within a social plan.[32] Such a treatment also pursues the legitimate aim to protect younger workers and facilitate their reintegration into employment. On the other side, the Court positively found that the prohibition of discrimination on grounds of disability precludes the application of an occupational social security scheme under which the compensation to which workers older than 54 are entitled is calculated on the basis of the earliest possible date on which their pension will begin, with the result that the compensation paid is lower than the standard formula compensation. The measure at issue disregards those risks faced by severely disabled people, who generally face greater difficulties in finding new employment. Severely disabled people have specific needs stemming both from the protection their condition requires and from the need to anticipate possible worsening of their condition.[33]

This case shows that the concept of multiple and intersectional discrimination is not yet embodied in the reasoning of the CJEU. The Court did not take into account the intersectional aspect of discrimination and the fact that different grounds not only add to each other but intrinsically interact. The CJEU rightfully found discrimination on grounds of disability, but it did not expressly recognise the necessity to assess the interaction between several grounds when analysing discriminatory treatments.

[31] Opinion of AG Sharpston in Case C-152/11 *Odar v Baxter Deutschland*, para 50, ECLI:EU:C:2012:451.

[32] P Craig and G De Búrca, *EU Law: Text, Cases, and Materials*, 6th edn (Oxford, Oxford University Press, 2015) 947.

[33] *Odar v Baxter Deutschland* (n 29) 69.

IV. *Surjit Singh Bedi v Bundesrepublik Deutschland*: Collective Agreement and Intersectional Discrimination

Surjit Singh Bedi v Bundesrepublik Deutschland also relates to indirect discrimination on grounds of disability and age.[34]

The claimant had a severe disability and lost his job. According to the collective agreement, he was entitled to receive 'bridging assistance' providing him with a reasonable means of subsistence until retirement. The bridging assistance ended when the early payment of a retirement pension for severely disabled people started to be applicable, reducing his monthly income significantly. The CJEU was asked whether the Equality Framework Directive is compatible with a national provision which sets out that the right to bridging assistance ends when the individual becomes entitled to an early retirement pension for severely disabled people.

The Court did not find any direct discrimination in this case, given that not only severely disabled workers but other groups of workers are entitled to early payment of a retirement pension, therefore the termination of payments of bridging assistance does not concern severely disabled workers alone.[35] On the contrary, with regard to indirect discrimination, the Court outlined that a non-disabled person would be entitled to receive the bridging assistance for a longer time than the claimant and would have a higher income. As a result, the Court concluded that a provision in a collective agreement under which the payment of bridging assistance must cease once that worker is entitled to early payment of a retirement pension for severely disabled persons is not in line with the Equality Framework Directive and represents a difference in treatment which is indirectly based on disability.[36]

In this judgment, the Court remarkably pointed out 'the risk that severely disabled persons may have financial requirements arising from their disability which cannot be adjusted and/or that, with advancing age, those financial requirements may increase'.[37] The CJEU seems to implicitly recognise the interplay between the different grounds of age and disability when assessing discrimination.[38] However, the Court failed to explicitly find the existence of intersectional discrimination, showing that EU law would need to be revised and improved to address intersectional and multiple forms of discrimination.

[34] C-312/17 *Surjit Singh Bedi v Bundesrepublik Deutschland*, ECLI:EU:C:2018:734.

[35] ibid, paras 46–47.

[36] ibid, para 80.

[37] ibid, para 75.

[38] A Gerards and R Xenidis, 'Algorithmic discrimination in Europe: Challenges and opportunities for gender equality and non-discrimination law' European network of legal experts in gender equality and non-discrimination (Luxembourg, Publications Office of the European Union, 2021).

V. The Case of *Z v A Government Department*: Gender and Disability

The request for a preliminary ruling in this case originated from national proceedings between Ms Z, a commissioning mother who had a child through surrogacy, and an Irish government department and the board of management of a community school.[39] The dispute concerned the refusal to grant Ms Z paid leave equivalent to maternity leave or adoption leave following the birth of her child. Ms Z was employed as a post-primary school teacher in a school managed by the board of management in accordance with the employment conditions of the government department. She had a rare disease preventing her from supporting a pregnancy. For this reason, Ms Z and her husband decided to have a child through a surrogacy arrangement and turned to a specialist agency in California. In vitro fertilisation occurred in Ireland and the egg transfer to the surrogate mother took place in California. According to California law, Ms Z and her husband are regarded as legitimate parents of the child. By contrast, Irish law does not regulate surrogacy arrangements and there is no provision covering maternity or adoption leave following the birth of a child under surrogacy. Ms Z made an application to the government department to obtain adoption leave, but the government refused that request because she did not meet the requirements established by the maternity or adoption leave scheme.

Ms Z started an action against the government department before the Equality Tribunal. The claimant argued that she has been discriminated against on grounds of gender, family status and disability. Moreover, she claimed that the government department failed to reasonably accommodate her as a person with a disability.[40] In light of these circumstances, the Equality Tribunal decided to refer some fundamental questions to the CJEU for a preliminary ruling. The first question concerned whether Directive 2006/54/EC (the so-called Equal Treatment Directive) has to be interpreted as meaning that there is discrimination on grounds of sex where a woman, whose genetic child has been born through a surrogacy arrangement, is refused paid leave from employment equivalent to maternity leave or adoption leave. Then, the CJEU was asked whether Directive 2000/78/EC (Equality Framework Directive) must be interpreted as meaning that there is discrimination on grounds of disability where a woman, who suffers from a disability which prevents her from giving birth, is refused paid leave from employment. Finally, the Equality Tribunal asked if the CRPD is capable of being relied on for the purposes of interpreting and challenging the validity of the Equality Framework Directive.

[39] Case C-363/12 *Z v A Government Department and The Board of Management of a Community School*, ECLI:EU:C:2014:159.

[40] ibid, para 44.

A. The Court's Findings

The first question addressed by the Court was the issue of discrimination on grounds of sex with regard to Directive 2006/54/EC on the implementation of the principle of equal opportunities and equal treatment of men and women in matters of employment and occupation.[41] Article 4 of that Directive provides that, for the same work or for work to which equal value is attributed, direct and indirect discrimination on grounds of sex with regard to all aspects and conditions of remuneration is to be eliminated. In this context, the Court selected a male comparator to assess whether the refusal to grant maternity leave constitutes unlawful discrimination on grounds of sex.

The CJEU noted that, under the national legislation applicable in the main proceedings, a commissioning father who has had a baby through a surrogacy arrangement is treated in the same way as a commissioning mother in a comparable situation.[42] It follows that a commissioning father is not entitled to paid leave equivalent to maternity leave. The Court therefore found that the refusal of Ms Z's request was not based on a ground that applies exclusively to workers of one sex at the expense of women. Further, the CJEU stated that the claimant could not be subject to less favourable treatment relating to her pregnancy because she had not been pregnant. The Court declared that Directive 2006/54/EC does not undermine the right of Member States to provide distinct rights to paternity and/or adoption leave. It preserves the freedom of Member States to grant or not to grant adoption leave, and the conditions for the implementation of such leave. In view of these considerations, the Court concluded that a refusal to provide paid leave equivalent to maternity leave to a female worker who had a baby through a surrogacy arrangement does not constitute discrimination on grounds of sex.

The second issue regarded the interpretation of the prohibition of discrimination on grounds of disability as defined by Directive 2000/78/EC. The CJEU referred to the Advocate General's opinions according to which 'the inability to have a child by conventional means does not in itself, in principle, prevent the commissioning mother from having access to, participating in or advancing in employment'.[43] This stance stressed that the claimant's conditions did not prevent Ms Z from carrying out her work or constitute a hindrance to the exercise of her professional activity. The Court failed to underline the importance of assessing the functional link between the personal impairment and the rule preventing her effective participation in professional life. In doing so, Ms Z was not recognised as 'disabled' within the meaning of the Equality Framework Directive and therefore the application of the duty to provide reasonable accommodation was ruled out.

[41] Directive 2006/54/EC (n 22).
[42] *Z v A Government Department* (n 39) para 52.
[43] ibid, para 81.

The last question concerned the validity of the Directive in light of the UN Convention. The Court argued that EU case law shows that an EU act may be challenged if it is incompatible with the provisions of international law.[44] The validity of the Directive can be assessed only where the provisions of the international agreement appear to be 'unconditional and sufficiently precise'. Such a condition is fulfilled 'where the provision relied on contains a clear and precise obligation which is not subject, in its implementation or effects, to the adoption of any subsequent measure'.[45] The CJEU considered the CRPD as a 'programmatic' international agreement. To support this argument, it expressly referred to Article 4(1) of the UN Convention that obliges States Parties to adopt all appropriate legislative, administrative and other measures for the implementation of the rights enshrined in that Convention. The Court also highlighted Article 4(3) of the CRPD, which requires the involvement of persons with disabilities, through their representative organisations, in the development and implementation of legislation and policies to apply the Convention. In those circumstances, the Convention's provisions were not recognised as unconditional and sufficiently precise within the meaning of EU case law. The Court merely laid down that 'the validity of that directive cannot be assessed in the light of the UN Convention, but that directive must, as far as possible, be interpreted in a manner that is consistent with that Convention'.[46]

B. How to Deal with Multiple and Intersectional Discrimination under EU Law

The Court's judgment reveals a weak and inadequate approach in dealing with discrimination based on multiple and intersectional grounds. The arguments used by the CJEU reflect a flaw in the EU legal system which is characterised by a single-ground equality paradigm. It would indeed appear that multiple and intersectional discrimination occurs frequently in the EU labour market and a new holistic approach is needed to accommodate the individual experience of multiple disadvantages.[47] Kimberle Crenshaw argues that 'neither the gender aspect of racial discrimination nor the racial aspects of gender discrimination are fully comprehended within human rights discourses'.[48]

[44] Case C-366/10 *Air Transport Association of America and Others* [2011] ECR I-13755, para 50; and Joined Cases C-335/11 and C-337/11 *HK Danmark* [2013] ECR, para 28.

[45] *Z v A Government Department* (n 39) para 86.

[46] ibid, para 91.

[47] H Bielefeldt, *Tackling Multiple Discrimination Practices, Policies and Laws* (Luxembourg, Office for Official Publications of the European Communities, 2007) 47.

[48] K Crenshaw, 'Background Paper for the Expert Meeting on the Gender-Related Aspects of Race Discrimination', UN Division for the Advancement of Women (DAW) Office of the High Commissioner for Human Rights (OHCHR) United Nations Development Fund for Women (UNIFEM) Expert Group Meeting on 'Gender and Racial Discrimination' (Zagreb, 21–24 November 2000).

Similarly, EU anti-discrimination law does not take into account the disability aspect of gender discrimination or the gender aspect of disability discrimination. In one judgment, the Court denied legal protection to a woman who suffered from discrimination on multiple and different grounds. In the case of *Z*, the CJEU ruled that there was no sex or gender discrimination, no disability discrimination and no violation of EU provisions concerning maternity leave. The lack of a legal instrument which takes into account the intersection of two or more grounds of discrimination may compromise the effective protection of vulnerable individuals.

To give an example, in this case the claimant was obliged to bring an allegation of sex discrimination separately from the allegation of disability discrimination. This practice implies the impossibility of assessing the inextricable link between the two grounds that brings about discrimination. As a result, the claimant, as a woman with disabilities, was not able to find protection under either the Equal Treatment Directive or the Equality Framework Directive. The Court found that a commissioning father was not entitled to such leave either and that the refusal did not put female workers at a particular disadvantage compared with male workers. At the same time, it did not recognise the situation experienced by Z as falling within the personal scope of Directive 2000/78/EC that prohibits discrimination on grounds of disability. It is noteworthy that the Court operated a comparison with male workers, as opposed to other women. In doing so, it did not compare the situation of a commissioning mother with that of a woman who has given birth or an adoptive mother. This framework of analysis shows that EU law does not always provide the necessary legal tools to identify the proper comparator and tackle multiple and intersectional discrimination. It seems evident that EU law does not accommodate those multiple disadvantages stemming from the combination of vulnerable characteristics such as sex and disability. In such cases, the correct comparator would have been a 'non-disabled woman' entitled to obtain the grant of maternity leave.

It may be argued that the most complex issue concerns the identification of an adequate group with whom to operate a comparison with the disadvantaged individual. EU equality law is still deeply linked to the formal idea of comparison which narrows the circumstances for challenging discrimination.[49] The failure to adopt a comprehensive piece of legislation to combat multiple and intersectional discrimination leaves a significant gap in the EU legal system and contributes to enhancing the hierarchy of equalities.

[49] C Sheppard, 'Multiple Discrimination in the World of Work' (2011) Working Paper no 66, International Labour Office, Programme for the Promotion of the ILO Declaration on Fundamental Principles and Rights at Work (Declaration) (Geneva, ILO, 2011).

C. The Failure to Apply the Human Rights Model of Disability

The case of *Z* also confirms the CJEU's hesitancy in embracing the social-contextual model of disability.[50] The Court did not recognise the status of disability of the claimant under Directive 2000/78/EC. It wrongly hailed the Advocate General's Opinion according to which the incapacity to have a child by conventional means does not in itself prevent the commissioning mother from having access to, participating in, or advancing in employment. The Court therefore concluded that 'it is not apparent from the order for reference that Ms Z's *condition* by itself made it impossible for her to carry out her work or constituted a hindrance to the exercise of her professional activity'.[51]

Again, the CJEU's reasoning emphasised the personal condition of the claimant without taking into account the crucial interaction between the individual impairment and the external barriers. This understanding is not convincing as it moves away from the social paradigm of disability and unjustifiably narrows the protection of Directive 2000/78/EC. Asserting that the individual condition does not jeopardise the claimant's effective participation in professional life is erroneous and echoes a remote medical model of disability. The Court should have noted that the claimant's *infertility*, in interaction with the *external rule* preventing her from taking maternity leave, represents an evident and unlawful hindrance to her professional life.[52]

The analysis of this case indicates that the CJEU's jurisprudence is failing to fully apply the social model of disability in the EU legal framework. The Court seems to have gradually left behind the project to promote a judicial approach to disability equality law in compliance with international human rights law.

D. The Complex Interplay between International Law and EU Law

The *Z* case raises questions regarding the relationship between international law and the EU legal order. As far as international agreements are concerned, EU law lays down that international law is an integral part of the EU legal order. According to Article 216(2) of the TFEU, 'agreements concluded by the Union are binding on the institutions of the Union and on its Member States'. At first sight, it would appear that EU law has embraced a monistic approach with respect to

[50] S Favalli and D Ferri, 'Defining Disability in the European Union Non-Discrimination Legislation: Judicial Activism and Legislative Restraints' (2016) 22 *European Public Law* 541.

[51] *Z v A Government Department* (n 39) para 81.

[52] C O'Brien, 'Driving Down Disability Equality?' (2014) 21 *Maastricht Journal of European and Comparative Law* 723, 728.

its relationship with international law.[53] The 'monist' term refers to a conception that views EU law and international law as one unitary and coherent system. By contrast, the 'dualist' approach considers international law and EU law as distinct and separate legal spheres.[54]

The CJEU's case law shows that the relationship between EU law and international law is highly complicated.[55] On several occasions, the Court emphasised the necessity to verify the nature of the international agreement in order to admit its direct applicability in the EU legal order. The term 'direct applicability' means that international rules can be applied to EU law without a specific implementation measure, while 'direct effect' implies that relevant norms of EU law can be effectively invoked by individuals in judicial proceedings.

In the case of *Z*, the CJEU ruled that the CRPD's provisions are not unconditional and sufficiently precise and therefore do not have direct effect under EU law. The Court, in accordance with the Opinion of the Advocate General, excluded that the UN Convention may be relied on to challenge the validity of Directive 2000/78/EC.[56] The Advocate General submitted that Articles 5, 6 and 28 of the UN Convention are not specifically related to employment and occupation as they lay down general obligations addressed to the contracting parties to take steps to ensure that the aims of the UN Convention are achieved.[57] In addition, the Advocate General argued that Article 27(l)(b) of the CRPD leaves it to the discretion of contracting parties to determine the measures which may be adopted to safeguard and promote the realisation of the right to work of persons with disabilities on an equal basis with others. According to this stance, Article 27(l)(b) of the CRPD gives wide leeway to the EU institutions to take legislative measures to promote the realisation of rights enshrined in the UN Convention.

The CJEU embraced the Advocate General's observations and reached a 'surprising conclusion'[58] by focusing on Article 4(1) of the UN Convention that imposes on States Parties the general duty to adopt all appropriate measures for implementing the CRPD's rights. For the first time, the Court stated that the CRPD does not produce direct effect because it is drafted in a programmatic form. This judgment reflects the narrow approach adopted by the Court in *Air Transport Association of America*.[59] In this instance, the CJEU denied the possibility of

[53] B Van Vooren and RA Wessel, *EU External Relations Law: Text, Cases and Materials* (Cambridge, Cambridge University Press, 2014) 229.

[54] G de Búrca, 'The European Court of Justice and the International Legal Order After Kadi' (2010) 51 *Harvard International Law Journal* 1.

[55] See Case 181/73 *Haegeman v Belgian State* [1974] ECR 449; Joined Cases C-402/05 P and C-415/05 P *Kadi and Al Barakaat International Foundation v Council and Commission* [2008] ECR I-6351.

[56] Case C-363/12 *Z v A Government Department and The Board of Management of a Community School*, Opinion of AG Wahl, para 114, ECLI:EU:C:2013:604.

[57] ibid, para 116.

[58] Craig and de Búrca (n 32) 368.

[59] Case C-366/10 *Air Transport Association of America v Secretary of State for Energy and Climate Change*, ECLI:EU:C:2011:864.

relying directly on Article 2(2) of the Kyoto Protocol to contest the validity of Directive 2008/101/EC. The content of the international provision was regarded as not 'unconditional and sufficiently precise so as to confer on individuals the right to rely on it in legal proceedings'.[60]

Several national courts also consider the CRPD as a programmatic instrument that only outlines general policy objectives which have to be implemented by the States Parties.[61] However, it is worth noting that the CPRD enshrines a binding framework and includes both legal provisions and programmatic standards. *In primis*, all States Parties have the clear legal obligation to implement the CRPD in their national systems by adopting legislative and administrative measures. Article 4 of the CRPD sets out a positive obligation on States Parties to ensure and promote the full realisation of all human rights without discrimination of any kind on the basis of disability.[62] Furthermore, the CJEU and national courts have the legal duty to interpret EU and secondary legislation in line with the Convention. The CRPD constitutes an interpretative tool to guide the judicial interpretation of EU and national legislation. This approach has often been confirmed at national level as domestic courts widely rely on the CRPD to interpret domestic law.[63]

The CJEU instead exhibits a particularly 'protectionist' and 'minimalist' approach with regard to the direct effect of international agreements in the EU legal framework. The reasoning of the Court strongly relies on an obsolete 'dualist' paradigm that privileges the autonomy of the EU legal order over its integration into an overarching international legal regime. The Court also avoids explaining the meaning of those conditions required to assess whether the content of an international treaty is 'unconditional and sufficiently precise'.

E. The Incongruous CJEU Reasoning: Time for a Change

The CJEU has reduced the chances of invoking international norms with the purpose of challenging rules of EU law. It certainly demands the assessment of 'unconditional and sufficiently precise' international provisions. Such a condition is merely fulfilled where the international norm relied on contains a clear and precise obligation which is not subject, in its implementation or effects, to the adoption of any subsequent measures.

[60] ibid, para 77.

[61] L Waddington and A Lawson, *The UN Convention on the Rights of Persons with Disabilities in Practice: A Comparative Analysis of the Role of Courts* (Oxford, Oxford University Press, 2018).

[62] V Della Fina, R Cera and G Palmisan, *The United Nations Convention on the Rights of Persons with Disabilities: A Commentary* (New York, Springer International Publishing, 2017) 142.

[63] Waddington and Lawson, *The UN Convention on the Rights of Persons with Disabilities in Practice* (n 61) 555.

The application of this 'test' appears inappropriate because it does not take into consideration the fact that every international human rights instrument needs specific mechanisms and measures to be implemented at EU and national levels. It may be suitable with respect to international agreements that only set out technical regulations and standards, but it results are inadequate in relation to human rights treaties including complex and sensitive legal provisions. To give an example, the Court recognised those provisions of the Open Skies Agreement establishing certain rules designed to apply directly and immediately to airlines as unconditional and sufficiently precise.[64] The Court inaccurately applied the same 'test' in the case of *Z* to verify the direct effect of the CRPD's provisions in the EU legal order. The CRPD represents an overarching human rights treaty that cannot be compared to an international air transport agreement. The peculiar legal nature of human rights treaties requires a more specific and coherent approach to assess their direct applicability at EU level.

In light of these observations, the Court's approach can be considered insufficient and incongruous as it purely aims at limiting the direct invocation of international agreements in the EU. The Court should therefore provide a comprehensive range of criteria and guidelines to further clarify the relationship between EU law and international human rights law. In doing so, it should revise the conditions necessary to examine the validity of an EU act in light of the rules of international law by taking into account the specific nature of human rights treaties.

The decision in the case of *Z* remains controversial because it also disregards the progressive legal developments led by the CRPD. As examined in chapter one, the UN Convention not only introduces general obligations, but also specific substantive rights affecting education, health, participation, work and employment, standard of living and social protection. In that regard, Article 27 of the CRPD sets out specific and precise guidelines to promote and implement the rights of persons with disabilities to work on an equal basis with others. For instance, it states the prohibition of discrimination with regard to all matters concerning all forms of employment, including conditions of recruitment, hiring and employment, continuance of employment, career advancement and safe and healthy working conditions.[65] It also imposes the duty to enable persons with disabilities to have effective access to general technical and vocational guidance programmes, placement services and vocational and continuing training. It furthermore sets out the specific obligation to promote the employment of persons with disabilities in the private sector through appropriate policies and measures, which may include affirmative action programmes, incentives and other measures. This Article provides clear objectives and identifies the appropriate means to achieve the scope of the UN Convention.

[64] Case C-366/10 *Air Transport Association of America, American Airlines Inc, Continental Airlines Inc, United Airlines Inc v Secretary of State for Energy and Climate Change* [2012] OJ C 49.

[65] Art 27(a) CRPD.

The CRPD adopts a substantive equality framework characterised by cross-cutting provisions for implementing disability rights, such as the duty to provide reasonable accommodation.[66] Against this backdrop, it is worth noting that labelling the CRPD as a mere programmatic instrument is highly simplistic. This judgment underlines the complexity of the relationship between international and EU law, but also the importance of further investigating the interaction between the UN Convention and EU law in order to define this controversial relationship.

[66] JE Lord and R Brown, 'The Role of Reasonable Accommodation in Securing Substantive Equality for Persons with Disabilities: The UN Convention on the Rights of Persons with Disabilities' in MH Rioux, LA Basser and M Jones (eds), *Critical Perspectives on Human Rights and Disability Policy* (The Hague, Martinus Nijhoff, 2011).

5

EU Governance and the Framework for Monitoring the CRPD

The current chapter will explore the role performed by EU institutions in the ratification and implementation process of the Convention on the Rights of Persons with Disabilities (CRPD) in order to identify how EU governance architecture has changed to deal with the CRPD, 10 years after its ratification. This chapter will show the interplay between Article 33 of the CRPD and the existing EU governance mechanisms and will investigate the structure of the independent framework for monitoring the CRPD crafted by the European Union (EU). This chapter can be approached from two perspectives. First, it aims at analysing the EU institutional balance and the role performed by the EU institutions in the CRPD's implementation process. Second, it seeks to assess the efficiency of the EU governance system.

I. Ratifying and Implementing the UN Convention: Winners and Losers in the EU Institutional Game

On 30 March 2007, the EU signed the UN Convention on the Rights of People with Disabilities on its opening day for signature (CRPD). The CRPD has been signed and ratified by all 28 EU countries and a further 150 states worldwide. On 23 December 2010, the EU formally ratified the Treaty. In doing so, it was the first, and so far only international organisation to have become a party to the Convention.[1] The accession by the EU to the CRPD represents an unprecedented event in international and EU law. It is the first time that the EU as a whole signed and ratified a comprehensive human rights treaty.

The EU's capacity to negotiate and conclude international agreements on its own behalf is set out in Article 216 of the Treaty on the Functioning of the European Union (TFEU):

> The Union may conclude an agreement with one or more third countries or international organisations where the Treaties so provide or where the conclusion of an agreement is

[1] Art 43 of the CRPD states that 'the present Convention shall be subject to ratification by signatory States and to formal confirmation by signatory regional integration organizations. It shall be open for accession by any State or regional integration organization which has not signed the Convention'.

> necessary in order to achieve, within the framework of the Union's policies, one of the objectives referred to in the Treaties, or is provided for in a legally binding Union act or is likely to affect common rules or alter their scope.

The Treaties lay down that agreements concluded by the Union are binding on its institutions and its Member States. Interestingly, the CPRD's conclusion is said to constitute a 'mixed' agreement to the extent that the EU and Member States are separate contracting parties and have 'concurrent powers' to conclude such an agreement.[2] As a consequence, EU institutions are bound to the provisions falling within EU competence, and Union secondary legislation must be enacted in compliance with the Convention's rules.

II. The Negotiations of the CRPD and the EU

The EU played a significant role in the process of negotiating and drafting the CRPD. The main institution involved in this procedure was the Commission, which had lobbied for the adoption of an international instrument to protect the rights of persons with disabilities since 2003.[3] The Commission released a Communication 'Towards a United Nations legally binding instrument to promote and protect the rights and dignity of persons with disabilities' in order to emphasise the importance of reinforcing the existing international framework for the protection of persons with disabilities.[4] In May 2004, the Council authorised the Commission to conduct negotiations on behalf of the then European Community (EC). The Commission acknowledged that persons with disabilities are often marginalised because of physical, technical and social obstacles that prevent them from fully enjoying their rights in all regions of the world. The Commission proposed that 'rather than create new law, the instrument should tailor the existing human rights implementation standards to the specific circumstances of people with disabilities, thereby improving access for people with disabilities to their rights'.[5] The Commission Communication highlighted the goal of putting in place a legally binding instrument that could reinforce the prohibition of non-discrimination and the principle of equality:[6]

> Equal access to the human rights can be guaranteed by ensuring that people with disabilities are not discriminated against on the grounds of their disability. The legally

[2] M Rhinard and M Kaeding, 'The International Bargaining Power of the European Union in "Mixed" Competence Negotiations: The Case of the 2000 Cartagena Protocol on Biosafety' (2006) 44 *Journal of Common Market Studies* 1023.

[3] G de Búrca, 'The EU in the Negotiation of the UN Disability Convention' (2010) 35 *European Law Review* 174.

[4] Commission, 'Communication to the Council and the European Parliament of 24 January 2003 towards a United Nations legally binding instrument to promote and protect the rights and dignity of persons with disabilities' COM (2003) 16 final.

[5] ibid, Introduction.

[6] L Waddington, 'Breaking New Ground: The Implications of Ratification of the UN Convention on the Rights of Persons with Disabilities for the European Community' in O Arnardóttir and

binding instrument should protect people with disabilities from discrimination in having access to and enjoying human rights.[7]

The EU's position in favour of an international binding treaty based on equality and non-discrimination has often been considered restrictive and prudent. For instance, Gráinne de Búrca argued that while the EU promoted a strong disability agenda, the Commission appeared sceptical with regard to the adoption of a separate convention including substantive rights for disabled persons. On the contrary, the emphasis placed by the Commission on the principle of equality derived from the need to identify the legal basis of Community competence to negotiate the CRPD.[8] The Commission mentioned Article 13 of the EC Treaty because this provision (now Article 19 TFEU) enabled the Community to combat discrimination on grounds of sex, racial or ethnic origin, religion or belief, disability, age and sexual orientation, in the areas of Community competence. In doing so, the Commission confirmed the leading role of the EC at international level in carrying out an overall strategy concerning disability, which also represents a shared commitment by all Member States.

A. The Commission's Contribution to the Drafting of the CRPD

The Commission promoted the realisation of an international instrument that enshrines the full spread of human rights including political and civil/fundamental rights as well as economic, social and cultural rights. The Commission Communication hailed the 'human rights' approach according to which states should take action to ensure that in reality people with disabilities are in a position to exercise their rights.[9] It also encouraged the establishment of a strong monitoring mechanism to successfully implement the new international instrument.[10] The Commission's stance did not aim at obstructing the adoption of a substantive rights-based convention. It rather pushed for introducing relevant provisions of EU equality law within the CRPD's framework. The Communication outlined the goal of bringing the Community's experience in the field of combating discrimination to an international level. In particular, the Commission set out those guiding principles that should have informed the Convention, drawing on the experience of Directive 2000/78/EC concerning equal treatment in employment and occupation, which embodies specific provision for people with disabilities.[11] The Commission's

G Quinn (eds), *The United Nations Convention on the Rights of Persons with Disabilities: European and Scandinavian Perspectives* (Leiden, Martinus Nijhoff, 2009) 119.

[7] 'Communication to the Council and the European Parliament of 24 January 2003' (n 4).

[8] Waddington, 'Breaking New Ground' (n 6) 119.

[9] 'Communication to the Council and the European Parliament of 24 January 2003' (n 4).

[10] ibid.

[11] Directive 2000/78/EC of the Council of 27 November 2000 establishing a general framework for equal treatment in employment and occupation [2000] OJ L303/16.

contribution mainly sought to ensure consistency between EU law and international legal standards in relation to the protection of disabled persons.

The work of the Commission during the negotiations also decisively helped in strengthening the EU role on the international stage. The European Commission's officials indeed explicitly demanded the insertion of an Article in the Convention's final draft to recognise the accession of international organisations to the CRPD. The action carried out by the Commission successfully culminated with the introduction of Articles 43 and 44, which provide the possibility for regional integration organisations to become parties to the CRPD. It may be argued that the Commission, acting on behalf of the EC (now EU), substantively contributed to the development of the existing UN binding instrument to safeguard the rights and dignity of persons with disabilities.

B. Ensuring Coordination between Various EU Actors

The negotiations revealed how various institutional and non-institutional EU identities interact with each other. In this regard, the Commission's role was not merely confined to the external representation of the EU. During the CRPD's drafting, the work of the Member States was concretely coordinated by the Commission in order to present a common position. It provided relevant expertise for the Member States in relation to EU disability law.[12] The Commission also clarified the legal contents of Directive 2000/78/EC with the purpose of supporting the work of national delegations and avoiding discrepancies with EU law. Its coordinating function at the pre-sessional meetings was essential to pursue a consensus position among the then 27 Member States with different political interests and legal approaches. Along with the Commission, the EU presidency of the Council was committed to driving forward the work of the Member States within the pre-sessional meetings. Importantly, the discussion between the EU Member States was coordinated by the representatives of the country holding the presidency of the Council of the EU.[13]

The synergy between the Commission, the Council and the Member States facilitated the negotiations for the CRPD's adoption and contributed to the development of a European shared strategy. Ultimately, EU participation in the negotiations of the CRPD was also characterised by a pioneering alliance between the Commission and civil society organisations (CSOs). In particular, the European Disability Forum (EDF) acted to support the EU's position enhancing its role as a global actor. The EDF contributed to promoting and protecting EU interests before other international actors.

[12] de Búrca (n 3) 181.

[13] The presidency of the Council of the European Union (EU) rotates among the EU Member States every six months and the country holding the presidency drives forward the Council's work.

At the end of this process, on 27 February 2007, the Commission presented a proposal for a Council Decision on the signing, on behalf of the EC, of the CRPD and its Optional Protocol.[14] The Council Decision, dated 27 March 2007, authorised the Community to sign the CRPD and issued a declaration on the Optional Protocol stating that the Council of the European Union shall reconsider the question of signing the Optional Protocol by the European Community as soon as possible.[15] As previously noted, the EU signed the CRPD on 30 March 2007.

C. The Commission and the Union's External Policy Representation

The negotiations of the Convention offer an interesting case study into the EU institutional architecture and the relationship between the EU institutions. The Commission performed a steering role to shape EU external policy with regard to disability and prevent internal divergences between Member States. It may be said that the Commission, as guardian of the Treaties, excellently interpreted its role because it ensured the application of the Treaties and of EU legislation. It promoted those values, legal provisions and objectives enshrined in Directive 2000/78/EC. To the same extent, the Commission improved internal coordination so that the EU and its Member States acted efficiently together and spoke with one voice. The Commission's nomination as the only EU negotiator correctly reflects the content of Article 218 of the TFEU according to which:

> [T]he Commission, or the High Representative of the Union for Foreign Affairs and Security Policy where the agreement envisaged relates exclusively or principally to the common foreign and security policy, shall submit recommendations to the Council, which shall adopt a decision authorising the opening of negotiations and, depending on the subject of the agreement envisaged, nominating the Union negotiator or the head of the Union's negotiating team. The Council may address directives to the negotiator and designate a special committee in consultation with which the negotiations must be conducted.

This provision, in contrast with previous Article 300 EC,[16] does not identify the Commission as the unique negotiator, but leaves the Council the power to nominate

[14] Commission, 'Proposal for a Council Decision concerning the conclusion, by the European Community, of the United Nations Convention on the Rights of Persons with Disabilities' COM (2008) 530 final.

[15] Council, 'Decision (EC) on the signing, on behalf of the European Community, of the United Nations' Convention on the Rights of Persons with Disabilities' [2010] OJ L23.

[16] Art 300 EC identified the Commission as the only negotiator: 'Where this Treaty provides for the conclusion of agreements between the Community and one or more States or international organisations, the Commission shall make recommendations to the Council, which shall authorise the Commission to open the necessary negotiations. The Commission shall conduct these negotiations in consultation with special committees appointed by the Council to assist it in this task and within the framework of such directives as the Council may issue to it'.

it depending on the subject of the agreement envisaged.[17] Notwithstanding this vague language, it seems evident that only the Commission and the High Representative can be nominated as negotiators. In this regard, the Commission should be appointed as negotiator when the international agreement entails matters of internal policymaking not related to the common foreign and security policy (CFSP). This provision should be read together with Article 17 of the TFEU that establishes the duty of the Commission to ensure the Union's external representation with the exception of the CFSP. It is clear that the Treaties confer on the Commission the delicate function of ensuring consistency between international agreements and EU law. The Commission had the institutional capacity to fit a complex international human rights instrument, such as the CRPD, into the wider EU law framework.

III. Monitoring the CRPD's Implementation: New Governance Mechanisms

After analysing the role of the EU institutions in the negotiations of the CRPD, the mechanisms adopted by the EU to monitor the correct implementation of the Convention will be now examined. The Convention introduces a unique mechanism of regional and national monitoring of its implementation.[18] Article 33 of the CRPD sets outs a 'three-tier' monitoring framework which includes a national or regional focal point, an independent mechanism to promote, protect and monitor the implementation of the Convention, and the involvement of civil society:[19]

> 1. States Parties, in accordance with their system of organization, shall designate one or more focal points within government for matters relating to the implementation of the present Convention, and shall give due consideration to the establishment or designation of a coordination mechanism within government to facilitate related action in different sectors and at different levels.
> 2. States Parties shall, in accordance with their legal and administrative systems, maintain, strengthen, designate or establish within the State Party, a framework, including one or more independent mechanisms, as appropriate, to promote, protect and monitor implementation of the present Convention. When designating or establishing such a mechanism, States Parties shall take into account the principles relating to the status and functioning of national institutions for protection and promotion of human rights.
> 3. Civil society, in particular persons with disabilities and their representative organizations, shall be involved and participate fully in the monitoring process.

[17] P Eeckhout, *EU External Relations Law* (Oxford, Oxford University Press, Oxford European Law Library, 2011) 196.

[18] G de Beco, 'Article 33(2) of the UN Convention on the Rights of Persons with Disabilities: Another Role for National Human Rights Institutions?' (2011) 29 *Netherlands Quarterly Human Rights* 84.

[19] J Arsenjeva, 'Implementation of the UN Convention on the Rights of Persons with Disabilities in the EU's External Relations', Briefing Paper for the Directorate-General for External Policies of the Union (European Parliament, Brussels, 2013).

This new system complements the traditional mechanism provided at international level by the UN Committee on the Rights of Persons with Disabilities, which has competence to receive and consider communications from or on behalf of individuals or groups of individuals subject to its jurisdiction who claim to be victims of a violation by that State Party of the provisions of the Convention.[20] Article 33 of the CRPD is therefore the most complete and peculiar provision on national level implementation and monitoring ever drafted in a human rights international agreement.[21] It provides for the creation of independent national mechanisms as well as traditional international human rights mechanisms. By doing so, Article 33 includes a set of provisions that resembles the new governance architecture of the EU.

The concept of new EU governance stresses a shift away from the monopoly of traditional politico-legal institutions and highlights the governing legitimacy and capacity of a broad sphere of actors.[22] The new EU governance model therefore includes 'regulatory approaches which are less rigid, less prescriptive, less committed to uniform outcomes, and less hierarchical in nature'.[23] This approach implies the prevalence of voluntary and non-binding norms over coercive instruments, along with the involvement of stakeholders in the decision-making process.

A. The Experimentalist Paradigm

The CRPD embodies significant characteristics of the so-called 'experimentalist' governance regime.[24] Experimentalist governance constitutes a form of political cooperation based on open-ended and participatory procedures that promote interaction between local and transnational actors.[25] Experimentalist governance usually informs the treaty-body monitoring systems of the UN human rights regime and the transnational certification of environmental standards.[26] This model focuses on the establishment of open-ended goals which are implemented by lower-level actors. Final results are subject to peer review and practices are

[20] Art 1 of the Optional Protocol to the Convention on the Rights of Persons with Disabilities.

[21] G de Beco, *Study on the Implementation of Article 33 of the UN Convention on the Rights of Persons with Disabilities* (Regional Office for Europe of the UN High Commissioner for Human Rights, 2014).

[22] G de Búrca and J Scott, 'Introduction: New Governance, Law and Constitutionalism' in G de Búrca and J Scott (eds), *Law and New Governance in the EU and the US* (Oxford, Hart Publishing, 2006). See also C Scott, 'Governing without Law or Governing without Government? New-ish Governance' (2009) 15 *European Law Journal* 160.

[23] de Búrca and Scott, 'Introduction: New Governance, Law and Constitutionalism' (n 22) 3.

[24] de Búrca (n 3) 174. See also: CF Sabel and J Zeitlin, 'Learning from Difference: The New Architecture of Experimentalist Governance in the European Union' (2008) 14 *European Law Journal* 271; J Heymann, MA Stein and G Moreno, *Disability and Equity at Work* (Oxford, Oxford University Press 2014) 417.

[25] G de Búrca, RO Keohane and C Sabel, 'New Modes of Pluralist Global Governance' (2013) New York University Public Law and Legal Theory Working Papers No 386.

[26] ibid, 26.

systematically evaluated in light of the data collected. The experimentalism architecture requires the participation of stakeholders in the implementation process, an influential role of national monitoring mechanisms, and regular reviews of the system. Article 33 of the CRPD may be said to reflect the main features of the experimentalist system to the extent that: (i) states should designate one or more independent mechanisms to promote, protect and monitor implementation of the Convention; (ii) stakeholders, in particular persons with disabilities and their representative organisations, shall be involved and participate fully in the monitoring process; (iii) States Parties shall take into account the status and functioning of national institutions for protection and promotion of human rights (NHRIs). In addition, the CRPD adopts a flexible approach with regard to several provisions and allows States Parties an appropriate degree of freedom to develop minimum standards, guidelines and benchmarks in consultation with civil society.[27]

Article 31 of the CRPD furthermore sets out that States Parties have to collect appropriate information, including statistical and research data, to enable them to formulate and implement policies to give effect to the Convention. It seems clear that the CRPD includes innovative mechanisms of experimentalism governance and enhances the involvement of stakeholders in all areas of the Convention's implementation. The systematic interaction between different actors, coupled with continuous feedback and monitoring initiatives, represent key aspects of the CRPD's implementation.

B. The Open Method of Coordination (OMC)

Civil society's performance was crucial not only in the CRPD's negotiations, but also in its implementation strategy. Article 33 of the CRPD embraces the principle of 'participation' that underpins the model of good governance proposed in the White Paper by the European Commission.[28] This concept aims, inter alia, at improving the quality, relevance and effectiveness of EU policies by means of 'wide participation throughout the policy chain from conception to implementation'.[29] Participation should entail an inclusive approach in the process of developing and implementing EU policies. The aim is to create more confidence in the final result and in the institutions which deliver policies.

[27] TJ Melish, 'The UN Disability Convention: Historic Process, Strong Prospects, and Why the US Should Ratify' (2007) 15 *Human Rights Brief* 37. For instance, Art 3 CRPD sets out sets general and broad principles such as 'respect for dignity, full participation and inclusion, non-discrimination, respect for difference, equal opportunity, accessibility, gender equality, and respect for the evolving capacities of children'.

[28] Commission, 'European Governance, A White Paper', COM (2001) 428 final.

[29] ibid, 10.

The fundamental mandate conferred upon civil society by the CRPD, along with the provisions on national implementation and monitoring, mirror some essential characteristics of the open method of coordination (OMC).[30]

The OMC is often considered the ideal model of experimentalist governance since it is a system for coordinating policies among Member States through procedures of soft law to achieve EU objectives.[31] This form of intergovernmental policymaking does not result in binding legislative measures and takes place in areas which fall within the competence of EU countries, such as employment, social protection, education, youth and vocational training. The participation of different actors is widely recognised as an excellent landmark in the decisional and implementing process.[32]

The OMC's emphasis on broad participation reveals striking similarities with the structure of those independent mechanisms required by Article 33 of the CRPD. This provision expressly demands the full participation of civil society in the monitoring process. National independent institutions shall therefore include stakeholders and persons with disabilities in their organisations. Such independent mechanisms have to promote, protect and monitor the implementation of the CRPD.

At EU level, the OMC also promotes decentralised reciprocal learnings and voluntary participation of Members States within an open network, in which benchmarks, peer review, multilateral surveillance, scoreboards and trend charts are essential tools to spread transnational policies and promote policy learning.[33] To the same extent, the CRPD includes a familiar obligation on States Parties to collect and research data in order to formulate and implement effective policies with regard to persons with disabilities. Moreover, Article 40 of the CRPD contains the general duty on the States Parties to meet regularly in a conference for the purpose of considering and reviewing any matter in relation to the CRPD's implementation.

The objective of this governance model is not merely the involvement of civil society in policymaking, but it seeks to carry out periodic evaluation, monitoring and peer review of policies in order to exchange best practices. To this end, it facilitates experimentation and diffusion of new knowledge.[34] To conclude, it may be argued that the CRPD's monitoring system combines several aspects of EU governance mechanisms.

[30] JW Reiss, 'Innovative Governance in a Federal Europe: Implementing the Convention on the Rights of Persons with Disabilities' (2014) 20 *European Law Journal* 107.

[31] CM Radaelli, *The Open Method of Coordination: A new governance architecture for the European Union* (Swedish Institute for European Policy Studies, 2003).

[32] J Scott and DM Trubek, 'Mind the Gap: Law and New Approaches to Governance in the European Union' (2002) 8 *European Law Journal* 1.

[33] M Heidenreich and G Bischoff, 'The Open Method of Coordination: A Way to the Europeanization of Social and Employment Policies?' (2008) 46 *Journal of Common Market Studies* 497.

[34] Scott and Trubek, 'Mind the Gap' (n 32).

C. The Focal Point

The first requirement of Article 33 of the CRPD is the establishment of one or more focal points for matters relating to the implementation of the Convention, given due consideration to the designation of a coordination mechanism within national governments to facilitate related actions in different sectors and at different levels. To this end, Council Decision 2010/48/EC lays down that, with respect to matters falling within the Community's competence, the Commission shall be a focal point for matters relating to the CRPD's implementation.[35] The Code of Conduct between the Council, Member States and the Commission setting out internal arrangements for the implementation by and representation of the EU relating to the CRPD provides additional details regarding the general functions of the EU focal point.[36]

The Commission holds the power to convene, on its own initiative or at the request of a Member State's focal point, a coordination meeting with the focal points of the Member States.[37] Moreover, in respect of matters falling within the Union's competence, the Commission is in charge of drafting the Union report, and may agree with Member States on the information they provide to enable it to do so.[38] The Union report is a fundamental tool to monitor the work of the EU in relation to the CRPD's implementation because it analyses each legislative act adopted by the Union that address those matters governed by the Convention. The Code of Conduct emphasises the necessity to strengthen cooperation between Member States and the Commission. In particular, they are called upon to provide information to each other, before submitting the report to the UN Committee on the Rights of Persons with Disabilities.[39]

The above-mentioned instruments however do not identify the Commission service responsible for performing the tasks of the EU focal point. De facto, the Unit JUST D.3 'Rights of Persons with Disabilities' has taken up the role of coordinating the work of the Commission in this field and implementing the European Disability Strategy 2010–2020.[40]

The Commission has always pointed out the need for a new approach to implementing disability rights which focuses on the identification and removal of the various barriers preventing disabled people from achieving equality of opportunity and full participation in all aspects of life. The Commission has committed itself to

[35] Council, 'Decision of 26 November 2009 concerning the conclusion, by the European Community, of the United Nations Convention on the Rights of Persons with Disabilities' [2010] OJ L/23/35.

[36] Code of Conduct between the Council, the Member States and the Commission setting out internal arrangements for the implementation by and representation of the European Union relating to the United Nations Convention on the Rights of Persons with Disabilities [2010] OJ C 340 (2010/C 340/08).

[37] ibid, para 11(d) of the Code of Conduct.

[38] ibid, para 12(c) of the Code of Conduct.

[39] ibid, para 12(d) of the Code of Conduct.

[40] Arsenjeva (n 19) 21.

review its socio-economic policies, programmes and projects in order to include the rights and concerns of people with disabilities. Despite that, the Commission experienced significant difficulties in carrying out its function because disability represents a cross-cutting issue that falls under different legal areas and touches several competences. As a consequence, the Commission engaged all relevant Directorates-General in the Inter-Service Group on Disability with the purpose of improving its own internal machinery and supporting exchanges between its departments. The group promotes an effective inter-sectoral cooperation within the Commission in the field of disability to exchange information and develop proposals for better cross-sectoral coordination.

The designation of the Commission, as the focal point for the implementation of the Convention at EU level, is the logical outcome of its relevant contribution to the CRPD's drafting. The role conferred on the Commission is in line with its mission to promote the general interests of the European Union, which the Commission accomplishes by participating in the decision-making process and overseeing the correct implementation of the Treaties and EU law. The Commission again emerges as one of the most important EU actors for implementing disability rights. The Commission's role seems also to be in compliance with the UN Committee's recommendations to withdraw from the independent monitoring mechanism and focus on acting as the focal point for the implementation of the CRPD.[41]

D. Coordination Mechanism between the EU and the Member States

The governance mechanisms that have been designated for ensuring coordination within national governments and facilitating action in different sectors and at different levels will now be outlined. The designation of a coordination mechanism between the EU and the Member States is a crucial step forward in the process of monitoring and implementing the CRPD.[42] This approach seeks to promote cooperation between ministries in order to avoid the adoption of discordant and isolated measures by policymakers.

As proposed by the Commission in its Communication on 30 July 1996, the High Level Group on Disability (HLGD) was set up to monitor the latest policies and priorities of governments concerning people with disabilities.[43] The HLGD

[41] A Hoefmans, 'The EU Framework for Monitoring the CRPD' in D Ferri and A Broderick (eds), *Research Handbook on EU Disability Law* (Cheltenham, Edward Elgar Publishing, 2020) 79. See also, UN Committee on the Rights of Persons with Disabilities, 'Concluding Observations on the Initial Report of the European Union', UN Doc. CRPD/C/EU/CO/1 (2015) paras 72–73.

[42] Commission, 'Report on the implementation of the UN Convention on the Rights of Persons with Disabilities (CRPD) by the European Union', SWD (2014) 182 final.

[43] Commission, 'Communication of the Commission on equality of opportunity for people with disabilities. A New European Community Disability Strategy' COM (96) 406 final.

provides significant involvement of representatives of people with disabilities in the follow-up of relevant policies and actions in their favour. This group constitutes a network of experts, representatives of the Member States, national focal points and non-governmental organisations (NGOs) to pool information and experience. The meetings take place in Brussels twice a year by invitation of the Commission.[44] The HLGD releases recommendations to the Commission on methods for reporting and addressing the situation of persons with disability in the EU. Furthermore, the Commission and the HLGD annually publish a joint report concerning the CRPD's implementation. The reports encompass information on developments made in the establishment of the governance structures and processes foreseen by Article 33 of the CRPD. In these ways, the Commission and Member States reinforce cooperation in the field of disability and promote the exchange of good practice in the EU context. The HLGD, as a Commission expert group, encourages dialogue between the EU and national actors by means of flexible and non-binding interactions. Indeed, it lacks the formal tools to shape the CRPD's implementation at European or national level and does not participate in the approval of the initial report to the UN Committee on the Rights of Persons with Disabilities by the EU.

Similarly, the Commission's goal to support mutual learning and exchange of good practice is also pursued within the Work Forum on the Implementation of the Convention that has met every year since 2010. The Forum's composition reflects that of the HLGD and brings together representatives of the governance mechanisms provided by Article 33 of the CRPD, such as civil society, focal points, coordination and monitoring mechanisms. The Work Forum represents a platform for sharing experiences on the practical implementation and monitoring of the CRPD in order to promote solutions to common challenges.[45]

Political coordination is guaranteed within the Council Working Party on Human Rights (COHOM), which deals with the human rights aspects of the external relations of the EU and supports the Council's decision-making process in this area.[46] According to the Code of Conduct, coordination meetings between the Member States and the Commission are held within the competent Council Working Group, composed of the representatives of foreign ministers of the Member States.[47] Coordination meetings are convened at the presidency's own initiative or at the request of the Commission or a Member State, with possible reference to the HLGD in its area of competence. These meetings mainly focus

[44] Arsenjeva (n 19) 21.

[45] J Zeitlin, *Extending Experimentalist Governance? The European Union and Transnational Regulation* (Oxford, Oxford University Press, 2015) 313.

[46] The Working Party on Human Rights (COHOM) was created under the Council of the European Union in 1987 (with the extension of its mandate in 2003) and is responsible for human rights issues in the EU's external relations.

[47] Code of Conduct between the Council, the Member States and the Commission setting out internal arrangements for the implementation by and representation of the European Union relating to the United Nations Convention on the Rights of Persons with Disabilities (2010/C 340/08) para 6(a).

on the division of competences and tasks between the EU and Member States. In particular, the Commission and the Member States, during the coordination meetings, 'decide who will deliver any statement to be made on behalf of the Union and its Member States in cases where the respective competences are inextricably linked'.[48] The work within the COHOM is essential to ensure sincere cooperation and complementarity between the EU and its Member States.[49] In addition, the COHOM plays an important formal role in the approval of the European independent monitoring mechanism. It participates in the preparation of the Union's position ahead of the UN High-Level meeting on Disability and Development in New York and in the discussion on the initial report of the EU to the UN Committee on the Rights of Persons with Disabilities.[50]

This institutional context highlights the existence of governance mechanisms which privilege informal arenas, cooperative problem-solving and flexible instruments to facilitate exchange and mutual learning between the Member States and the EU.[51] Thus, the Commission does not have formal and binding tools to coordinate policies of national governments and facilitate action in different sectors and at different levels. The EU embraced a coordination mechanism based on mutual learning programmes and stakeholders' participation under the Commission's institutional umbrella in order to implement Article 33(1) of the CRPD.

IV. The EU Framework for Promoting, Protecting and Monitoring the CRPD

The EU introduced a monitoring framework that promotes, protects and monitors the implementation of the Convention in areas falling within its competences. 'Promotion' implies raising awareness of the Convention by organising public events and by providing training both to public officials and private citizens. 'Protection' requires the assessment of individual complaints with regard to the violations of rights of persons with disabilities. 'Monitoring' entails the evaluation of the compliance of legislation and practice with the CRPD.[52]

The Council put the Commission in charge of proposing an appropriate framework for one or several independent mechanisms, taking into account all relevant Union institutions, bodies, offices or agencies.[53] To this end, the Commission

[48] ibid, para 6(c).
[49] ibid, para 12.
[50] Arsenjeva (n 19) 22.
[51] See, for instance, J Corkin, 'Constitutionalism in 3D: Mapping and Legitimating Our Lawmaking Underworld' (2013) 19 *European Law Journal* 637.
[52] de Beco, *Study on the Implementation of Article 33 of the UN Convention on the Rights of Persons with Disabilities in Europe* (n 21).
[53] Code of Conduct between the Council, the Member States and the Commission setting out internal arrangements for the implementation by and representation of the European Union relating to the United Nations Convention on the rights of Persons with Disabilities [2010] OJ C340, para 13.

identified five existing EU institutions and bodies to perform the tasks required by Article 33(2) of the CRPD: the European Parliament's Petitions Committee (PETI), the European Ombudsman, the European Commission, the European Union Agency for Fundamental Rights (FRA) and the European Disability Forum (EDF). On 25 January 2012, the Commission's proposal was formally submitted to the Member States in the COHOM and was definitively adopted by the Council on 29 October 2012.[54] It is worth noting that, following the 2015 UN Committee's Concluding Observations on the initial report of the EU, the structure of the EU monitoring framework experienced significant changes leading to the removal of the Commission from the framework.[55]

The EU framework complements the national frameworks and independent mechanisms which bear the main responsibility for the promotion, protection and monitoring of the CPRD within the Member States.[56] The EU framework's action covers legislation and policies that fall under those areas where the Member States have transferred competences to the EU. This framework also carries out tasks with regard to the implementation of the Convention by the EU institutions in their capacity as public administration for the promotion, protection and monitoring of disability rights.

Figure 1 The EU Independent Framework's Composition

[54] Council Press Release 15491/12 (Luxembourg, 29 October 2012).

[55] L Waddington and A Broderick, 'The Post-2020 European Disability Strategy', study commissioned by the European Parliament's Policy Department for Citizens' Rights and Constitutional Affairs at the request of the PETI Committee (Brussels, 2020).

[56] Fifth High Level Group on Disability, *Report on the Implementation of the UN Convention on the rights of persons with disabilities* (Brussels, 2012).

A. The Commission's Experimentalist Approach

The Commission was initially fully integrated into the EU independent mechanism to promote, protect and monitor the CRPD. Informal meetings and soft policy instruments characterised the Convention's promotion within the EU. The Commission mainly supported mutual learning and the exchange of good practices through events and stakeholder engagement.[57] It released reports, disseminated information and organised training. In particular, the Commission had the duty, in cooperation with the HLGD, to prepare an annual report on the implementation of the Convention in the Member States and the EU. The report provides for a detailed analysis of the implementation of CRPD articles and statistical information on disability in the EU. The report systematically refers to and uses the Convention as a benchmark. It refers to legislative measures adopted under the scope of the CRPD and contributes to delineating a clear picture of the status of persons with disabilities in the EU.

Importantly, during the preparation of the report, the focal point constantly consults all the relevant stakeholders, including Members States within the COHOM. Furthermore, the HLGD's meetings are open to EU-level CSOs and disabled people's organisations (DPOs). The crucial interactions between the Commission and NGOs are reinforced by the financial support provided to CSOs, in particular DPOs that promote and raise awareness of the Convention. Stakeholders' involvement and mutual learning are also achieved through the annual conference that celebrates the European Day of Persons with Disabilities on 3 December. Moreover, the Commission organises training for legal practitioners and policymakers, arranges information sessions on the UN Committee on the Rights of Persons with Disabilities for staff, sets up an annual Work Forum for all concerned actors at EU level, in the Member States and from civil society and DPOs.[58]

The Commission's experience in the framework was characterised by the prevalence of mechanisms reflecting the 'experimentalist' architecture of the CRPD and the fundamental principles of 'good governance' adopted in the White Paper. The Commission has systematically encouraged the development of tools to share good practice and the participation of all relevant stakeholders in the process of promoting and monitoring the CRPD at EU level. This 'soft' model was integrated by the traditional powers of the Commission, which may initiate an infringement procedure according to Article 258 of the TFEU.[59] The Commission may intervene

[57] Commission, 'Commission non-paper on Setting-up the EU framework prescribed by article 33.2 of the UN Convention on the Rights of Persons with Disabilities' (2012).

[58] ibid.

[59] Art 258 TFEU: 'If the Commission considers that a Member State has failed to fulfil an obligation under the Treaties, it shall deliver a reasoned opinion on the matter after giving the State concerned the opportunity to submit its observations. If the State concerned does not comply with the opinion within the period laid down by the Commission, the latter may bring the matter before the Court of Justice of the European Union'.

where a Member State has failed to fulfil their treaty obligations.[60] This means that the Commission can ensure compliance with the UN Convention and monitor Members States' legislation in situations where they are implementing EU law.

However, the Commission's role in the monitoring framework has been the subject of intense discussion and concern. In 2015, the Concluding Observations of the UN Committee on the Rights of Persons with Disabilities pointed out the incompatibility with the Paris Principles of the Commission's dual role, as EU focal point (Article 33.1 CRPD) and a member of the Monitoring Framework (Article 33.2 CRPD).[61] According to the Paris Principles, the representatives of government departments should participate in the deliberations only in an advisory capacity.[62] Therefore, the UN Committee on the Rights of Persons with Disabilities recommended that the EU remove the Commission from the mechanism to monitor the CRPD's implementation. To comply with the Committee's recommendation, the Commission immediately expressed its intention to withdraw from the EU independent framework even before the finalisation of any legal and institutional procedures.[63] In 2017, the Council later adopted the revised EU-level framework that formally removed the Commission's functions.[64] Since its withdrawal, the Commission has continued to be involved in the work of monitoring the CRPD by sharing information with other bodies of the EU independent framework.[65]

B. The European Parliament and the Protection of Disability Rights

The European Parliament participates in the EU independent mechanism required by Article 33 of the CRPD, but it lacks adequate structures to monitor, promote

[60] M Mendrinou 'Non-compliance and the European Commission's role in integration' (1996) 3 *Journal of European Public Policy* 1.

[61] UN Committee on the Rights of Persons with Disabilities, 'Concluding Observations' (n 41) para 77: 'The Committee recommends that the European Union take measures to decouple the roles of the European Commission in the implementation and monitoring of the Convention, by removing it from the independent monitoring framework, so as to ensure full compliance with the Paris Principles, and ensure that the framework has adequate resources to perform its functions. The Committee also recommends that the European Union consider the establishment of an interinstitutional coordination mechanism and the designation of focal points in each European Union institution, agency and body'.

[62] UN General Assembly, 'Principles relating to the Status of National Institutions adopted by General Assembly Resolution 48/134 of 20 December 1993', UN Doc A/RES/48/134 (Paris Principles).

[63] During a public hearing at the European Parliament on the CRPD implementation held on 15 October 2015, the Commission representative underlined that 'the Commission prepares for the withdrawal of the Framework as a member'. See also, Hoefmans (n 41) 79; I Anglmayer, 'EU Implementation of the UN Convention on the Rights of Persons with Disabilities (CRPD)' (Brussels, European Parliamentary Research Service 2016).

[64] Council of the European Union, 3515th meeting of the Foreign Affairs Council, 16 January 2017, List of A-items, non-legislative activities.

[65] Hoefmans (n 41) 79.

and protect the UN Convention in the EU. The function to protect the CRPD is performed by the PETI in its capacity of hearing petitions and analysing issues of non-compliance.[66] According to Article 227 of the TFEU:

> Any citizen of the Union, and any natural or legal person residing or having its registered office in a Member State, shall have the right to address, individually or in association with other citizens or persons, a petition to the European Parliament on a matter which comes within the Union's fields of activity and which affects him, her or it directly.

The right of petition is a fundamental right of EU citizens and represents a simple means of contacting the institutions with a request or complaint. The petition must relate to an area falling within the sphere of activity of the EU and concern the petitioner directly. The PETI has the authority to provide non-judicial remedies, table questions to the Council and Commission, issue reports and resolutions. The PETI does not coordinate the work between national CRPD mechanisms and the UN Committee on the Rights of Persons with Disabilities. However, it is empowered to receive complaints concerning EU law before their submission to the Committee. According to the Parliamentary Rules of Procedure, the petition may take the form of a request arising from a general need, an individual grievance or an application to the European Parliament to take a position on a matter of public interest.[67] In this regard, any citizen of the European Union and any natural or legal person residing or having its registered office in a Member State shall have the right to address a petition to the Parliament, individually or in association with other citizens or persons.[68]

The PETI's work is highly linked to the other EU institutions. The UN Committee on the Rights of Persons with Disabilities may request assistance from the Commission in the form of information on the application and documents relevant to the petition. The Committee may also ask the President to forward its opinion or recommendation to the Commission, the Council or the Member State authority concerned for action or response.[69] Against this background, it is worth noting that the Committee does not have the competence to overrule competent legal authorities and impose binding remedies.[70] Despite that, in 2015 the Committee received a significant number of petitions regarding disability rights and contributed to improving the protection of persons with disabilities at the EU level.

[66] M Priestley, M Raley and G de Beco, *The protection role of the Committee on Petitions in the context of the implementation of the UN Convention on the Rights of Persons with Disabilities, study for the Directorate General for Internal Policies Policy Department C Citizens' Rights and Constitutional Affairs Petition* (Brussels, European Parliament, 2015).

[67] Rules of Procedure (Arts 215–18), 8th Parliamentary Term, July 2014.

[68] ibid, Art 215.

[69] ibid, Art 216(6).

[70] Priestley, Raley and de Beco (n 66) 22.

The European Parliament congratulated the UN Committee on the work it had undertaken in relation to petitions received on issues relating to disability.[71] It noted that considerable efforts had been made to ensure the successful launch of the EU framework under the terms of Article 33 of the CRPD and recognised the willingness of the Committee to continue to support this activity. Moreover, in the 2015 report the Parliament highlighted the necessity to adequately resource the EU framework in line with the requirements of the Convention.[72] The Parliament called for enhancing the capacity of the PETI and its Secretariat in order to fulfil its protection role. To this end, it proposed 'the establishment of a designated officer responsible for the processing of disabilities-related issues'.[73] The Parliament also emphasised the need for further efforts and action on behalf of the Committee in the protection of people with disabilities, such as actions directed to promote the swift ratification of the Marrakesh Treaty.[74]

The establishment of a specific officer dealing exclusively with disability issues would facilitate and improve the CRPD's protection in the EU. In practice, petitioners cannot always directly present their cases to the PETI because of a lack of meeting time and human resources at the Committee Secretariat. In addition, the new designated officer should support the use of video-conferencing, or of any other means enabling petitioners and persons with disabilities to become actively involved in the work of the PETI. In doing so, the EU would comply with Article 13 of the CRPD that aims to ensure effective access to justice for persons with disabilities, through the provision of procedural and age-appropriate accommodation, in order to facilitate their effective role as direct and indirect participants in all legal proceedings. To conclude, it may be said that the appointment of a specific body dedicated to the protection of persons with disabilities will simplify and clarify the functioning of the EU independent monitoring framework.

i. The PETI's Main Tasks and Achievements

The PETI's contribution to the effective improvement of the rights of persons with disabilities has been particularly relevant. For instance, Dan Pescod (British), on behalf of the European Blind Union and the Royal National Institute of Blind People, presented Petition 0924/2011 relating to the access for blind people to books and other printed products. The petition promoted accession to the Marrakesh Treaty, an international copyright agreement that aims at facilitating access to published works for persons who are blind, visually impaired, or otherwise print disabled. The PETI examined the petition and invited the Parliament's

[71] European Parliament, 'Report on the activities of the Committee on Petitions 2013' (A7-0131/2014).
[72] European Parliament, Report on the activities of the Committee on Petitions 2014' (A8-0361/2015).
[73] ibid, para 22.
[74] Marrakesh Treaty to Facilitate Access to Published Works for Persons Who Are Blind, Visually Impaired, or Otherwise Print Disable, Word Intellectual Property Organization, WIPO (27 June 2013).

President to formally contact the Council and the Commission in order to accelerate the procedure of accession to the Treaty by the EU. It also proposed to submit an Oral Question to Plenary and requested a meeting with the Commissioner of the Internal Market and Service.[75]

On 28 January 2016, the European Parliament released a motion for a Resolution on the ratification of the Marrakesh Treaty underlying 'that seven EU Member States have formed a minority block which is impeding the process of ratifying the Treaty' and calling 'on the Council and the Member States to accelerate the ratification process, without making ratification conditional on revision of the EU legal framework or the decision of the Court of Justice of the European Union'.[76] Importantly, the Parliament recalled Articles 24 and 30 of the CRPD, which set out the rights of persons with disabilities to education, without discrimination and on the basis of equal opportunity, while ensuring that laws protecting intellectual property rights do not constitute an unreasonable or discriminatory barrier to access by persons with disabilities to cultural materials. As a consequence, on 1 October 2018 the Treaty was successfully signed and ratified by the EU.

The PETI plays a remarkable role in the EU framework for the promotion of disability rights. It does not have the competence to provide judicial remedies, and the effectiveness of its work depends on the intervention of other institutional actors. Yet it has contributed to increasing the awareness of disability rights in the EU and constitutes an effective channel to exercise pressure on the main EU institutions. As such, in this context, CSOs and individuals have the possibility to perform lobbying and advocacy activities to ensure that public authorities understand and support their cause. Indeed, the most significant petitions have been supported by NGOs and CSOs engaged in public campaigns for combating stereotypes, prejudices and harmful practices relating to persons with disabilities.[77] To give another example, on 8 July 2020, following a petition from the NGO Inclusion Europe, the PETI drafted a Resolution on the rights of persons with intellectual disabilities in the COVID-19 crisis that has been positively approved by the European Parliament.[78] The Resolution points out 'the disproportionate impact of the COVID-19 crisis on persons with intellectual disabilities … and emphasises that persons with disabilities should not become further isolated when they emerge from the lockdown phase'.[79]

[75] Priestley, Raley and de Beco (n 66) 29.

[76] European Parliament, 'Motion for a Resolution, pursuant to Rule 216(2) of the Rules of Procedure on the ratification of the Marrakesh Treaty, based on petitions received, notably Petition 924/2011, 28.1.2016' (2016/2542(RSP).

[77] Priestley, Raley and de Beco (n 66) 40.

[78] European Parliament, 'Resolution of 8 July 2020 on the rights of persons with intellectual disabilities in the COVID-19 crisis' (2020/2680(RSP)), Brussels, 8 July 2020, B9-0204/2020.

[79] ibid, para 1.

ii. The Disability Intergroup of the European Parliament

The European Parliament's monitoring duties are also carried out by the Disability Intergroup, an informal group of Members of the European Parliament (MEPs) who are interested in promoting disability policy in their work at EU and national level. Their priorities are defined by the Intergroup Bureau, which meets regularly to approve the work programme of the Disability Intergroup. The Work Programme for 2020–22 outlines the importance of adopting the so-called Horizontal Equal Treatment Directive implementing the principle of equal treatment, aiming to extend the protection against discrimination beyond employment, to social protection and healthcare, social advantages, access to and supply of goods and other services available to the public, including housing and education.[80] The Disability Intergroup also calls for a more ambitious 'European Disability Strategy (Disability Rights Agenda 2020–2030)' with a specific budget for its implementation and monitoring and the regular involvement of organisations of persons with disabilities.

The Disability Intergroup ensures that the European Parliament agenda takes into account disability and contributes to awareness-raising of the CRPD. However, the Disability Intergroup is not financially supported by the European Parliament and is not involved in its official activities. It only represents a voluntary initiative to promote an exchange of views between political groups from all Member States. This body does not formally express the Parliament's views and has no capacity to effectively influence the legislative process. It seems that the Disability Intergroup, acting on behalf of the European Parliament, does not have sufficient tools to fulfil the delicate function of monitoring the CPRD. According to Rule 34 of the European Parliament's Rules of Procedure, individual members may form 'Intergroups' to hold informal exchanges of views on specific issues across different political groups and promote contact between members and civil society. Nonetheless, such groupings 'may not engage in any activities which might result in confusion with the official activities of Parliament or of its bodies'. This means that the Disability Intergroup is an informal forum for policy dialogue with a limited political mandate; it therefore cannot properly monitor the CRPD on behalf of the Parliament.

C. The European Ombudsman

The European Ombudsman is an independent and impartial body that investigates complaints about maladministration in EU institutions, bodies, offices and agencies.[81] According to Article 228 of the TFEU, the Ombudsman is empowered

[80] Disability Intergroup of the European Parliament, 'Work Programme 2020–2022'. The Disability Intergroup approved the workplan 2020–22 during a meeting on 13 February 2020.

[81] LC Reif, *The Ombudsman, Good Governance, and the International Human Rights System* (Leiden, Brill, 2004).

to receive complaints from any citizen of the Union or any natural or legal person residing or having its registered office in a Member State concerning instances of maladministration in the activities of the Union institutions, bodies, offices or agencies. Only the Court of Justice of the European Union (CJEU), when acting in its judicial role, does not fall within the Ombudsman's mandate. The Ombudsman examines such complaints and reports on them. Moreover, he or she has the duty to 'conduct inquiries for which he finds grounds, either on his own initiative or on the basis of complaints submitted to him directly or through a Member of the European Parliament' (Article 228(2) TFEU). In case the Ombudsman finds an instance of maladministration, he or she shall refer the matter to the institution, body, office or agency concerned, who shall have a period of three months to inform him of their views. The Ombudsman shall then forward a report to the European Parliament and the institution, body, office or agency concerned. The work of the Ombudsman may be said to be characterised by the use of soft law instruments which do not give rise to substantive legal rights.[82] Despite that, on 4 July 2007 the Ombudsman reviewed the actions undertaken by the EU Commission in the area of disability rights to assess whether or not they were consistent with its legal obligations.

i. *The Ombudsman's Own Initiatives*

The Ombudsman opened an own-initiative inquiry concerning the integration of persons with disabilities by the Commission with the purpose of verifying that these citizens were not discriminated against in their relations with the institution.[83] To this end, the Ombudsman started an open and transparent dialogue with all relevant stakeholders such as individuals with disabilities, representative groups and other ombudsmen at national and regional levels. The Ombudsman stated that the Commission made significant progress to integrate people with disabilities. In particular, the employment of persons with disabilities by all EU institutions respects the prohibition of non-discrimination on grounds of disability and the duty to provide reasonable accommodation.

Another significant Ombudsman's own initiative inquiry focused on European schools' treatment of disabled children with special educational needs (SEN children).[84] The Ombudsman regretted that the financial support and assistance given to officials with disabled family members was insufficient and encouraged the adoption of a new policy based on inclusion, and pointed out

[82] M Smith, *Centralized Enforcement, Legitimacy and Good Governance in the EU* (New York, Routledge, 2010). See also, PG Bonnor, 'The European Ombudsman: A Novel Source of Soft Law in the European Union' (2000) 1 *European Law Review* 39.

[83] European Ombudsman, 'Decision of the on own-initiative inquiry OI/3/2003/JMA concerning the European Commission', 4 July 2007.

[84] Integration of children with disabilities by the European Schools, Case OI/3/2003/JMA, Opened 19 November 2003, Decision 4 July 2007.

that the integration of SEN children should comply with the obligation to provide inclusive, non-discriminatory education for all enshrined in the CRPD. The Ombudsman concluded that the Commission should try to strengthen its own role in the European Schools' SEN policy.

The EU Ombudsman intervened in relation to the use of the European Structural and Investment Fund (ESI) that are the European Union's main investment policy tool.[85] It stated that a Member State used ESI funds to renovate a large institution housing disabled persons. By contrast, ESI funds are meant to finance the closure of such institutions and the transition to community-based living.[86] The Ombudsman found a violation of Article 19 of the CRPD, which promotes the deinstitutionalisation of persons with disabilities. The Ombudsman emphasised that the Commission should dissuade Member States from breaching fundamental rights when their activities are funded by the EU cohesion policy. To this end, the Ombudsman proposed guidelines for improvement to the Commission. For instance, the Commission should initiate infringement proceedings against a Member State if its actions in the framework of the cohesion policy amount to a violation of EU law. The suspension of funding constitutes an effective deterrent in case of violations of specific provisions of Regulation 1303/2013.[87] In addition, it recommended the creation of a clear and transparent framework to encourage the participation of civil society in monitoring and implementing the ESI funds. In this regard, the Commission should launch an online platform to involve small CSOs, report abuses of fund and Charter violations and submit complaints. The Ombudsman also suggested setting up mixed working parties composed of Commission representatives, Member States and civil society.[88]

ii. The Ombudsman's Limited Mandate

As noted above, the Ombudsman does not have the power to impose binding measures on the EU institutions in order to correct an instance of maladministration. Maladministration includes non-compliance with EU law and human rights

[85] European Ombudsman, 'Decision of the closing her own-initiative inquiry OI/8/2014/AN concerning the European Commission', 11 May 2015.

[86] Art 9(9) Regulation (EU) no 1303/2013 of the European Parliament and of the Council of 17 December 2013. See also, G Quinn and S Doyle, 'Taking the UN Convention on the Rights of Persons with Disabilities Seriously: The Past and Future of the EU Structural Funds as a Tool to Achieve Community Living' (2012) 9 *Equal Rights Review* 69.

[87] Regulation (EU) No 1303/2013 of the European Parliament and of the Council of 17 December 2013 laying down common provisions on the European Regional Development Fund, the European Social Fund, the Cohesion Fund, the European Agricultural Fund for Rural Development and the European Maritime and Fisheries Fund [2013] OJ L347/320.

[88] European Ombudsman, 'Decision of the closing her own-initiative inquiry OI/8/2014/AN' (n 85) para 48.

obligations under the UN Charter of Fundamental Rights.[89] The Ombudsman performs protection tasks through investigation of complaints and own-initiative inquiries. The Ombudsman's proposals aim at achieving friendly solutions and persuading EU institutions to improve their administrative practices.

If an institution fails to comply with his recommendations, the Ombudsman can criticise it publicly or if the issue is serious enough, may release a special report to the Parliament.[90] By contrast, the Ombudsman cannot start any procedures with regard to the implementation of EU law by Member States and cannot evaluate the compatibility of EU legislation with the Convention. In this context, the Ombudsman's role is limited because its mandate does not reflect those strategic requirements of Article 33(2) of the CRPD concerning the promotion and protection of the Convention. The Ombudsman's contribution is more significant in the process of monitoring the CRPD, as the specific reports and initiative inquiries show the extent to which the EU institutions and agencies are compliant with the Convention. The monitoring component is crucial to foster accountability and strengthen the capacity of EU institutions to fulfil their commitments.

D. The Monitoring Role of the EU Agency for Fundamental Rights

The FRA was established by Council Regulation (EC) 168/2007 in order to provide the EU relevant institutions, bodies, offices and agencies and its Member States with assistance and expertise relating to fundamental rights when implementing EU law.[91] The FRA cannot perform any functions to protect disability rights as it lacks the competence to investigate or examine complaints. Nevertheless, it represents a vital part of the EU independent mechanism to promote and monitor the CRPD's implementation. The Agency can formulate and publish conclusions and opinions on specific thematic topics, for the Union institutions and the Member States when implementing EU law. It also publishes an annual report on fundamental rights issues for highlighting examples of good practice. The FRA has the duty to develop a communication strategy and encourage dialogue with civil society in order to raise public awareness of fundamental rights.[92] In doing so, the

[89] European Parliament, 'Decision on the Regulations and General Conditions Governing the Performance of the Ombudsman's Duties 94/262/ECSC. See also LC Reif, 'Ombudsman Institutions and Article 33(2) of the United Nations Convention on the Rights of Persons with Disabilities' (2014) 65 *University of New Brunswick Law Journal* 213.

[90] European Ombudsman, 'Strategy for the mandate', September 2010. See also L Waddington, 'Reflections on the Establishment of a Framework to Promote, Protect and Monitor Implementation of the UN Convention on the Rights of Persons with Disabilities (Article 33(2) CRPD) by the European Union' (2011) Maastricht Faculty of Law Working Paper 2011/3.

[91] Art 2 of Council Regulation (EC) No 168/2007 of 15 February 2007 establishing a European Union Agency for Fundamental Rights [2007] OJ L53/1.

[92] ibid, Art 2(h).

FRA's activities may be essential for promoting disability rights and raising awareness of the CRPD.

It is not however clear if the Convention falls under the scope of the FRA's action.[93] The founding Regulation 168/2007 lays down that the Agency should, in its own work, refer to those fundamental rights within the meaning of Article 6(2) of the Treaty on European Union (TEU), including the European Convention on Human Rights and Fundamental Freedoms and the Charter of Fundamental Rights. Article 6 of the TEU underlines the EU fundamental rights *acquis* and does not make reference to the CRPD's conclusion. Notwithstanding, the Convention's ratification by the EU and the recent CJEU judgments signal that the CRPD forms an integral part of the EU fundamental rights *acquis*, as it prevails over instruments of EU secondary law.[94] As a consequence, the CRPD may be considered as the benchmark of the FRA's mandate. This means that the FRA should refer in its monitoring work to those fundamental rights enshrined by the CRPD.

Moreover, it is noteworthy to recall Article 26 of the EU Charter of Fundamental Rights, which provides that the 'Union recognises and respects the right of persons with disabilities to benefit from measures designed to ensure their independence, social and occupational integration and participation in the life of the community'. To the same extent, the Multiannual Framework 2013–2017 for the FRA establishes that the Agency shall carry out its tasks in the area of discrimination based on disability.[95] To this end, the FRA has to collect, analyse and disseminate reliable and comparable information and data. It has to develop methods and standards to improve the comparability, objectivity and reliability of data at the European level.[96]

The development of standards and data constitutes a fundamental tool to evaluate and monitor national practice and legislation with regard to disability rights. For instance, the FRA developed human rights indicators in order to allow EU Member States and all stakeholders to assess the fulfilment of Article 19 of the CRPD on the transition from institutional care to community-based support for persons with disabilities.[97] A human rights indicator can be described as

> specific information on the state or condition of an object, event, activity or outcome that can be related to human rights norms and standards; that addresses and reflects

[93] Waddington, 'Reflections' (n 90) 8.

[94] See Joined Cases C-335/11 and C-337/11 *HK Danmark, acting on behalf of Jette Ring v Dansk almennyttigt Boligselskab; HK Danmark, acting on behalf of Lone Skouboe Werge v Dansk Arbejdsgiverforening, acting on behalf of Pro Display A/S* (C-337/11) ECLI:EU:C:2013:222, para 29: 'primacy of international agreements concluded by the European Union over instruments of secondary law means that those instruments must as far as possible be interpreted in a manner that is consistent with those agreements'.

[95] Art 2(g) of Council Decision No 252/2013/EU of 11 March 2013 establishing a Multiannual Framework for 2013–2017 for the European Union Agency for Fundamental Rights [2013] OJ L79/1.

[96] Art 4 (a), (b) Regulation (EC) 168/2007.

[97] Indicators available online at: fra.europa.eu/en/project/2014/rights-persons-disabilities-right-independent-living/indicators.

> human rights principles and concerns; and that can be used to assess and monitor the promotion and implementation of human rights.[98]

The FRA's indicators cover important topics such as non-discrimination, reasonable accommodation, accessibility of support services, budget allocation, complaints and redress mechanisms, awareness-raising measures and training. They are fundamental part of a systematic process to implement, monitor and realise rights. They may contribute to assess violations of international and national human rights norms by national and EU tribunals, CSOs and policymakers. In this regard, the FRA's work is necessary to carry out those tasks enshrined in Article 31 of the CRPD that require the collection of statistical and research data.

In 2016, the FRA released an important opinion concerning the requirements under Article 33(2) of the CRPD within the EU context. It was emphasised that the EU independent framework 'is not based on an easily accessible and legally binding act' that clarifies the tasks of the actors involved.[99] To improve its working arrangements, the FRA recommended ensuring diversity of relevant societal groups and actors in the EU framework 'through procedures allowing for effective cooperation with these groups and actors, as well as by establishing consultative committees.'[100] In addition, the FRA suggested enhancing collaboration among the members of the framework, including the national frameworks, the European Commission, the coordination mechanisms, the UN Committee on the Elimination of Discrimination against Women and NHRIs.[101]

It may be argued that the FRA's role will be more effective in promoting and monitoring the CRPD because its current methods of operation reflect the key features of the OMC (continuous feedback, reporting, peer reviews, revising practices, data gathering and analysis).

E. The EDF's Challenge to Open Up the EU Decision-Making Process

The inclusion of the EDF in the EU independent monitoring system symbolises one of the most remarkable aspects of the governance mechanism adopted by the EU according to Article 33 of the CRPD. Indeed, the designation of the EDF complies with the international requirement to involve civil society in the monitoring process and it represents a concrete application of new governance paradigms. The EDF is the main disability rights organisation in Europe, and

[98] Office of the United Nations High Commissioner for Human Rights (OHCHR), 'Human rights indicators A Guide to Measurement' (New York, 2012).

[99] FRA, 'Opinion of the European Union Agency for Fundamental Rights concerning requirements under Article 33(2) of the UN Convention on the Rights of Persons with Disabilities within the EU context' (Vienna, 3/2016).

[100] ibid, 4.

[101] Hoefmans (n 41) 84.

has lobbied for achieving fundamental political objectives, such as the clause on combating discrimination on the grounds of disability in Article 13 of the Treaty of Amsterdam[102] and the inclusion of the concept of reasonable accommodation in the Equality Framework Directive.

The EDF plays a central role in promoting the Convention's implementation through awareness-raising campaigns, media activities and organisations of public events. The EDF conducts those specific tasks that are expressly required by Article 8 of the CRPD on awareness-raising. For instance, the EDF campaigned for the adoption of the European Accessibility Act to improve the functioning of the internal market for accessible products and services and remove barriers created by divergent rules in Member States.[103] Crucially, the EDF raises awareness throughout society to foster respect for the rights and dignity of persons with disabilities. It encourages all organs of the media to portray persons with disabilities in a manner consistent with the CRPD and aims at combating stereotypes, prejudices and harmful practices. To this end, it initiates effective public awareness campaigns to develop positive perceptions towards persons with disabilities, in particular with regard to their contribution to the workplace and the labour market. The EDF organises awareness-training programmes concerning the rights of persons with disabilities in order to strengthen the technical knowledge and advocacy capacity of CSOs.[104]

The EDF is also responsible for monitoring the EU's implementation of the CRPD. This strategic duty implies the examination of the legislative proposals and policy of the EU and the assessment of development or retrogression of rights of persons with disabilities in the EU legal context. In this regard, the EDF is involved in a continuous dialogue with the EU institutions. The EDF every year meets the bureau of the Disability Intergroup of the European Parliament to discuss the progress on the work programme and the political priorities of the year (eg, the effects of COVID-19 on persons with disabilities; the role of the Parliament in the follow-up of the UN's Concluding Observations on the Rights of Persons with Disabilities; the impact of austerity measures on persons with disabilities; and the situation of refugees and migrants with disabilities). For example, the MEPs of the Disability Intergroup endorsed the EDF's proposal to hold a fourth European Parliament of Persons with Disabilities in 2017, co-organised by the EDF and the European Parliament.

The European Parliament of Persons with Disabilities is an event to mainstream at EU level the situation of the most vulnerable groups of individuals such

[102] Treaty of Amsterdam amending the Treaty on European Union, the Treaties establishing the European Communities and certain related acts, signed in Amsterdam on 2 October 1997, entered into force on 1 May 1999.

[103] Directive (EU) 2019/882 of the European Parliament and of the Council of 17 April 2019 on the accessibility requirements for products and services [2019] OJ L151/70.

[104] Commission, 'Staff Working Document, Report on the implementation of the UN Convention on the Rights of Persons with Disabilities' (CRPD) by the European Union, Brussels, SWD (2014) 182 final, 49.

as women, youth, children and people with disabilities. To mainstream implies that the needs of disadvantaged people must be taken into account in the design and implementation of all policies and measures. This forum is shaped according to the rules governing the plenary sitting of the European Parliament. The event involves the participation of delegates from DPOs who vote on a resolution calling on the EU institutions, the Member States, social partners, civil society and other stakeholders to take appropriate steps towards the CRPD's implementation. It aims at reinforcing the link between national representatives of organisations of persons with disabilities and EU decision-makers. Such an event may constitute a considerable contribution to EU governance as it helps the European Parliament to individuate work priorities and develop long-term policy perspectives.

To give another example, on 17 February 2016 the EDF participated in the meeting of the European Parliament's Employment Committee focusing on the implementation of the UN's recommendations to the EU on the promotion of the rights of persons with disabilities.[105] The European Ombudsman and the FRA, as members of the EU Monitoring Framework along with the EDF and the Parliament, also took part in the debate. The EDF emphasised that the UN's recommendations set out a clear roadmap and a list of actions to be adopted in line with the CRPD: review of the European Disability Strategy; revision of EU laws; and adoption of the European Accessibility Act. This meeting represents another decisive moment in the constructive relationship between the Parliament and EFD because MEPs have the opportunity to share and exchange ideas with key EU bodies and the European disability movement. Thus, the EDF can effectively monitor to what extent the EU will address the UN's recommendations and implement the CRPD.

This framework has enabled the European Parliament and its committees to gradually improve the quality of their policy deliberation through regular consultation and public hearings with the EDF. The need for reinforcing the culture of consultation and dialogue is a central guideline of the Commission's White Paper. The principle of good governance indeed demands measures to consolidate the consultative process in the European Parliament, given its role in representing the citizens. In particular, public hearings are expressly required to enhance dialogue between the Parliament and civil society. The consultative process within the Parliament and its committees with regard to the CRPD's implementation demonstrates the emergence of a strong interplay between the European Parliament and the EDF.

The fundamental rules, processes and behaviours that characterise the way in which powers are exercised by EU actors within the independent framework have been described above. The analysis of the EU system created in accordance with Article 33 of the CRPD to implement the Convention has been done through the

[105] UN Committee on the Rights of Persons with Disabilities, 'Concluding Observations on the Initial Report of the European Union', UN Doc CRPD/C/EU/CO/1 (adopted by the Committee at its fourteenth session, 17 August–4 September 2015).

lens of the experimentalist approach to governance. This chapter will now offer an overview of the main weaknesses and positive aspects of the governance mechanism designed by the EU. The final objective is to assess whether the open method of coordination, as an ideal model of experimentalist governance, is appropriate for implementing the CRPD.

F. Focal Point and Coordination Mechanism: Innovative or Inefficient Practices?

The European Commission had originally been appointed both as a focal point (Article 33.1) for implementation and as an actor of the mechanism for monitoring the CRPD's implementation until 2015 (Article 33.2). As a focal point, the Commission is responsible for the implementation of the Convention on behalf of the EU and for Union examination by the UN Committee on the Rights of Persons with Disabilities. It ensures cross-sectoral coordination within its own institution, between all EU bodies and with the Member States.[106]

To achieve *internal* coordination, the Inter-Service Group on Disability involves all relevant Directorates-General in order to share policy initiatives between different departments. This internal mechanism is crucial to ensure dialogue between Directorates-General and facilitate the fulfilment of common goals.[107] For instance, the new European Disability Strategy 2021–2030 aims to boost the access of people with disabilities to quality and sustainable jobs, and improve access to justice, legal protection, freedom and security.[108] The coordination mechanism developed within the Commission's Inter-Service Group on Disability may be not sufficient to achieve these ambitious objectives. This structure seems necessary to put together departments that work in different areas, but further and stronger coordination is needed to implement the Disability Strategy in a systematic way. The Inter-Service Group's role is mainly consultative and is not informed by clear procedures for the adoption of common proposals or policy instruments. The Commission, as a focal point, will face significant obstacles to effectively achieve cross-sectoral coordination within its own institutions. It may be argued that the lack of a permanent and specific department dealing with the Disability Strategy and the CRPD's implementation will slow down EU action.

In a different way, a *vertical* coordination mechanism has been informally developed to coordinate all EU bodies and the Member States. The vertical coordination mechanism should foster related actions in different sectors and at different levels,

[106] Anglmayer (n 63).

[107] E Flynn, *From Rhetoric to Action: Implementing the UN Convention on the Rights of Persons with Disabilities* (Cambridge, Cambridge University Press, 2011) 72.

[108] Commission, 'Union of Equality: Strategy for the Rights of Persons with Disabilities 2021–2030', COM(2021) 101 final.

but the EU has not formally nominated any bodies to carry out this duty.[109] Despite that, two main actors are involved in this process: the Council Working Party on Human Rights (COHOM) and the High Level Group on Disability (HLGD). They ensure coordination between the EU institutions and Member States. It is worth noting that this mechanism combines two opposite governance models: a traditional hierarchal approach and an experimentalist paradigm. The COHOM is part of the Council of the European Union and includes only representatives of foreign ministers of the Member States. By contrast, the HLGD promotes participation of national focal points and CSOs along with Member States representatives. The coexistence of a classic procedure of coordination with a new mode of governance may consolidate the effectiveness of the vertical mechanism. This 'hybrid' system represents a good practice to develop cooperation between EU and Member States taking into account the views of European DPOs and NGOs.

To conclude, the de facto vertical mechanism that links the EU institutions, national governments and private actors may be considered as highly innovative and efficient. It mixes bottom-up political dynamics with top-down structures in order to facilitate political coordination in a delicate sensitive area. However, the observations of the UN Committee on the Rights of Persons with Disabilities missed clarifying the exact interplay between the independent framework and the focal points and coordination mechanisms under Article 33(1) of the CRPD, leaving some doubts concerning the functioning of these mechanisms.[110]

V. Light and Shadow in the EU Independent Framework

Each member of the EU independent framework shares the common mission to promote, protect and monitor the Convention's implementation. All relevant EU institutions, agencies and bodies of the governance mechanism should work together to put into practice the requirements of Article 33 of the CRPD. Despite that, every member exercises its functions within the limits of those powers and competences conferred by the EU Treaties. The final part of this chapter will look at the main gaps existing in the EU independent framework and how its functioning and mechanisms could be improved.

A. The Commission's Withdrawal from the Framework: What Next?

As already mentioned in this chapter, the Concluding Observations of the UN Committee on the Rights of Persons with Disabilities pointed out the

[109] Anglmayer (n 63) 11.
[110] Hoefmans (n 41) 83.

incompatibility with the Paris Principles of the Commission's dual role, as EU focal point (Article 33.1 CRPD) and a member of the Monitoring Framework (Article 33.2 CRPD).[111] According to the Paris Principles, representatives of government departments should participate in the deliberations only in an advisory capacity.[112] Therefore, to comply with the Committee's recommendation, the Commission immediately resigned from the EU independent framework.[113] However, the withdrawal of the Commission has left a 'governance gap' in the framework, which is not yet fully in line with the Paris Principles.[114] Indeed, it is not clear which institutions would replace the role and functions exercised by the Commission, which was the only body capable of starting infringement procedures against Member States breaching EU law. Moreover, the Commission's withdrawal may have negative effects on the budget allocated for the framework, since several human rights bodies and NGOs need financial support for carrying out their work and mandate.

The brief experience of the Commission in the independent framework showed distinctive features of the new EU modes of governance. The procedures affecting the Commission's work have been characterised by the existence of structured channels for enhancing feedback and civil society's engagement. The continuous consultation of organised civil society within the HLGD represented a positive element of the mechanism to independently implement the CRPD. Consultation and dialogue not only contribute to foster the transparency and accountability of the EU institutions, but also help the Commission in developing long-term policy perspectives.[115] By contrast, a weak point of this governance mechanism was that the Commission had no clear authority to release formal recommendations to the Member States in case of non-compliance with the CRPD's objectives. The Commission independently monitored to what extent the Member States apply EU legislation falling under the scope of the CRPD and prepared an annual report on the application of the Convention in the Member States and the EU, but it failed to make recommendations for policy changes.

[111] UN Committee on the Rights of Persons with Disabilities, 'Concluding Observations on the Initial Report' (n 105) para 77: 'The Committee recommends that the European Union take measures to decouple the roles of the European Commission in the implementation and monitoring of the Convention, by removing it from the independent monitoring framework, so as to ensure full compliance with the Paris Principles, and ensure that the framework has adequate resources to perform its functions. The Committee also recommends that the European Union consider the establishment of an interinstitutional coordination mechanism and the designation of focal points in each European Union institution, agency and body'.

[112] Paris Principles (n 62).

[113] During a public hearing at the European Parliament on the CRPD implementation held on 15 October 2015, the Commission representative underlined that 'the Commission prepares for the withdrawal of the Framework as a member'. See also, European Parliamentary Research Service, *EU Implementation of the UN Convention on the Rights of Persons with Disabilities (CRPD) European Implementation Assessment* (2016).

[114] Hoefmans (n 41) 80.

[115] O de Schutter, 'Europe in Search of its Civil Society' (2002) 8 *European Law Journal* 198.

On the contrary, according to the European Employment Strategy (EES), the most interesting example of the OMC, the Commission has the power to issue recommendations for policy change when the Member States' performances are not in line with the EES guidelines.[116] The EES emerged in the 1990s when the EU Member States decided to set up common objectives and targets for employment policy. Currently, the Member States and the Commission agree on the establishment of initial goals, general guidelines and a series of indicators to promote the creation of more and better jobs in the European Union.[117] In this context, national governments have the duty to submit National Reform Programmes (NRPs) that are analysed by the Commission. Crucially, based on the assessment of the NRP, the Commission publishes a series of country reports and issues country-specific recommendations. Neither the recommendations nor the guidelines are legally binding, but they are part of a comprehensive strategy to share information and good practice.[118] The NRPs circulate between the Member States to exchange feedback. At the same time, indicators ensure transparent data and reliable benchmarks to assess positive results. This system assures a multilateral surveillance mechanism based on the involvement of the Member States, the Commission and the EU Council.

The EES model may be also appropriate with regard to the monitoring of the CRPD's implementation and the EU should consider reforming the monitoring system to effectively put the CRPD's objectives into practice.

The EU may consider introducing a new monitoring mechanism based on the submission of NRPs by national governments and the final analysis by the Commission for compliance with the CRPD. The Commission should not only publish a series of country and Union reports, but also release specific recommendations to promote legislative improvements. The Code of Conduct should therefore confer on the Commission the power to release country reports and country-specific recommendations to encourage Member States to follow the guidelines agreed with the EU institutions and avoid negative peer reviews. The Commission's role may benefit from the adoption of those main rules and procedures that inform the open method of coordination.

B. Is the European Parliament Marginalised?

The European Parliament mainly performs its duty to implement the CRPD through political debates, informal meetings and public hearings. It examines legislative and policy documents for assessing their compliance with the CRPD

[116] DM Trubek and LG Trubek, 'Hard and Soft Law in the Construction of Social Europe: the Role of the Open Method of Co-ordination' (2005) 11 *European Law Journal* 343.

[117] The Employment Guidelines, proposed by the Commission, have finally been approved by the EU Council.

[118] Trubek and Trubek (n 116) 349.

and carries out several awareness-raising activities. The Parliament is represented in the independent framework by the PETI, the Committee on Employment and Social Affairs (EMPL) and the Committee on Civil Liberties, Justice and Home Affairs.

As previously noted, the PETI has the authority to protect the rights of persons with disabilities and monitor the CRPD's implementation. Despite the non-binding nature of its decisions, the PETI is effectively contributing to the enhancement of disability rights. It does so by hearing petitions from any EU citizen concerning EU legislation and reporting on the petitions it receives. Its competences are in line with the 'soft' policy mechanisms of the OMC. However, its role might be improved to better achieve the aims of Article 33 of the CRPD.

In primis, the appointment of a specific officer responsible for dealing with legal issues relating to disability is strongly required in order to strengthen the Committee's protection role. Second, the PETI should release an annual report on the main disability issues stemming from the petitions to facilitate the identification of possible legal solutions. Third, a systematic and periodic exchange of information should be set up between the PETI and national monitoring institutions. The lack of coordination between the PETI and national mechanisms constitutes a critical point in the functioning of the governance system to implement the CRPD. In this regard, the interplay between EU and domestic actors is essential to carry out the sensitive task of protecting the rights of persons with disabilities. The PETI may potentially address the CRPD's broad scope, but it needs a comprehensive and enhanced capacity to perform its protection role.

With the exception of the PETI, the European Parliament does not have any formal structure to implement the CRPD. Nevertheless, the EMPL is crucially promoting the implementation of the UN's recommendations to the EU and the role of the European Parliament in this context. The European Parliament has drafted a report on the UN's recommendations in order to tackle crucial issues such as the adoption of the Accessibility Act and the effects of austerity measures on persons with disabilities.[119] The EDF and members of civil society have been constantly involved in public hearings and events organised by the EMPL. This report is a spontaneous initiative of the Parliament and symbolises a remarkable starting point to lead efforts for the CRPD's implementation. Importantly, the Parliament calls for the EU to ratify the Optional Protocol to the Convention and urges a cross-cutting review of EU legislation and funding programmes to comply fully with the CRPD. It also asks the Commission to update the declaration of competence in light of the Concluding Observations, to review the EDF and to develop a comprehensive EU CRPD strategy with a clear time frame, benchmarks and indicators.[120]

[119] Committee on Employment and Social Affairs, 'Draft Report on the implementation of the UN Convention on the Rights of Persons with Disabilities, with special regard to the Concluding Observations of the UN CRPD Committee' (2015/2258(INI)).

[120] ibid, 6.

The Parliament is gradually emerging from the institutional shadows by means of the political action of a proactive group of MEPs and claims a greater involvement in EU governance.[121] It is important to underline that the Parliament is excluded from the official drafting of the EU periodic report to the UN Committee on the Rights of Persons with Disabilities, which is still under the exclusive competence of the Commission. Moreover, the Parliament does not participate in any procedures of the de facto vertical and horizontal coordination system. It may therefore be said that the European Parliament's role has been marginalised within the EU independent framework.

This institutional scenario may jeopardise the adequate implementation of the CRPD at European level. The Parliament has always worked to mainstream the rights of persons with disabilities pushing for the adoption of the Horizontal Equal Treatment Directive. For this reason, the European Parliament should be more influential both in the coordination system and the implementation process. To this end, the Commission should invite the Parliament to take a full part in the debate concerning the implementation of the Convention within the HLGD.[122] In this way, the Parliament would be involved in the fundamental mechanism that ensures vertical coordination between the EU and Member States. The Parliament might also provide a relevant contribution to the internal coordination among the EU institutions. Currently, the EU mechanism does not provide for an inter-institutional coordination mechanism and the European Parliament may fill this governance gap. Good coordination among all the EU institutions is an essential condition to achieve the ambitious objectives of the Convention. Last, the Code of Conduct should be revised in order to expressly update the Parliament's role in the EU independent framework.[123] It may be recommended to formally recognise the Parliament's task to provide an annual report on the implementation of the CRPD by the EU and to present a periodic report to the UN Committee. However, the presence of the European Parliament in the independent framework should be further discussed at EU and international level, as it seems to not be formally in line with the Paris Principles which merely allow representatives of parliaments to be part of the NHRIs.[124]

This *excursus* on the procedures adopted by the EU to face the challenges posed by the CRPD's ratification highlights some controversial features of the EU institutional framework and governance. In particular, the mechanism established according to Article 33 of the CRPD brings about the obscuration of the European

[121] Significantly, MEPs Helga Stevens (ECR, BE) and Martina Anderson (GUE/NGL, UK) hosted, on 27 January 2016, the European Parliament's Public Hearing focusing on the UN's recommendations to the EU on how to better promote the rights of 80 million people with disabilities.

[122] HLGD includes only the European Commission, the Member States, Norway, the Council of Europe, EU-level NGOs, including organisations of people with disabilities.

[123] Para 14 of the Code of Conduct states: 'At the request of the Council, a Member Stare or the Commission. The arrangement will be reviewed, taking into account of experience gained during its operation'.

[124] Hoefmans (n 41) 80

Parliament, the closer body to the European citizens and civil society organisations. Nonetheless, the Parliament has extended its role in the framework and is taking a leading role in the Convention's implementation through the political initiatives of the EMPL.

C. Is the OMC Appropriate?

The governance system required by Article 33 of the CRPD employs those typical mechanisms and procedures of the experimentalist approach. The EU has responded to this challenge by crafting a governance model that mirrors the OMC. The European Commission first adopted the European Disability Strategy 2010–2020 in order to pursue its objectives by actions in eight priority areas and then the Disability Rights Strategy for 2021–2030.[125] The approach to achieve these shared goals is mainly based on voluntary political cooperation. Member States still retain a significant portion of autonomy in the adoption of national policies to accomplish EU objectives.[126] It would seem that the Member States are quite reluctant to confer political competence on the European Union in such a sensitive area as disability law that affects different legal sectors (equality law, access to justice, legal capacity and accessibility). Member States are also supported by the Commission's expertise and guidance in implementing strategic objectives. This 'soft' coordination system has already been applied in specific policy fields such as employment and growth, social protection and social inclusion, but never with regard to equality issues.[127] As a result, this new scenario raises several concerns in relation to the feasibility of the OMC in the disability sector.

i. An Overview of the Reporting Mechanism

The main weakness of the existing governance mechanism affects the reporting and benchmarking process. Peer review and reporting are central elements of the OMC. Indeed, governments should provide national plans to the Commission concerning the situation of persons with disabilities in their domestic system. To this end, Member States started to report on disability by means of the NRPs. The Member States were asked to follow the guidelines offered by the HLGD in a discussion paper on 'Disability mainstreaming in the new streamlined European social protection and inclusion processes'.[128] The HLGD, as a Commission expert

[125] See on this matter, Waddington and Broderick (n 55).

[126] M Priestley, 'Disability Policies and the Open Method of Coordination' (2012) 3 *European Yearbook of Disability Law* 7.

[127] ibid, 14.

[128] High Level Group on Disability Work Programme 2006–2007, High Level Group on Disability Discussion Paper. Subject: Disability mainstreaming in the new streamlined European social protection and inclusion processes.

group, supported mainstreaming disability into social protection and social inclusion, taking into account the EU Charter of Fundamental Rights and the CRPD. The HLGD outlined important strategic and key policy priorities such as overcoming discrimination, increasing the integration of people with disabilities into the labour market, tackling disadvantages in education, enhancing assistance to families with disabled members, ensuring decent housing, and improving access to quality services that are accessible and affordable. Notably, national reports have not mainstreamed disability in a systematic and coherent way. Several countries have not addressed the fundamental framework of guidance given by the HLGD. Some NRPs failed to report on the implementation progress made by the country or paid insufficient attention to core European policy concepts.[129] The majority of states did not provide clear and analytical evidence with regard to the implementation of disability policies. In doing so, the Commission could not carry out any rigorous assessment of the rights of persons with disabilities at national level.

The launch of the European Disability Strategy 2010–2020 and the entry into force of the CPRD slightly improved the reporting system. Disability strategies and action plans have been developed by some Member States to highlight areas which will be at the forefront of government action. For instance, in June 2011, Germany released a National Action Plan that covers crucial issues such as equality, social and political participation of persons with disabilities, empowerment and self-help. To the same extent, the Latvian government adopted the Guidelines for the Implementation of the CRPD 2014–2020, and Denmark launched a new National Action Plan on Disability in October 2013. Yet, most of the national disability plans does not take into consideration specific disability indicators or do not develop reliable data. Therefore, the EU institutions cannot promote the exchanging of good practice and benchmark progress by the Member States. This context reveals that the reporting mechanism should be more incisive in order to involve all EU Member States and improve the effectiveness of the OMC. National plans should not merely contain political guidelines, but should identify clear legislative actions and enforcement mechanisms.

Positively, the new Disability Strategy specifies that Member States are key actors to implement the CRPD and the Commission calls on Member States to adopt 'ambitious national strategies to foster the implementation of the UNCRPD and of this Strategy at national, regional and local level'.[130] To better work with Member States, regional and local authorities, the Commission will also establish the 'Disability Platform' in 2021 to replace the existing HLGD and support the implementation of the EU Strategy and national disability strategies.

[129] According to Mark Priestley's research, disability had limited or no visibility in the 2008 National Reform Programmes of several countries: Austria, Bulgaria, Finland, France, Germany, Lithuania, Malta, Poland and Romania. See Priestley (n 126) 19.

[130] Commission, 'Union of Equality Strategy' (n 108) 27.

This new platform will consist of national CRPD focal points, organisations of persons with disabilities and the Commission, and it will be used as a forum for exchanges on the UN's assessments of Member States' implementation of the CRPD.[131]

ii. *Enhancing the EU Independent Framework: Some Suggestions*

The OMC has not always been considered a proper tool to accelerate the process of EU integration because it is not based on a comprehensive system of sanctions, and the concrete achievement of its objectives depends on the extent to which national plans are implemented by governments.[132] The adoption of non-binding recommendations and atypical acts do not ensure the uniform application of EU rules in Member States. Moreover, fundamental EU institutions such as the European Parliament and the CJEU have a secondary role. The Court does not have a structural position in protecting rights under the CRPD, as it can intervene only in response to specific cases submitted by individuals.

It should be said that the establishment of an independent framework reflecting the experimentalist governance approach results from the international obligation under Article 33 of the CRPD. The absence of 'hard' sanctioning mechanisms should not constitute an obstacle in a governance architecture that incentivises reciprocal learnings.[133] As a consequence, the reporting methods and the coordination mechanisms of the OMC should be enhanced to mainstream disability in the EU.

First, the new Disability Platform, along with the Parliament's contribution, may promote the objectives of the new Disability Strategy 2021–2030 developing precise time frames and key performance indicators. This approach has been also recommended by the European Parliament's Resolution on the European Disability Strategy post-2020.[134] Such instruments will be useful for identifying good practice and for measuring countries' performances in the area of disability. In this regard, the FRA has already provided human rights indicators with regard to the right of political participation of people with disabilities. As a member of the EU independent framework, it may assist the Commission and the Parliament in adopting new policy strategies and indicators. The formulation of clear performance indicators by the EU institutions can facilitate the benchmarking process

[131] ibid.

[132] V Hatzopoulos, 'Why the Open Method of Coordination is Bad For You: A letter to the EU' (2007) 13 *European Law Journal* 309. See also S Sciarra, 'Experiments in the Open Method of Coordination: Measuring the Impact of EU Employment Policies' [2011] *Rivista Italiana di Diritto del Lavoro* 475.

[133] Radaelli (n 31) 52.

[134] European Parliament, 'Resolution of 18 June 2020 on the European Disability Strategy post 2020 (2019/2975(RSP), Brussels', P9_TA-PROV (2020) 0156, para 5.

and improve the reporting mechanism. By doing so, the Member States will be encouraged to elaborate statistics and data on the impact of their policy measures. At the same time, the EU institutions will have the necessary tools to share good practice and evaluate Member States' performance.

Second, the EU governance system designed to implement the CPRD should introduce procedures to penalise non-cooperation by the Member States. The Commission should formally release specific recommendations that emphasise poor performance and call on Member Sates to comply with EU guidelines and indicators. Recommendations will spur the Member States to participate in the reporting mechanisms in order to avoid negative publicity.[135] Moreover, this procedure will urge the non-compliant Member State to follow positive models and propose legislative reforms. The OMC does not provide tangible coercion mechanisms and infringement procedures to punish non-implementers.[136] However, 'peer pressure' and 'naming and shaming' by the EU Commission may represent 'soft' procedures and sanctions to foster learning and improvement mechanisms at domestic level.[137] No formal sanctions should be adopted against those Member States whose performances do not comply with agreed standards. Instead, Commission recommendations addressed to individual Member States may constitute powerful tools to influence national policy discourses.[138]

Third, the EU independent framework reveals excessive fragmentation. Unreasonable decentralisation may bring about poorly defined responsibilities and unclear competences.[139] It may be said that the EU governance mechanisms should be simplified in order to avoid the coexistence of multiple EU bodies with overlapping functions. To this end, precise duties and responsibilities should be conferred on the EU actors involved in the OMC. The OMC is not seen as a panacea to implement the CRPD, but the improvement of certain mechanisms may contribute to facilitate the achievement of the Disability Strategy objectives and the EU independent framework. In doing so, Member States will retain the main responsibility in a sensitive area where they are still reluctant to lose an important share of legislative power.

[135] Trubek and Trubek (n 116) 357.

[136] M López-Santana, 'The Domestic Implications of European Soft Law: Framing and Transmitting Change in Employment Policy' (2006) 13 *Journal of European Public Policy* 481.

[137] M Buch, 'The Open Method of Coordination as a "Two-level game"' (2008) 36 *Policy & Politics* 21.

[138] FW Scharpf, 'The European Social Model: Coping with the Challenges of Diversity' (2002) Max Planck Institute for the Study of Societies Working Paper 02/8.

[139] G Majone, 'The European Commission: The limits of Centralization and the Perils of Parliamentarization' (2002) 15 *Governance: An International Journal of Policy, Administration and Institutions* 375.

iii. Proposal to Upgrade and Simplify the EU Independent Framework to Implement the CRPD

An outline of the key recommendations to improve the EU governance architecture is offered below:

- Considering that the Commission is no longer a formal member of the independent framework, a reform of the Code of Conduct would be needed to introduce 'soft' procedures to sanction non-compliant behaviour by Member States.
- The Parliament should play a leading role with regard to EU external relations and internal policies. On the one hand, the Parliament should be in charge of preparing the annual report on the CRPD's implementation by the EU to the UN Committee. The Parliament has actively facilitated interactions and constructive dialogues between the EU and the UN Committee on the Rights of Persons with Disabilities. The European Parliament regularly organises events and public hearings to discuss the CRPD's review process and the list of issues released by the UN Committee on the Rights of Persons with Disabilities. Furthermore, the Parliament on a regular basis drafts reports and resolutions with regard to the Convention's implementation and the Concluding Observations of the UN Committee on the Rights of Persons with Disabilities. It may be said that the Parliament embodies the political capacity to act as the main contact point for the purpose of CRPD reporting. On the other hand, the Committee on Employment and Social Affairs, acting on behalf of the Parliament, should be acknowledged as the central internal coordinator between the EU institutions, EU agencies and civil society. It has a strong competence in the field of the rights of persons with disabilities and is promoting several political initiatives to improve their legal protection at EU level.
- The EU Ombudsman and PETI should formally monopolise the duty to ensure the implementation of the CRPD through an independent officer responsible for disability legal cases.
- The Agency for Fundamental Rights (FRA) should acquire an active role in the monitoring process. Its functions are highly relevant in supporting the work of the Commission in measuring the impact of the Disability Strategy 2021–2030. Indicators and data developed by the FRA should be used to systematically benchmark and evaluate national strategies concerning the rights of persons with disabilities.
- The European Disability Forum (EDF) is identified as the main NGO involved in the promotion of disability rights in the EU. It participates in all the main meetings and procedures of the EU independent framework. The central challenge is to improve the quality of EU policy deliberation ensuring regular consultation and public hearings with civil society. Its contribution may also be significant in assisting the European Parliament in drafting reports to the UN Committee and monitoring the CRPD's implementation.

Figure 2 The EU Independent Framework's recommended functions

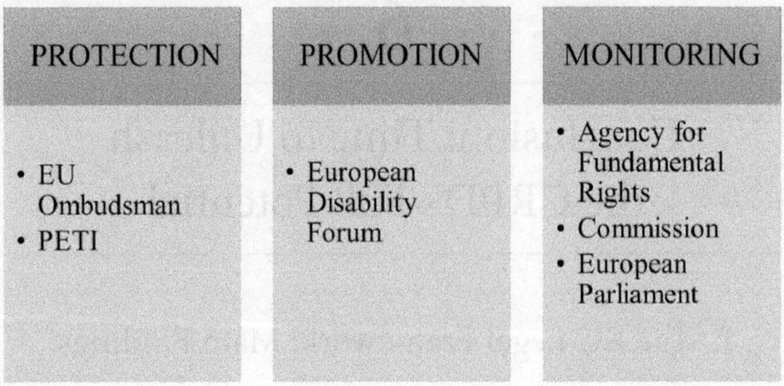

6

Conclusion: Time to Unleash the CRPD's Full Potential

I. The EU Legal Framework: Main Findings

This final chapter will summarise the main findings of the book concerning the impact of the UN Convention on the Rights of Persons with Disabilities (CPRD) on the EU legal framework 10 years after its ratification by the European Union. In particular, it will be shown that: (i) the Court of Justice of the European Union (CJEU) is failing to fully apply the 'human rights' model of disability enshrined in the CRPD; (ii) the CJEU's understanding of multiple and intersectional discrimination is not in line with the substantive model of equality; (iii) the CJEU is still embracing a 'protectionist' and 'minimalist' approach with regard to the status of the CRPD in the EU legal order.

A. The Definition of Disability: A Missed Opportunity

The case of *Ring and Skouboe Werge* marked a crucial development in the CJEU's case law on discrimination on grounds of disability.[1] It represents the first decision taken by the CJEU after the EU ratified the CRPD in 2010. In this case, for the first time the CJEU partially applied the social-contextual model of disability endorsed by the CRPD and focused its analysis on those external barriers that hinder the full and effective participation of persons with disabilities in professional life on an equal basis with other workers. The Court's reasoning was highly significant as it started to clarify the personal scope of the Equality Framework Directive, which still lacks a comprehensive definition of disability in compliance with the CRPD's provisions.[2] The CJEU rightfully set out that disability does not require the complete impossibility of working, but it does imply a hindrance to the exercise of a professional activity. The CJEU gradually embraced a social construct

[1] Joined Cases C-335/11 and C-337/11 *HK Danmark, acting on behalf of Jette Ring v Dansk almennyttigt Boligselskab* (C-335/11); *HK Danmark, acting on behalf of Lone Skouboe Werge v Dansk Arbejdsgiverforening, acting on behalf of Pro Display A/S* (C-337/11), ECLI:EU:C:2013:222.

[2] Directive 2000/78/EC of the Council of 27 November 2000 establishing a general framework for equal treatment in employment and occupation [2000] OJ L303/16.

of disability which considers the interplay between individual impairments and external barriers, in line with the Directive's objective to enable persons with disabilities to have access to or participate in employment. This interpretation was a significant development in comparison with the pre-CRPD judicial understanding of disability in *Chacón Navas*, when the CJEU applied an obsolete medical model of disability.

At first glance, it may be said that the CRPD has positively influenced the interpretation and implementation of EU equality law. However, the CJEU's approach to the concept of disability still shows some gaps that need to be addressed and better clarified. The Court has narrowly interpreted the definition of disability as limited to those individuals whose 'professional life' is hindered. On the contrary, the CRPD requires broadly to cover persons with disabilities whose full and effective participation in 'society' is undermined, including in all other areas and spheres of life.[3] In addition, the definition developed by the Court leaves out those persons who are disabled because of the mere existence of environmental and social barriers, such as false assumptions and prejudices.[4]

The struggle of the CJEU in fully applying the new human rights model of disability underpinning the CPRD is also evident in *Kaltoft*, where the Court had to decide whether obesity can be considered a disability covered by the Equality Framework Directive.[5] In this case, the CJEU's reasoning wrongfully focused on the physical constraints of the claimant to evaluate whether he fell within the Directive's personal scope. This judgment symbolises a controversial step back with regard to the interpretation of the concept of disability. The Court disregarded the interactions between the claimant's personal characteristic and the external barriers that hindered his full participation in professional life. Similarly, in the later case of *Ruiz Conejero* the CJEU reiterated that if the obesity of the worker, on account of reduced mobility or the onset of medical conditions, prevents his work or causes discomfort during his professional activity, such a state is covered by the definition of disability under EU law.[6] By doing so, the CJEU restored the medical model of disability in EU equality law by classifying disability as a medical condition merely located within the individual.

The failure to concretely implement the human rights model of disability emerges in *Z* as the Court concluded that the impossibility to have a child by conventional means does not in itself prevent the commissioning mother (the claimant) from having access to, participating in, or advancing in employment.

[3] L Waddington and A Broderick, *Realising equality: A comparison of the UN Convention on the Rights of Persons with Disabilities and EU equality and non-discrimination law* (Luxembourg, Publications Office of the European Union, 2018) 88.

[4] ibid.

[5] Case C-354/13 *FOA, acting on behalf of Karsten Kaltoft v Kommunernes Landsforening (KL), acting on behalf of the Municipality of Billund* [2014] Opinion of AG Jääskinen, para 30(4), ECLI:EU:C:2014:2106.

[6] Case C-270/16 *Carlos Enrique Ruiz Conejero v Ferroser Servicios Auxiliares SA and Ministerio Fiscal*, ECLI:EU:C:2018:17.

The Court pointed out that 'it is not apparent from the order for reference that Ms Z's *condition* by itself made it impossible for her to carry out her work or constituted a hindrance to the exercise of her professional activity'.[7] The Court once again referred to the medical definition of disability and concentrated its analysis on the personal characteristic of the claimant to trigger the protection of the Equality Framework Directive.

The CJEU's problematic assessment of the concept of disability has been also confirmed in the case law beyond the prohibition of discrimination in the field of employment. In *Glatzel*,[8] the Court based its reasoning principally on the nature of the individual impairments (the claimant suffered from unilateral amblyopia) and the medical standards required by Directive 2006/126/EC to release a driving licence.[9] The Court incorrectly abandoned a social model understanding of disability according to which disability must not be exclusively understood with regard to the *degree of the deficiency at issue*, but must be determined on the basis of the *final outcome provoked by* that deficiency in a given social context.

This case law analysis suggests that the CJEU encounters several difficulties in applying the social understanding of disability in practice and still retains some aspects of a medical approach which defines functional limitations as the final result of a physical condition. The CJEU has so far missed the opportunity to provide a legal definition of disability which thoroughly reflects the human rights model adopted by the CRPD. Despite the UN Convention having become 'a clear point of reference in the reasoning of the European judges', it seems clear that the Court's reasoning is not yet aligned with the latest legal developments under international law.[10]

B. The Legal Gaps in Addressing Multiple and Intersectional Discrimination

The CJEU adopted an inadequate approach to address discrimination based on multiple grounds. The CJEU's reasoning relating to the legal protection of women with disabilities echoes the main gaps of EU equality law which is characterised by a single-ground equality paradigm.[11] In particular, EU equality norms fail to contemplate the disability dimension of gender discrimination or the gender aspect

[7] Case C-363/12 *Z v A Government Department and The Board of Management of a Community School* [2013] ECR, para 81, ECLI EU:C:2014:159.

[8] Case C-356/12 *Wolfgang Glatzel v Freistaat Bayer* [2014] ECR, ECLI: EU:C:2014:350.

[9] Directive 2006/126/EC of the European Parliament and of the Council of 20 December 2006 on driving licences [2006] OJ L403/18.

[10] D Ferri and S Favalli, 'Tracing the Boundaries between Disability and Sickness in the European Union: Squaring the Circle?' (2016) 23 *European Journal of Health Law* 5.

[11] See for instance, R Xenidis 'Multiple Discrimination in EU Anti-Discrimination Law: Towards Redressing Complex Inequality?' in U Belavusau and K Henrard (eds), *EU Anti-Discrimination Law Beyond Gender* (Oxford Hart Publishing, 2018).

of disability discrimination. In the case of *Z*, the Court denied legal protection to a woman who suffered from discrimination on multiple and different grounds. In the same judgment, the CJEU ruled that there was no sex or gender discrimination, no disability discrimination and no violation of EU provisions concerning maternity leave. This judgment proves that the lack of adequate legal instruments which recognise the intersection of two or more grounds of discrimination jeopardise the effective protection of vulnerable individuals.

The main flaw of EU law derives from the impossibility to group multiple grounds of discrimination in the same claim. In *Z*, the claimant was obliged to bring an allegation of sex discrimination separately from the allegation of disability discrimination. This framework impedes the determination of the inextricable link between the two grounds that brings about discrimination. As a result the claimant, as a woman with disabilities, was not able to find protection under the Equal Treatment Directive[12] and the Equality Framework Directive.[13] The Court found that a commissioning father was not entitled to such leave either and that the refusal did not put female workers at a particular disadvantage compared with male workers. Similarly, it did not find the situation experienced by Z to fall within the personal scope of the Equality Framework Directive that prohibits discrimination on grounds of disability. The Court wrongfully applied a comparison with male workers, instead of comparing it with a woman who has given birth or an adoptive mother.

It is clear that EU law does not provide the necessary legal tools to identify the proper comparator and tackle multiple and intersectional discrimination. This is strongly linked with a 'formal' comparative analysis that merely requires the identification of an adequate group with whom to carry out a comparison with the disadvantaged individual. This approach is very limited as it narrows the possibility to combat multiple and intersectional discrimination. On this matter, EU law does not comply with the CRPD, which under Article 6 requires multiple and intersectional discrimination against women and girls with disabilities to be addressed.

C. Indirect Discrimination and Reasonable Accommodation: Towards a Better Judicial Interpretation?

The CJEU's interpretation of the provisions concerning the prohibition of indirect discrimination and the duty to make reasonable accommodation highlights the positive impact of the CRPD on the Equality Framework Directive.

[12] Directive 2006/54/EC of the European Parliament and of the Council of 5 July 2006 on the implementation of the principle of equal opportunities and equal treatment of men and women in matters of employment and occupation (recast) [2006] OJ L204/23.

[13] Directive 2000/43/EC of the Council of 29 June 2000 implementing the principle of equal treatment between persons irrespective of racial or ethnic origin [2000] OJ L180/22.

Indirect discrimination is broadly interpreted by the CJEU in compliance with the CRPD. In *Ring and Skouboe Werge*, the Court pointed out the incompatibility with EU law of national legislation allowing for a shortened period of notice for those workers on sick leave for 120 days over a one-year period. It was rightfully recognised that this law potentially puts persons having a disability at a particular disadvantage compared with other persons without disability as they are more likely to accumulate days of absence on grounds of illness. Similarly, in *Ruiz Conejero* the CJEU properly clarified that Article 2(2)(b)(i) of Directive 2000/78/EC prohibits the dismissal of a worker on grounds of his intermittent absences from work, when those absences are the consequence of sickness linked to a disability. In addition, in the recent case of *DW v Nobel Plastiques Ibérica SA*, the Court concluded that, a dismissal based on three apparently neutral criteria such as 'workers' productivity rate, multi-skilling capacities and level of absenteeism', can result in placing at a disadvantage disabled workers who may have more difficulties in meeting these selection criteria.[14] This case law seems to point out that the CJEU has embraced a legal understanding of indirect discrimination that is compatible with the CRPD and can effectively protect the rights of persons with disabilities in the workplace.

The CJEU's interpretation of the obligation to provide reasonable accommodation also exhibits significant improvements even if some gaps still remain. In *Ring and Skouboe Werge*, the Court made clear that the 'adaptation of working hours' is an example of reasonable accommodation that can be adopted by employers to foster the rights of workers with disabilities. However, in the same case the CJEU stated that an accommodation is reasonable when it does not constitute a disproportionate burden on the employer. On the contrary, the definition of 'reasonableness' given by the Committee on the Rights of Persons with Disabilities is not based on the costs or available resources, but refers to a measure's 'relevance, appropriateness and effectiveness' for the person with a disability.[15]

Another important issue to examine is the lack of a specific provision under the Equality Framework Directive that explicitly defines an unjustified failure to make a reasonable accommodation as a form of discrimination.[16] In that regard, in *DW v Nobel Plastiques Ibérica SA* the Court recalled that 'under Article 2 of the UN Convention, discrimination on grounds of disability includes all forms of discrimination, including denial of reasonable accommodation'.[17] Regardless of the merits of this judgment, the Court's statement represents a critical judicial development that could pave the way for further elaboration on the nature of this concept in the case law of the Court and EU anti-discrimination law. According

[14] Case C-397/18 *DW v Nobel Plastiques Ibérica SA*, ECLI:EU:C:2019:703.

[15] UN Committee on the Rights of Persons with Disabilities (2018), General Comment No 6 on Equality and Non-Discrimination, UN Doc CRPD/C/GC/6 (adopted by the Committee at its nineteenth session (14 February–9 March 2018) para 24(b).

[16] On this matter, see Waddington and Broderick (n 3) 92.

[17] *DW v Nobel Plastiques Ibérica SA* (n 14) para 72.

to Lisa Waddington and Andrea Broderick, by classifying the failure to provide reasonable accommodation as discrimination, 'judges may be empowered or inclined to order more far-reaching sanctions and remedies in cases of discrimination than in cases of other wrong'.[18]

D. The Inclusive Equality Paradigm under the CRPD

This book has highlighted that the new 'inclusive' model of equality adopted by the CRPD has not yet been entirely incorporated into the EU legal framework. The CPRD provides an innovative and inclusive legal framework to tackle discrimination. It has pioneered a line of fundamental substantive 'equality-promoting' provisions that may improve the legal protection of persons with disabilities: (i) the prohibition of direct and indirect discrimination (Article 2); (ii) the obligation to provide reasonable accommodation (Article 5.3); (iii) the prohibition of multiple discrimination (Articles 6 and 7); and (iv) the duty to launch affirmative action programmes (Article 27).

The CPRD abandoned the formal model of equality (also known as the 'sameness' or 'symmetrical' approach) and opted in favour of a substantive approach according to which individuals in different situations should be treated differently. The substantive model has been further reinforced by a new 'inclusive' paradigm that requires understanding and accommodating the concrete differences of persons with disabilities, not only by considering their biological characteristics, but also by removing those environmental, attitudinal and legislative obstacles that jeopardise their full enjoyment of human rights.[19]

E. The Complicated Relationship between the CRPD and the EU Legal System

The ratification of the CRPD by the EU raises several and interesting questions regarding its legal status within the EU legal order. According to the Treaties, as far as international agreements are concerned international law is an integral part of the EU legal order. According to Article 216(2) Treaty on the Functioning of the European Union, 'agreements concluded by the Union are binding upon the institutions of the Union and on its Member States'. It would appear that EU law has embraced a 'monistic' approach to regulate its relationship with international

[18] L Waddington, 'Equal to the Task: Re-Examining EU Equality Law in Light of the United Nations Convention on the Rights of Persons with Disabilities' (2013) 4 *European Yearbook of Disability Law* 169, 190.

[19] UN Committee on the Rights of Persons with Disabilities, General Comment No 6 on equality and non-discrimination (n 15) para 24(b).

law. However, the CJEU's case law has revealed that the interplay between EU law and international human rights law is not yet properly defined.

In the case of *Z*, the CJEU ruled that the CRPD's provisions are not unconditional and sufficiently precise and therefore do not have direct effect under EU law. The same approach has been confirmed in the case of *Glatzel*. The Court excluded that the UN Convention may be relied on to challenge the validity of EU norms. The Court surprisingly concluded that the CRPD does not produce direct effects in the EU legal order since it is drafted in a programmatic form. In this respect, only those international treaties containing 'unconditional and sufficiently precise' provisions can produce direct effects. This condition is fulfilled where the international norm relied on enshrines a clear and precise obligation which is not subject, in its implementation or effects, to the adoption of any subsequent measures.

F. Key Recommendations for Improving the Interpretation of EU Equality Norms

The analysis of the CJEU's judgment reveals that the CRPD is not fully producing the expected results at EU level. A more coherent and progressive judicial approach is required in relation to the legal understanding of the concepts of disability, reasonable accommodation and multiple discrimination. Moreover, the CJEU is minimising the impact of the CPRD in the EU legal system without properly clarifying the relationship between EU law and international human rights law. The following recommendations aim to improve the judicial interpretation of the EU equality norms and identify the legal status of the CRPD.

In the first instance, the CJEU is showing an unreasonable reluctance and prudence in its assessment of the equality norms included under EU law. In doing so, it is again promoting the re-emergence of a medical or welfare model of disability according to which functional limitations are deemed to be a direct outcome of the individual impairment. Instead the CJEU should consider not only an individual's biomedical deficiency, but also those external circumstances that hamper the enjoyment of fundamental rights. The CRPD makes clear that disability represents a social construct that should be interpreted in a broad manner. The *ratio* of the inclusive model of equality is indeed to identify social barriers and address those relevant effects of the discriminatory treatment. To this end, it aims to ensure that differential characteristics are accommodated within the equality norms. The CJEU should not hesitate to recognise that structural disabling barriers are not located within the individual, but are often represented by environmental, attitudinal and legislative measures.

This author also recommends adopting a *functional* and *individualised* understanding of the duty to provide reasonable accommodation. Judges should first carry out an analysis to verify whether the accommodation requested by the employee is 'feasible and functional' for the person with a disability and then 'proportional and sustainable' for the organisation. The primary goal of such adjustments is to facilitate the achievement of equality in the workplace. Accommodating workers with disabilities does not represent a mere charitable goal, but a legally enforceable right to ensure the full participation of persons with disabilities in the workplace on an equal basis with others. Other factors including the size of the organisation, the costs of the measure and its impact on the general workplace should instead be examined to assess the presence of a 'disproportionate or undue burden' on the employer and the limit of the duty. This interpretative model may help correctly implement the concept of reasonable accommodation at national level. This legal obligation is often new for nearly all Member States and its implementation may frustrate the scope of inclusive equality.

In addition, the Court's judgment in relation to multiple and intersectional discrimination negatively mirrors the limits of the single-ground equality model of EU law. Multiple and intersectional discrimination against women with disabilities occurs frequently in the labour market and a new holistic approach is needed to accommodate the individual experience of multiple disadvantages. In this respect, the Court should abandon a *formalist* comparative approach when deciding cases of discrimination based on disability and gender. This approach fails to properly determine the *group* to which the claimant should be compared and the *object* of the comparison. The accommodation requested by the claimant (paid leave equivalent to maternity or adoption leave) was not provided to any member of other groups of individuals (male workers). The judicial analysis should therefore focus on the *adverse impact* on the claimant of the discriminatory treatment (the failure to provide paid leave) rather than on the differential treatment the individual receives in comparison with others. A new inclusive approach aimed at addressing the *effects* of discriminatory measures is greatly required to replace a 'formalistic' comparative model which is inadequate to tackle multiple and intersectional discrimination.

With regard to the legal status of the CRPD, the CJEU's reasoning demands the assessment of 'unconditional and sufficiently precise' provisions to ensure the direct effects of international treaties within the EU legal order. It may be said that the blanket application of this 'test' does not consider the legal complexity of an international human rights treaty such as the CRPD. This approach reflects the 'protectionist' scope of preserving the EU legal framework from the interference of international human rights law. This understanding of the relationship between EU law and international law conflicts with the formal openness of the EU Treaties to other legal orders. It is worth noting that the CRPD represents an overarching human rights treaty that cannot share the same characteristics of those international agreements setting out technical standards. Furthermore, the assumption that the CRPD's provisions are not precise enough is not fully accurate. The Convention not only introduces general obligations, but also specific substantive rights and implementation provisions which set forth explicit and well-defined obligations. Consequently, labelling the CRPD as a mere programmatic instrument is highly reductive. With this background, the CJEU should identify new criteria to assess the direct applicability of international provisions. To this end, the peculiar legal nature of the CPRD in comparison with other international agreements should be acknowledged. The CJEU should also consider the CRPD's provisions as having direct effects because they set out specific substantive rights, obligations and procedures.

II. EU Governance: Main Findings

With regard to the impact of the CPRD on EU governance, this book has highlighted the following key findings: (i) one of the main flaws of existing governance mechanisms is the 'reporting and benchmarking' process; (ii) the EU independent framework reveals excessive fragmentation; and (iii) the European Parliament is marginalised and the role of civil society organisations (CSOs) should be enhanced.

The governance mechanism put in place by the EU to comply with Article 33 of the CRPD mirrors the open method of coordination (OMC). Since 2010, the European Parliament's Petitions Committee, the European Ombudsman, the European Commission, the EU Agency for Fundamental Rights and the European Disability Forum have been actively involved as part of the EU independent framework to monitor the CRPD's implementation. In addition, in 2010, the European Commission launched the European Disability Strategy 2010–2020 in order to pursue its objectives with actions in eight priority areas, and in March 2021 the new Strategy for the Rights of Persons with Disabilities 2021–2030 was adopted.[20]

The approach to achieving EU shared goals has been so far based on voluntary political cooperation. Member States still retain a significant portion of autonomy in the adoption of national policies to accomplish EU objectives. Member States are supported by the Commission's expertise and guidance in implementing strategic objectives. This framework raises several concerns in relation to the feasibility of the OMC in the disability sector. The main weakness of the EU governance mechanisms is represented by the 'reporting and benchmarking' process. Peer review and reporting are fundamental aspects of the OMC. Accordingly, governments should systematically release national plans to the Commission concerning the situation of persons with disabilities in their domestic system. National reports however have not mainstreamed disability in a comprehensive and coherent way. The majority of states did not provide clear and analytical evidence with regard to the implementation of disability policies. In doing so, the Commission cannot carry out any rigorous assessment of the rights of persons with disabilities at national level.

[20] See C O'Mahony and S Quinlivan, 'The EU Disability Strategy and the Future of EU Disability Policy' in D Ferri and A Broderick (eds), *Research Handbook on EU Disability Law* (Cheltenham, Edward Elgar Publishing, 2020).

It has also been argued that the EU independent framework reveals excessive fragmentation and decentralisation of competences and responsibilities. The EU governance mechanisms should be simplified in order to confer clear duties to those EU actors involved in the OMC and avoid the coexistence of several EU bodies with overlapping functions. In particular, the role of the European Parliament is marginal within the EU independent framework as it lacks formal structures to monitor the CRPD's implementation.

The Parliament is officially excluded from the drafting of the EU periodic report to the UN Committee on the Rights of Persons with Disabilities and it does not participate in any procedures of the de facto vertical and horizontal coordination system between the EU institutions and Member States. Despite that, the European Parliament promoted several political initiatives to foster the CRPD's implementation at EU level and encourage the participation of governmental and non-governmental stakeholders in decision-making. To give an example, in 2016 the European Parliament released a Resolution on the implementation of the CRPD as a follow up to the UN Recommendations to the EU. The European Parliament urged a cross-cutting review of EU legislation and funding programmes to fully comply with the CRPD, an update of the declaration of competence in light of the Concluding Observations, a review of the European Disability Strategy and the development of a comprehensive EU CRPD strategy with a clear time frame, benchmarks and indicators. Moreover, the European Parliament and its committees have gradually improved the quality of their policy deliberation by means of regular consultations and public hearings with the European Disability Forum and other NGOs.

The participation of CSOs is a fundamental principle of good governance which aims to open up the decision-making process and promote dialogue between the EU institutions and civil society. The consultative process within the European Parliament and its committees with regard to the CRPD's implementation shows the emergence of a beneficial interaction between the European Parliament and NGOs. However, the involvement of CSOs in the policy chain should be adequately resourced and structured to perform the crucial function of monitoring the CPRD's implementation in the EU.

A. The Importance of Reforming the EU Independent Framework

The OMC is perhaps not the most suitable tool to accelerate the implementation of the CRPD in the European Union. It is not based on a comprehensive system of sanctions and the concrete achievement of its objectives depends on the extent to which national plans are implemented by governments. The adoption of non-binding recommendations and atypical acts do not ensure the uniform application of EU rules in the Member States. Still, the lack of hard sanctioning mechanisms should not represent an obstacle in a governance architecture that incentivises reciprocal learnings. The reporting methods and coordination mechanisms of the OMC should be reinforced to promote the CRPD's implementation in the EU. The OMC is not seen as a panacea to implement the CRPD, but the improvement of certain mechanisms may contribute to facilitate the achievement of those objectives pursued by the EU independent framework and the Disability Strategy. In doing so, Member States will remain responsible for a sensitive area where they are still reluctant to lose important parts of legislative power.

B. Key Recommendations for Improving EU Governance Mechanisms

The Commission should develop precise time frames and key performance indicators. Such instruments will be useful for identifying good practice and for measuring countries' performances in the area of disability. In this regard, the European Agency for Fundamental Rights may assist the Commission and the Parliament in adopting new policy strategies and indicators. The formulation of clear performance indicators by the EU institutions can facilitate the benchmarking process and improve the reporting mechanism. By doing so, Member States will be encouraged to deliver data on the impact of their policy measures. At the same time, the EU institutions will have the necessary tools to share good practice and evaluate Member State performance. In conclusion, the EU governance system designed to implement the CPRD should provide clear procedures to penalise non-cooperation by Member States.

C. Good Governance and Participatory Democracy: The CPRD's Positive Practice

A key finding of this book is that the CPRD's adoption proves that there are beneficial effects from increasing participation of CSOs within international political processes. The contribution of CSOs to the drafting and monitoring of the CRPD's implementation represents good practice of participatory democracy that may be replicated at EU level.

CSOs and NGOs have adequate advocacy and policy instruments to properly support stakeholders' concerns and provide specific information, expertise, analysis and reports to decision-makers. In this respect, NGOs have advanced influential proposals, criticisms and perspectives for building an effective framework for the protection of persons with disabilities. Their advocacy initiatives have significantly impacted the final draft of the CPRD. The most successful contributions of CSOs concerned the participatory democracy approach (Article 4.3), the social model of disability (Article 1) and the acknowledgment of multi-discrimination against women with disabilities (Article 6). The participation of CSOs has been regulated by structured and formalised procedures that ensured the effective functioning of the entire decision-making process. First, the participation of NGOs in the Ad Hoc Committee's work has been granted to all NGOs enjoying consultative status within the UN Economic and Social Council. Second, their participation has been enlarged to those organisations which could prove they carry out relevant activities in respect of the work of the Committee.

With this background, a key recommendation is that the ex ante establishment of certain requirements for structuring the participation of civil society is an essential precondition for putting good governance at EU level into practice. Inclusive and open procedures necessitate the involvement of actors in a high representative capacity. This assessment should be based on qualitative criteria, such as NGO capacity to represent common interests and carry out effective advocacy activities. A structured participation would not jeopardise the independence of CSOs, and would create the conditions needed to promote the participation of representative groups of individuals that can advance constructive dialogue and bring relevant expertise to the decision-making process. The model of participatory democracy adopted by the CRPD may be feasible for improving the EU decision-making process in those sensitive and technical areas relating to human rights law.

III. Time to Unleash the CRPD's Full Potential

The CRPD has undoubtedly influenced the judicial interpretation of equality norms at EU and national level. However, 10 years after its ratification by the European Union, the CRPD's full potential has still not been unleashed in order to achieve its ambitious goal to effectively foster equality for persons with disabilities in the EU legal framework. To this end, the judiciary and policymakers must transpose the human rights model of disability and the inclusive approach towards equality into concrete judicial and legal practices. Moreover, the improvement of the EU independent framework is an essential requirement to boost the effective monitoring of the CRPD's implementation in the EU and its Member States. It is clear that equality is still far from being achieved, but the emergence of positive judicial approaches towards non-discrimination norms may facilitate and accelerate the translation of the CRPD's provisions into the EU legal system.

BIBLIOGRAPHY

Academic Sources

Books

Arambulo, K, *Strengthening the Supervision of the International Covenant on Economic, Social and Cultural Rights: Theoretical and Procedural Aspects* (Antwerp, Intersentia, 1999)

Aristotle, '3 Ethica Nicomachea, 112–117, 1131a–1131b, JL Ackrill and JO Urmson (eds), W Ross, *Translation* (Oxford University Press, 1980)

Arnardóttir, OM, *Equality and Non-Discrimination under the European Convention on Human Rights* (Leiden, Martinus Nijhoff Publishers, 2003)

Arnardóttir, OM and Quinn, G, *The UN Convention on the Rights of Persons with Disabilities: European and Scandinavian Perspectives* (Leiden, Martinus Nijhoff, 2009)

Barnard, C, *EC Employment Law* (Oxford, Oxford University Press, 2006)

—— *The Substantive Law of the EU: The Four Freedoms*, 4th edn (Oxford, Oxford, University Press, 2013)

Bebbington, J, Unerman, J and O'Dwyer, B, *Sustainability Accounting and Accountability* (London, Routledge, 2014)

Blanck, P and Flynn, E, *Routledge Handbook of Disability Law and Human Rights* (London, Routledge, 2017)

Bogg, A and Costello, C, *Research Handbook on EU Labour Law* (Cheltenham, Edward Elgar Publishing, 2016)

Broderick, A and Ferri, D, *International and European Disability Law and Policy: Text, Cases and Materials* (Cambridge, Cambridge University Press, 2019)

Cabrelli, D, *Employment Law in Context: Text and Materials* (Oxford, Oxford University Press, 2016)

Craig, P and de Búrca, G, *EU Law: Text, Cases, and Materials*, 6th edn (Oxford, Oxford University Press, 2015)

Della Fina, V, Cera, R and Palmisano, G, *The United Nations Convention on the Rights of Persons with Disabilities: A Commentary* (New York, Springer International Publishing, 2017)

Dzehtsiarou, K et al (eds), *Human Rights Law in Europe: The Influence, Overlaps and Contradictions of the EU and the ECHR* (London, Routledge, 2014)

Eeckhout, P, *EU External Relations Law* (Oxford, Oxford University Press, Oxford European Law Library, 2011)

Flynn, E, *From Rhetoric to Action: Implementing the UN Convention on the Rights of Persons with Disabilities* (Cambridge, Cambridge University Press, 2011)

Fredman, S, *Discrimination Law* (Oxford, Clarendon Law Series, 2001)

—— *Human Rights Transformed: Positive Rights and Positive Duties* (Oxford, Oxford University Press, 2008)

—— *Discrimination Law*, 2nd edn (Oxford University Press, 2011)

Gramsci, A, *Quaderni dal Carcere, 1929–1935* (Roma, Istituto della Enciclopedia Italiana, 2017)

Heymann, J, Stein, MA and Moreno, G, *Disability and Equity at Work* (Oxford, Oxford University Press, 2014)

Howard, E, *The EU Race Directive: Developing the Protection against Racial Discrimination within the EU* (London, Routledge, 2010)

Hutchinson, T, Re*searching and Writing in Law*, 3rd edn (Reuters Thomson, 2010)

Jackson, K and Banerjee, L, *Disability Discrimination Law and Case Management* (The Law Society, March 2014)

Joseph, S, *Blame it on the WTO? A Human Rights Critique* (Oxford, Oxford Scholarship Online, 2011)

Kelsen, H, *Introduction to the Problems of Legal Theory* (Oxford, Clarendon Press, 1992)
Kurtz, LR, *Encyclopedia of Violence, Peace, & Conflict* (Amsterdam, Elsevier, 2008)
Lawson, A, *Disability and Equality Law in Britain: The Role of Reasonable Adjustment* (Oxford, Hart Publishing, 2008)
Loenen, T and Rodrigues, PR, *Non-Discrimination Law: Comparative Perspectives* (Leiden, Martinus Nijhoff Publishers, 1999)
Macpherson, CB, *The Life and Times of Liberal Democracy* (Oxford, Oxford University Press, 1977)
Majone, G, *Regulating Europe* (London, Routledge, 1996)
McColgan A., *Discrimination, Equality and the Law* (Hart Publishing, 2014)
Meron, T, *Human Rights Law-Making in the United Nations: A Critique of Instruments and Processes* (Oxford, Clarendon Press, 1986)
Numhauser-Henning, A, *Elder Law: Evolving European Perspectives* (Cheltenham Edward Elgar Publishing, 2017)
O'Brien, R, *Crippled Justice: The History of Modern Disability Policy in the Workplace* (Chicago, Ill, University of Chicago Press, 2001)
Oliver, M, *Understanding Disability: From Theory to Practice* (Basingstoke, Macmillan, 1996)
Pateman, C, *Participation and Democratic Theory* (Cambridge, Cambridge University Press, 1970)
Peers, S and Rogers, N, *EU Immigration and Asylum Law: Text and Commentary* (Leiden Martinus Nijhoff Publishers, 2006)
Peers, S et al (eds), *The EU Charter of Fundamental Rights: A Commentary* (Oxford, Hart Publishing, 2009)
Reif, LC, *The Ombudsman, Good Governance, and the International Human Rights System* (Leiden Brill, 2004)
Rondinelli, DA and Shabbir Cheema, G (eds), *Reinventing Government in the Twenty-First Century: State Capacity in a Globalizing Society* (West Hartford, CT, Kumarian Press, 2003)
Scharpf, F, *Governing in Europe* (Oxford, Oxford University Press, 1999)
Schiek, D and Chege, V, *European Union Non-Discrimination Law: Comparative Perspectives on Multidimensional Equality Law* (London, Routledge, 2009)
Schiek, D and Lawson, A, *European Union Non-Discrimination Law and Intersectionality Investigating the Triangle of Racial, Gender and Disability Discrimination* (Farnham, Ashgate Publishing, 2011)
Shakespeare, T, *Disability Rights and Wrongs* (Abingdon, Routledge, 2006)
Smit, JM, *Elgar Encyclopedia of Comparative Law*, 2nd edn (Cheltenham Edward Elgar Publishing, 2006)
Smith, M, *Centralized Enforcement, Legitimacy and Good Governance in the EU* (Routledge, New York 2010)
Vandenhole, W, *Non-Discrimination and Equality in the View of the UN Human Rights Treaty Bodies* (Antwerp, Intersentia, 2005)
Van Vooren, B and Wessel, RA, *EU External Relations Law: Text, Cases and Materials* (Cambridge, Cambridge University Press, 2014)
Waddington, L and Lawson, A, *The UN Convention on the Rights of Persons with Disabilities in Practice: A Comparative Analysis of the Role of Courts* (Oxford, Oxford University Press, 2018)
Wendell, S, *The Rejected Body: Feminist Philosophical Reflections on Disability* (New York, Routledge, 1996)
Weiss, TG, Thakur, R and Ruggie, JG, *Global Governance and the UN: An Unfinished Journey* (Bloomington, IND, Indiana University Press, 2010)
Zeitlin, J, *Extending Experimentalist Governance? The European Union and Transnational Regulation* (Oxford, Oxford University Press, 2015)

Book Chapters

Arnardóttir, OM, 'A Future of Multidimensional Disadvantage Equality? in OM Arnardóttir and G Quinn (eds), *The UN Convention on the Rights of Persons with Disabilities: European and Scandinavian Perspectives* (Leiden, Martinus Nijhoff, 2009)

Broderick, A and Watson, P, 'Disability in EU Non-discrimination Law' in D Ferri and A Broderick (eds), *Research Handbook on EU Disability Law* (Cheltenham, Edward Elgar Publishing, 2020)

Chamon, M, 'Negotiation, Ratification and Implementation of the CRPD and its Status in the EU Legal Order' in D Ferri and A Broderick (eds), *Research Handbook on EU Disability Law* (Cheltenham, Edward Elgar Publishing, 2020)

Clifford, J, 'Equality' in D Sheldon (ed), *The Oxford Handbook of International Human Rights Law* (Oxford, Oxford University Press, 2013)

Dahl, R, 'Can International Organizations Be Democratic? A Skeptic's View' in I Shapiro and C Hacker-Cordon (eds), *Democracy's Edges* (Cambridge, Cambridge University Press, 1999)

De Búrca, G, 'Fundamental Rights and Citizenship' in B de Witte (ed), *Ten Reflections on the Constitutional Treaty for Europe* (Florence, European University Institute, 2003)

De Búrca, G and Scott, J, 'Introduction: New Governance, Law and Constitutionalism' in G de Búrca and J Scott (eds), *Law and New Governance in the EU and the US* (Oxford, Hart Publishing, 2006)

Degener, T, The Impact of the UN Convention on the Rights of Persons with Disabilities on EU Anti-Discrimination Law in T Giegerich, *The European Union as Protector and Promoter of Equality* (Springer, 2020) 349–362

—— A New Human Rights Model of Disability in V Della Fina, R Cera, G Palmisano, *The United Nations Convention on the Rights of Persons with Disabilities* (Springer, 2020) 41–59

Ferri, D, 'Participation in EU Governance: A "Multi-Level" Perspective and a "Multifold" Approach in C Fraenkel-Haeberle et al (eds), *Citizen Participation in Multi-Level Democracies* (Leiden, Brill – Nijhoff, 2015)

—— 'Disability in the EU Charter of Fundamental Rights' in D Ferri and A Broderick (eds), *Research Handbook on EU Disability Law* (Cheltenham, Edward Elgar Publishing, 2020)

Fredman, S, 'Positive Rights and Positive Duties: Addressing Intersectionality in D Schieck and V Chege (eds), *European Union Non-Discrimination Law: Comparative Perspectives on Multidimensional Equality Law* (Abingdon, Routledge-Cavendish, 2009)

Hasler, F, 'Developments in the Disabled People's Movement in J Swain et al (eds), *Disabling Barriers, Enabling Environments* (London, Sage, 1993)

Herzog, P, 'Giving Shape to a European Civil Society and Opening Up the Institutional System (2001) in O De Schutter, N Lebessis and J Paterson (eds), *Governance in the European Union* (Luxembourg, Office for Official Publications of the European Communities, 2001)

Hoefmans, A, 'The EU Framework for Monitoring the CRPD' in D Ferri and A Broderick (eds), *Research Handbook on EU Disability Law* (Cheltenham, Edward Elgar Publishing, 2020)

Kimber, CJM, 'Equality or Self Determination' in C Gearty and A Tomkins (eds), *Understanding Human Rights* (London, Mansell Publishing, 1996)

Koch, IE, 'From Invisibility to Indivisibility: The International Convention on the Rights of Persons with Disabilities in O Arnardóttir and G Quinn (eds), *The United Nations Convention on the Rights of Persons with Disabilities: European and Scandinavian Perspectives* (Leiden, Martinus Nijhoff, 2009)

Lawson, A, 'The UN Convention on the Rights of Persons with Disabilities and European Disability Law: A Catalyst for Cohesion? in OM Arnardóttir and G Quinn (eds), *The United Nations Convention on the Rights of Persons with Disabilities: European and Scandinavian Perspectives* (Leiden, Martinus Nijhoff, 2009)

Lord, JE and Brown, R, 'The Role of Reasonable Accommodation in Securing Substantive Equality for Persons with Disabilities: The UN Convention on the Rights of Persons with Disabilities' in MH Rioux, LA Basser and M Jones (eds), *Critical Perspectives on Human Rights and Disability Policy* (The Hague, Martinus Nijhoff, 2011)

O' Brien, C, 'Article 26 – Integration of Persons with Disabilities' in S Peers et al (eds), *The EU Charter of Fundamental Rights: A Commentary* (Oxford, Hart Publishing, 2014)

O'Mahony, C and Quinlivan, S, 'The EU Disability Strategy and the Future of EU Disability Policy' in D Ferri and A Broderick (eds), *Research Handbook on EU Disability Law* (Cheltenham, Edward Elgar Publishing, 2020)

Pech, L, 'France: Rethinking "Droits-Creances"' in M Langford (ed), *Socio-Economic Rights Jurisprudence: Emerging Trends in Comparative and International Law* (Cambridge, Cambridge University Press, 2007)

Peters, A, 'The Transparency of Global Governance' in M Pazartzis et al (eds), *Reconceptualising the Rule of Law in Global Governance, Resources, Investment and Trade* (Oxford, Hart Publishing, 2015)

Quinlivan, S and Bruton, C, 'Disability, EU Law and the CRPD: A New Dawn?' in C O'Mahony and G Quinn (eds), *Disability Law and Policy: An Analysis of the UN Convention* (Dublin, Clarus Press, 2017)

Schmidt, JD and Hersh, J, 'The Past has No Future: Revisiting Danish Flexicurity. Globalization and Labour Market Dynamics' in PK Chopra (ed), *Globalisation and Labour Market Dynamics* (Leeds, Wisdom House Publications, 2016)

Shelton, DL, 'Prohibited Discrimination in International Law' in A Constantinides and N Zaikos (eds), *The Diversity of International Law: Essays in Honour of Professor Kalliopi K Koufa* (Leiden, Brill – Nijhoff, 2009)

Stein, MA and Lord, JE, 'Participation in International Agreements as Transformative Social Change: The UN Convention on the Rights of Persons with Disabilities' in J Heymann (ed), *Making Rights Real* (Cambridge, Cambridge University Press, 2012)

Steiner, HJ, 'Subsidiarity under the Maastricht Treaty' in D O'Keeffe and PM Twomey (eds), *Legal Issues of the Maastricht Treaty* (Chichester, John Wiley & Sons, 1994)

Ventegodt Liisberg, M, 'Flexicurity and Employment of Persons with Disability in Europe in a Contemporary Disability Human Rights Perspective' in L Waddington et al (eds), *European Yearbook of Disability Law Vol 4* (Cambridge, Intersentia, 2013)

Waddington, L, 'Breaking New Ground: The Implications of Ratification of the UN Convention on the Rights of Persons with Disabilities for the European Community' in O Arnardóttir and G Quinn (eds), *The United Nations Convention on the Rights of Persons with Disabilities: European and Scandinavian Perspectives* (Leiden, Martinus Nijhoff, 2009)

Xenidis, R, 'Multiple Discrimination in EU Anti-Discrimination Law: Towards Redressing Complex Inequality?' in U Belavusau and K Henrard (eds), *EU Anti-Discrimination Law Beyond Gender* (Oxford Hart Publishing, 2018)

Journal Articles

Alston, P, 'Conjuring up New Human Rights: A Proposal for Quality Control' (1984) 78 *American Journal of International Law* 607

Areheart, BA, 'When Disability Isn't "Just Right": The Entrenchment of the Medical Model of Disability and the Goldilocks Dilemma (2008) 83 *Indiana Law Journal* 183

Barnard, C and Hepple, B, 'Substantive Equality' (2010) 59 *Cambridge Law Journal* 562

Barnes, C, 'Review of *The Rejected Body*, by Susan Wendell' (1998) 13 *Disability and Society* 145

Bayefsky, A, 'The Principle of Equality and Non-Discrimination in International Law' (1990) 11 *Human Rights Law Journal* 1

Bell, M, 'The Implementation of European Anti-Discrimination Directives: Converging towards a Common Model?' (2008) 79 *Political Quarterly* 36

Besson, S, 'The Principle of Non-Discrimination in the Convention on the Rights of the Child' (2005) 13 *International Journal of Children's Rights* 433

Bonnor, PG, 'The European Ombudsman: A Novel Source of Soft Law in the European Union' (2000) 1 *European Law Review* 39

Brake, DL, 'When Equality Leaves Everyone Worse Off: The Problem of Leveling Down in Equality Law' (2004) 46 *William & Mary Law Review* 513

Bribosia, E, Ringelheim, J and Rorive, I, 'Reasonable Accommodation for Religious Minorities: A Promising Concept for European Antidiscrimination Law?' (2010) 17 *Maastricht Journal of European and Comparative Law* 137

Broderick, A, '*Ruiz Conejero*: (Re-)Conceptualizing Disability-based Discrimination and Sickness Absence at Work' (2019) 5 *International Labor Rights Case Law* 1

Bryan, I, 'Equality and Freedom from Discrimination: Article 13 EU Treaty' (2002) 24 *Journal of Social Welfare and Family Law* 223

Buch, M 'The Open Method of Coordination as a "Two-level game"' (2008) 36 *Policy & Politics* 21

Butler, M, 'Obesity As A Disability: The Implications or Non-Implications Of Kaltoft' (2014) 20(3) *Web Journal of Current Legal Issues*
Butlin, F, 'The UN Convention on the Rights of Persons with Disabilities: Does the Equality Act 2010 Measure up to UK International Commitments?' (2011) 40 *Industrial Law Journal* 428
Corkin, J, 'Constitutionalism in 3D: Mapping and Legitimating Our Lawmaking Underworld' (2013) 19 *European Law Journal* 637
Cullen, H and Morrow, K, 'International Civil Society in International Law: The Growth of NGO Participation' (2001) 1 *Non-State Actors & International Law* 7
De Beco, G, 'Article 33(2) of the UN Convention on the Rights of Persons with Disabilities: Another Role for National Human Rights Institutions? (2011) 29 *Netherlands Quarterly Human Rights* 84
De Búrca, G, 'The EU in the Negotiation of the UN Disability Convention' (2010) 35 *European Law Review* 174
—— 'After the EU Charter of Fundamental Rights: The Court of Justice as a Human Rights Adjudicator?' (2013) 20 *Maastricht Journal of European and Comparative Law* 168
—— 'The European Court of Justice and the International Legal Order After Kadi' (2010) 51 *Harvard International Law Journal* 1
De Sadeleer, N, 'Principle of Subsidiarity and the EU Environmental Policy' (2012) 9 *Journal for European Environmental Planning* 63
De Schutter, O, 'Europe in Search of its Civil Society' (2002) 8 *European Law Journal* 198
Degener, T, 'Disability in a Human Rights Context' (2016) 5 *Laws* 35
Dhanda, A, 'Constructing a New Human Rights Lexicon: Convention on the Rights of Persons with Disabilities' (2008) 5 *SUR International Journal of Human Rights* 42
Emmett, T and Alant, E, 'Women and disability: exploring the interface of multiple disadvantage' (2006) 23 *Development Southern Africa* 445
Favalli, S and Ferri, D, 'Defining Disability in the EU Non-Discrimination Legislation: Judicial Activism and Legislative Restraints' (2016) 22 *European Public Law* 541
Felne, E, 'Closing the "Escape Hatch": A Toolkit to Monitor the Progressive Realization of Economic, Social, and Cultural Rights' (2009) 1 *Journal of Human Rights Practice* 402
Ferri, D, 'The Conclusion of the UN Convention on the Rights of Persons with Disabilities and the EC/EU: A Constitutional Perspective' (2010) 2 *European Yearbook of Disability Law* 47
—— 'European Citizens … Mind the Gap! Some Reflections on Participatory Democracy in the EU' (2013) 5 *Perspectives on Federalism* 56
—— 'L'accomodamento ragionevole per le persone con disabilità in Europa: dal Transatlantic Borrowing alla Cross-Fertilization' (2017) 2 *Diritto Pubblico Comparato ed Europeo* 381
—— 'Reasonable Accommodation as a Gateway to the Equal Enjoyment of Human Rights: From New York to Strasbourg' (2018) 6 *Social Inclusion* 40
Ferri, D and Favalli, S, 'Tracing the Boundaries between Disability and Sickness in the European Union: Squaring the Circle?' (2016) 23 *European Journal of Health Law* 5
Finke, B, 'Civil Society Participation in EU Governance' (2007) 2 *Living Reviews in European Governance* 4
Franck, TM, 'The Emerging Right to Democratic Governance' (1992) 86 *American Journal of International Law* 46
Fredman, S, 'Transformation or Dilution: Fundamental Rights in the EU Social Space' (2006) 12 *European Law Journal* 41
Greenawalt, K, 'How Empty is the Idea of Equality?' (1983) 83 *Columbia Law Review* 1167
Harbo, TI, 'The Function of the Proportionality Principle in EU Law' (2010) 16 *European Law Journal* 158
Harpur, P, 'Embracing the New Disability Rights Paradigm: The Importance of the Convention on the Rights of Persons with Disabilities' (2012) 27 *Disability & Society* 1
Hart, N et al, 'Making Every Life Count: Ensuring Equality and Protection for Persons with Disabilities in Armed Conflicts' (2014) 40 *Monash University Law Review* 148
Hatzopoulos, V, 'Why the Open Method of Coordination is Bad For You: A Letter to the EU' (2007) 13 *European Law Journal* 309

Sciarra, S, 'Experiments in the open method of coordination: measuring the impact of EU employment policies' [2011] *Rivista Italiana di Diritto del Lavoro* 475

Heidenreich, M and Bischoff, G, 'The Open Method of Coordination: A Way to the Europeanization of Social and Employment Policies?' (2008) 46 *Journal of Common Market Studies* 497

Hendriks, AC, 'UN Convention on the Rights of Persons with Disabilities' (2007) 14 *European Journal of Health Law* 273

—— 'The UN Disability Convention and Multiple Discrimination: Should EU Nondiscrimination Law be Modeled Accordingly?' (2010) 2 *European Yearbook of Disability Law* 7

Hepple, B, 'The New Single Equality Act in Britain' (2010) 5 *Equal Rights Review* 11

Hosking, DL, 'Fat Rights Claim Rebuffed: *Kaltoft v Municipality of Billund*' (2015) 44 *Industrial Law Journal* 460

Howard, E, 'The EU Race Directive: Time for Change?' (2007) 8 *International Journal of Discrimination and the Law* 237

Iglesias Sánchez, S, 'The Court and the Charter: The Impact of the Entry into Force of the Lisbon Treaty on the ECJ's Approach to Fundamental Rights (2012) 49 *Common Market Law Review* 1565

Kanter, AS, 'The Promise and Challenge of the United Nations Convention on the Rights of Persons with Disabilities' (2006–07) 34 *Syracuse Journal of International Law & Commerce* 287

Kayess, R and French, P, 'Out of Darkness into Light? Introducing the Convention on the Rights of Persons with Disabilities' (2008) 8 *Human Rights Law Review* 1

Kohler-Koch, B and Rittenberger, B, 'Review Article: The Governance Turn in EU Studies' (2006) 3 *Journal of Common Market Studies* 205

Lang, R, 'Human rights and Disability – New and Dynamic Perspective with the United Nations Convention on Disability' (2006) 17 *Asia Pacific Disability Rehabilitation Journal* 3

Lang, R, 'The United Nations Convention on the right and dignities for persons with disability: A panacea for ending disability discrimination? La Convention des Nations Unies sur les droits des personnes handicapées: une solution pour mettre fin à la discrimination contre le handicap?' (2009) 3 *ALTER European Journal of Disability Research* 266

Lawson, A, 'The EU Rights Based Approach to Disability: Strategies for Shaping an Inclusive Society' (2005) 6 *International Journal of Discrimination and the Law* 4269

—— 'New Era of False Dawn?' (2006–07) 34 *Syracuse Journal of International Law & Commerce* 562

—— 'Disability and Employment in the Equality Act 2010: Opportunities Seized, Lost and Generated' (2011) 40 *Industrial Law Journal* 359

Leckie, S, 'Another Step towards Indivisibility: Identifying the Key Features of Violations of Economic, Social and Cultural Rights' (1998) 20 *Human Rights Quarterly* 81

López-Santana, M, 'The Domestic Implications of European Soft Law: Framing and Transmitting Change in Employment Policy' (2006) 13 *Journal of European Public Policy* 481

Mabbett, D, 'The Development of Rights-based Social Policy in the European Union: The Example of Disability Rights' (2005) 43 *Journal of Common Market Studies* 97

Majone, G, 'Europe's Democratic Deficit' (1998) 4 *European Law Journal* 237

—— 'The European Commission: The Limits of Centralization and the Perils of Parliamentarization' (2002) 15 *Governance: An International Journal of Policy, Administration and Institutions* 375

McKay, D, 'The Convention on the Rights of Persons with Disabilities: A Benchmark for Action' (2007) 56 *International Rehabilitation Reviews* 2

McTigue, P, 'From Navas to Kaltoft: The European Court of Justice's Evolving Definition of Disability and the Implications for HIV-Positive Individuals' (2015) 15 *International Journal of Discrimination and the Law* 1

Melish, TJ, 'The UN Disability Convention: Historic Process, Strong Prospects, and Why the US Should Ratify' (2007) 15 *Human Rights Brief* 37

Mendrinou, M, 'Non-compliance and the European Commission's role in Integration' (1996) 3 *Journal of European Public Policy* 1

Meron, T, 'On a Hierarchy of International Human Rights' (1986) 80 *American Journal of International Law* 1

Mogami, T, 'The United Nations System as an Unfinished Revolution' (1990) 15 *Alternatives* 177
Moravcsik, A, 'Is there a "Democratic Deficit" in World Politics? A Framework for Analysis' (2004) 39 *Government and Opposition* 336
Nanz, P and Steffek, J, 'Global Governance, Participation and the Public Sphere' (2004) 39 *Government and Opposition* 314
O'Brien, C, 'Driving Down Disability Equality?' (2014) 21 *Maastricht Journal of European and Comparative Law* 723
Otto, D, 'Nongovernmental Organizations in the United Nations System: The Emerging Role of International Civil Society' (1996) 18 *Human Rights Quarterly* 107
Oulton, R, 'When is a Clone not a Clone?' (2009) 159 *New Law Journal* 1158
Pech, L, 'La solution au "déficit démocratique": une nouvelle gouvernance pour l'Union Européenne? (2003) 2 *Journal of European Integration* 131
—— 'Between Judicial Minimalism and Avoidance: The Court of Justice's Sidestepping of Fundamental Constitutional Issues in *Römer and Dominguez*' (2012) 49 *Common Market Law Review* 1841
Perju, V, 'Impairment, Discrimination, and the Legal Construction of Disability in the European Union and the United States' (2011) 44 *Cornell International Law Journal* 280
Pothier, D, 'Tackling Disability Discrimination at Work: Toward a Systemic Approach' (2010) 4 *McGill Journal of Law and Health* 1
Priestley, M, 'Disability Policies and the Open Method of Coordination' (2012) 3 *European Yearbook of Disability Law* 7
Quinn, G, The United Nations Convention on the Rights of Persons with Disabilities: Toward a New International Politics of Disability' (2009–10) 15 *Texas Journal on Civil Liberties & Civil Rights* 33
Quinn, G and Doyle, S, 'Taking the UN Convention on the Rights of Persons with Disabilities Seriously: The Past and Future of the EU Structural Funds as a Tool to Achieve Community Living' (2012) 9 *Equal Rights Review* 69
Quinn, G and Flynn E, 'Transatlantic Borrowings: The Past and Future of EU Non-Discrimination Law and Policy on the Ground of Disability' (2012) 60 *American Journal of Comparative Law* 23
Redish, MH, 'The Federal Courts, Judicial Restraint, and the Importance of Analyzing Legal Doctrine' (1985) 85 *Columbia Law Review* 1378
Reif, LC, 'Ombudsman Institutions and Article 33(2) of the United Nations Convention on the Rights of Persons with Disabilities' (2014) 65 *University of New Brunswick Law Journal* 213
Reiss, JW, 'Innovative Governance in a Federal Europe: Implementing the Convention on the Rights of Persons with Disabilities' (2014) 20 *European Law Journal* 107
Rhinard, M and Kaeding, M, 'The International Bargaining Power of the European Union in "Mixed" Competence Negotiations: The Case of the 2000 Cartagena Protocol on Biosafety' (2006) 44 *Journal of Common Market Studies* 1023
Richardson, L, 'Economic, Social and Cultural Rights (and Beyond) in the UN Human Rights Council' (2015) 15 *Human Rights Law Review* 409
Sabel, CF and Zeitlin, J, 'Learning from Difference: The New Architecture of Experimentalist Governance in the European Union' (2008) 14 *European Law Journal* 271
Samuel, G, 'Comparative Law and Jurisprudence' (1998) 47 *International and Comparative Law Quarterly* 817
Shapiro, MA, 'Labor Goals and Antidiscrimination Norms: Employer Discretion, Reasonable Accommodation, and the Costs of Individualized Treatment' (2013) 32 *Yale Law & Policy Review* 1
Scott, C, 'Governing without Law or Governing without Government? New-ish Governance' (2009) 15 *European Law Journal* 160
Scott, J and Trubek, DM, 'Mind the Gap: Law and New Approaches to Governance in the European Union' (2002) 8 *European Law Journal* 1
Shakespeare, T and Watson, N, 'The Social Model of Disability: An Outdated Ideology?' (2002) 2 *Research in Social Science and Disability* 9
Sohn, L, 'The New International Law: Protection of the Rights of Individuals rather than States' (1982) 32 *American University Law Review* 1
Stein, MA, 'The Law and Economics of Disability Accommodations' (2003) 53 *Duke Law Journal* 88
Stein, MA et al, 'Accommodating Every Body' (2014) 82 *University of Chicago Law Review* 690

Stein, MA and Lord, JE, 'Participation in International Agreements as Transformative Social Change: The UN Convention on the Rights of Persons with Disabilities' (2008) 83 *Washington Law Review* 449

Stein, M and Stein, P, 'Beyond Disability Rights' (2007) 58 *Hastings Law Journal* 1203

Toth, AG, 'The Principle of Subsidiarity in the Maastricht Treaty' (1992) 29 *Common Market Law Review* 1079

Trubek, DM and Trubek, LG, 'Hard and Soft Law in the Construction of Social Europe: The Role of the Open Method of Co-ordination' (2005) 11 *European Law Journal* 343

Uccellari, P, 'Multiple Discrimination: How Law can Reflect Reality' (2008) 1 *Equality Rights Review* 24

Van Hoecke, M, 'Methodology of Comparative Legal Research' [2015] *Law and Method* 1

Vierdag, EW, 'The Legal Nature of the Rights Granted by the International Covenant on Economic, Social and Cultural Rights (ICESCR)' (1978) 9 *Netherlands Yearbook of International Law* 69

Waddington, L, 'Case C-13/05, Chacón Navas v Eurest Colectividades SA, Judgement of the Grand Chamber of 11 July 2006' (2007) 44 *Common Market Law Review* 487

—— 'Case C-303/06, S Coleman v Attridge Law and Steve Law, Judgement of the Grand Chamber of the Court of Justice of 17 July 2008, not yet reported' (2009) 46 *Common Market Law Review* 665

—— 'The European Union and the United Nations Convention on the Rights of Persons with Disabilities: A Story of Exclusive and Shared Competences' (2011) 18 *Maastricht Journal of European & Comparative Law* 431

—— 'Equal to the Task: Re-Examining EU Equality Law in Light of the United Nations Convention on the Rights of Persons with Disabilities' (2013) 4 *European Yearbook of Disability Law* 169

—— 'Fine-tuning Non-discrimination Law: Exceptions and Justifications Allowing for Different Treatment on the Ground of Disability' (2014) 15 *International Journal of Discrimination and the Law* 11

—— 'Saying All the Right Things and Still Getting It Wrong: The Court of Justice's Definition of Disability and Non-Discrimination Law' (2015) 22 *Maastricht Journal of European and Comparative Law* 576

Waddington, L and Bell, M, 'More Equal than Others: Distinguishing European Union Equality Directives' (2001) 38 *Common Market Law Review* 587

Waddington, L and Hendriks, A, 'The Expanding Concept of Employment Discrimination in Europe: From Direct and Indirect Discrimination to Reasonable Accommodation Discrimination' (2002) 18 *International Journal of Comparative Labour Law and Industrial Relations* 403

Waldschmidt, A, 'Disability Policy of the European Union: The Supranational Level' (2009) 4 *ALTER European Journal of Disability Research* 8

Westen, P, 'The Empty Idea of Equality' (1982) 95 *Harvard Law Review* 537

Whittle, R, 'The Framework Directive for Equal Treatment in Employment and Occupation: An Analysis from a Disability Rights Perspective' (2002) 27 *European Law Review* 303

Woodburn, H, 'Nothing about us without Civil Society: The Role of Civil Society Actors in the Formation of the UN Convention on the Rights of Persons with Disabilities' (2013) 7 *Political Perspectives* 75

Miscellaneous Sources (Reports, Research Series and Other)

Anglmayer, I, 'EU Implementation of the UN Convention on the Rights of Persons with Disabilities (CRPD)' (Brussels, European Parliamentary Research Service, 2016)

Arnade, S and Haefner, S, *Standard Interpretation of the UN Convention on the Rights of Persons with Disabilities (CRPD) from a Female Perspective, Position and Reference Paper on the Significance of References to Women and Gender in the Convention on the Rights of Persons with Disabilities* (Berlin, Netzwerk Artikel, 2011)

Arsenjeva, J, 'Implementation of the UN Convention on the Rights of Persons with Disabilities in the EU's External Relations', Briefing Paper for the Directorate-General for External Policies of the Union (European Parliament, Brussels, 2013)

Bielefeldt, H, *Tackling Multiple Discrimination Practices, Policies and Laws* (Luxembourg, Office for Official Publications of the European Communities, 2007)

Brodsky G., Day S., and Peters Y., Accommodation in the 21st Century, Canadian Human Rights Commission, (March, 2012)

Carrera, S, De Somer, M and Petkova, B, 'The Court of Justice of the European Union as a Fundamental Rights Tribunal: Challenges for the Effective Delivery of Fundamental Rights in the Area of Freedom, Security and Justice' (2012) 49 CEPS, Justice and Home Affairs Liberty and Security in Europe Papers

Chopin, I and Germaine-Sahl, C, *European Anti-Discrimination Law Review* (Luxembourg, Publications Office of the European Union, 2009)

—— *European Anti-Discrimination Law Review* (Luxembourg, Publications Office of the European Union, 2013)

—— *European Anti-Discrimination Law Review* (Luxembourg, Publications Office of the European Union, 2014)

Committee on Employment and Social Affairs, 'Draft Report on the implementation of the UN Convention on the Rights of Persons with Disabilities, with special regard to the Concluding Observations of the UN CRPD Committee' (2015/2258(INI))

Council of Europe, 'Action Plan to promote the rights and full participation of people with disabilities in society: improving the quality of life of people with disabilities in Europe 2006–2015, Rec(2006)5

Council Press Release 15491/12 (Luxembourg, 29 October 2012)

Crenshaw, K, 'Background Paper for the Expert Meeting on the Gender-Related Aspects of Race Discrimination', United Nations Division for the Advancement of Women (DAW) Office of the High Commissioner for Human Rights (OHCHR) United Nations Development Fund for Women (UNIFEM) Expert Group Meeting on 'Gender and Racial Discrimination' (Zagreb, 21–24 November 2000)

De Beco, G, *Study on the Implementation of Article 33 of the UN Convention on the Rights of Persons with Disabilities in Europe* (Regional Office for Europe of the UN High Commissioner for Human Rights, 2014)

De Búrca, G, 'The Decline of EU Anti-Discrimination Law? (2016) Note for the Colloquium on Comparative and Global Public Law (NYU)

De Búrca, G, Keohane, RO and Sabel, C, 'New Modes of Pluralist Global Governance' (2013) New York University Public Law and Legal Theory Working Papers No 386

De Vos, M, *Beyond formal equality: Positive action under Directive 2000/43/EC and Directive 2000/78/EC* (Luxembourg, Office for Official Publications of the European Communities, European Commission, 2007)

Deutsches Institut fuer menschenrechte, *Anhang: Überblick über die Organisationen der Verbändekonsultationen der Monitoring-Stelle zur UN-Behindertenrechtskonvention* (Stand, November 2014)

Estrada-Tanck, D, 'Human rights of persons with disabilities in international and EU law' (2016) Working Paper EUI AEL, 2016/01

European Commission, 'Green Paper European Social Policy: Options for the Union' COM(93) 551 final

—— 'Communication of the Commission on equality of opportunity for people with disabilities. A New European Community Disability Strategy' COM(96) 406 final

—— 'Promoting the role of voluntary organisations and foundations in Europe', COM(97) 241 final [1998] OJ C 95

—— 'The Commission and Non-Governmental Organisations: building a stronger partnership', presented by President Prodi and Vice-President Kinnock (18 January 2000)

—— 'European Governance – A White Paper', COM 428 final ([2001] OJ C 287/1)

—— 'Communication to the Council and the European Parliament of 24 January 2003 towards a United Nations legally binding instrument to promote and protect the rights and dignity of persons with disabilities' COM (2003) 16 final

—— 'Equal opportunities for people with disabilities: A European Action Plan' (Communication) COM/2003/0650

—— 'Proposal for a Council Decision concerning the conclusion, by the European Community, of the United Nations Convention on the Rights of Persons with Disabilities' COM (2008) 530 final

—— 'Commission non-paper on Setting-up the EU framework prescribed by article 33.2 of the UN Convention on the Rights of Persons with Disabilities' (2012)

—— 'Report on the implementation of the UN Convention on the Rights of Persons with Disabilities (CRPD) by the European Union', SWD (2014) 182 final

—— 2014 *Report on the application of the EU Charter of Fundamental Rights* (Luxembourg, Publications Office of the European Union, 2015)

—— *2018 Report on the application of the EU Charter of Fundamental Rights* (Luxembourg, Publications Office of the European Union, 2019)

Commission, 'Union of Equality: Strategy for the Rights of Persons with Disabilities 2021–2030', COM(2021) 101 final

European Economic and Social Committee, 'The Role and contribution of civil society organisations in the building of Europe', CES 851/99 (22 September 1999)

—— 'The Commission and non-governmental organisations: building a stronger partnership', CES 811/2000 (13 July 2000)

European Ombudsman, 'Strategy for the mandate', September 2010

European Parliamentary Research Service, 'Implementing the principle of equal treatment between persons Complementary Impact Assessment of the proposed horizontal Directive on Equal Treatment' (Brussels, 2014)

—— 'EU Implementation of the UN Convention on the Rights of Persons with Disabilities (CRPD) European Implementation Assessment' (Brussels, 2016)

European Union Agency for Fundamental Rights (FRA), *National Human Rights Institutions in the EU Member States, Strengthening the fundamental rights architecture in the EU* (Luxembourg, Publications Office of the European Union 2010)

—— *Inequalities and Multiple discrimination in Access to and quality of healthcare* (Luxembourg, Publications Office of the European Union, 2013)

—— 'Opinion of the European Union Agency for Fundamental Rights concerning requirements under Article 33(2) of the UN Convention on the Rights of Persons with Disabilities within the EU context' (Vienna, 3/2016)

Fredman, S, 'Human Rights Transformed: Positive Duties and Positive Rights' (2006) Legal Research Paper Series, Paper No 38/2006

—— 'Anti-discrimination laws and work in the developing world: A thematic overview' Background paper for the world development report (World Bank, Washington, DC, 2013)

Fredman, S and Goldblatt, B, 'Gender Equality and Human Rights' (July 2015) Discussion Paper, UN Women

Groussot X, Lock T and Pech, L, 'EU Accession to the European Convention on Human Rights: A Legal Assessment of the Draft Accession Agreement of 14th October 2011' (2011) Foundation Robert Schuman, Policy Paper European issues no 218

High Level Disability Group Work Programme 2006–2007, Disability High Level Group Discussion Paper. Subject: Disability mainstreaming in the new streamlined European social protection and inclusion processes

Human Development Report 1998 published for the United Nations Development Programme (UNDP) (Oxford, Oxford University Press, 1998)

Interights, *Non-Discrimination in International Law: A Handbook for Practitioners* (London, 2011)

Jans, L and Stoppard, S, *Chartbook on Women and Disability in the United States*. An InfoUse Report (Washington, DC, US Department of Education, National Institute on Disability and Rehabilitation Research, 1999)

Krieger, LH, *Backlash Against the ADA: Reinterpreting Disability Rights* (Ann Arbor, MI, University of Michigan Press, 2003)

Leadership Council, Sustainable Development Solutions Network, *An Action Agenda for Sustainable Development: Report for the UN Secretary-General* (6 June 2013)

Memorandum of the Commission to the Council concerning the employment of disabled people in the European Community (COM 86(9) of 24 January 1986)

Office of the High Commissioner for Human Rights, *Monitoring the Convention on the Rights of Persons with Disabilities Guidance for human rights monitors* Professional training series No 17 (New York and Geneva, 2010)

—— 'Human rights indicators A Guide to Measurement' (New York, 2012)

Priestley, M, Raley, M and de Beco, G, *The protection role of the Committee on Petitions in the context of the implementation of the UN Convention on the Rights of Persons with Disabilities*, study for the Directorate General for Internal Policies Policy Department C Citizens' Rights and Constitutional Affairs Petition (Brussels, European Parliament, 2015)

Quinlivan, S, 'The United Nations Convention on the Rights of Persons with Disabilities: An Introduction' (2012) 13 *ERA Forum* 71

Quinn, G et al, *Human Rights and Disability: The current use and future potential of United Nations human rights instruments in the context of disability* (New York, United Nations Press, 2002)

Radaelli, CM, *The Open Method of Coordination: A new governance architecture for the European Union* (Swedish Institute for European Policy Studies, 2003)

Scharpf, FW, 'The European Social Model: Coping with the Challenges of Diversity' (2002) Max Planck Institute for the Study of Societies Working Paper 02/8

Scholte, JA, 'Civil Society and Democracy in Global Governance' (2001) Centre for the Study of Globalization and Regionalisation CSGR Working Paper No 65/01

Secretariat for the Convention on the Rights of Persons with Disabilities of the Department of Economic and Social Affairs; United Nations Population Fund; Wellesley Centers for Women, *Disability Rights, Gender, and Development: A Resource Tool for Action* (2008)

Sheppard, C, 'Multiple Discrimination in the World of Work' (2011) Working Paper no 66, International Labour Office, Programme for the Promotion of the ILO Declaration on Fundamental Principles and Rights at Work (Declaration) (Geneva, ILO, 2011)

Waddington, L, 'Reflections on the Establishment of a Framework to Promote, Protect and Monitor Implementation of the UN Convention on the Rights of Persons with Disabilities (Article 33(2) CRPD) by the European Union' (2011) Maastricht Faculty of Law Working Paper 2011/3

Waddington, L and Broderick, A, *Realising equality: A comparison of the UN Convention on the Rights of Persons with Disabilities and EU equality and non-discrimination law* (Luxembourg, Publications Office of the European Union, 2018)

—— 'The Post-2020 European Disability Strategy', study commissioned by the European Parliament's Policy Department for Citizens' Rights and Constitutional Affairs at the request of the PETI Committee (Brussels, 2020)

Waddington, L and Lawson, A, *Disability and non-discrimination law in the European Union: An analysis of disability discrimination law within and beyond the employment field* (Luxembourg, Publications Office of the European Union, 2009)

Weiwei, L, 'Equality and non-discrimination under international human rights law' (2004) Norwegian Centre for Human Rights, Research Notes 03/2004

Whittle, R, 'The concept of disability discrimination and its legal construction' in *Discrimination and affirmative action on the labour market – legal perspectives* (in preparation of the Swedish Presidency of the European Union) (National Institute for Working Life, Sweden, 6–7 November 2001)

INDEX

accountability:
European governance, 49, 140
European Ombudsman, 133
global governance, 37
NGOs' role, 38–39
Ad Hoc Committee on a Comprehensive and Integral International Convention on Protection and Promotion of the Rights and Dignity of Persons with Disabilities (Ad Hoc Committee), 40–42, 52–53
NGO participation, 41–42, 161
Working Group, 42
affirmative action, 10–11, 14, 17, 19, 28, 109, 155
CEDAW, 12, 12–13
CRPD, 14
ICERD, 11–13
margin of discretion, 11–12
monitoring processes, 46
age and disability discrimination:
Odar case, 99–101
Surjit Singh Bedi case, 101
associative discrimination:
applicability, 94–95
Coleman case, 91–94
equality as a fundamental principle of the EU, 92–93
Equality Framework Directive, 93–94
factual background, 91–92
protection of dignity and autonomy, 92–93
definition, 91
reasonable accommodation, 95–96
asymmetrical model of equality, *see* **substantive model of equality**
autonomy:
civil society organisations, 53
EU legal order, 58, 108
EU member states, 144, 158
personal autonomy
non-discrimination principle, 3, 92–93
***Chacón Navas v Eurest Colectividades SA*:**
medical model of disability, 63–64, 73–74, 82, 151
personal scope of Equality Framework Directive, 66–67
reasonable accommodation, 66–67
children with disabilities, 3, 22–23
see also UN Convention on the Rights of the Child
***Coleman v Attridge Law and Steve Law*:**
associative discrimination
factual background, 91–92
direct discrimination, 92–94, 95
equality as a fundamental principle of the EU, 92–93
Equality Framework Directive, 93–94
protection of dignity and autonomy, 92–93
Committee on Economic, Social and Cultural Rights (CESCR):
evolution of concept of intersectionality, 22
Committee on Employment and Social Affairs (EMPL), 142, 144
Council Working Group on Human Rights (COHOM), 122–23, 124, 125, 139
Court of Justice of the European Union (CJEU):
Chacón Navas case, 63–64, 66–67, 73–74, 82, 89, 151
Daouidi case, 81–83
disability defined, 65–66
intersectional and multiple discrimination
Odar case, 99–101
Surjit Singh Bedi case, 101
Z v A Government Department, 102–10, 151–52
Kaltoft case, 76–81, 151
promoter of disability rights, as a, 89–90
Ring and Skouboe Werge case, 67–76, 89–90, 150–51
Ruiz Conejero case, 83–85, 151
sickness and disability distinguished, 63–64
Wolfgang Glatzel case, 85–89, 152

***Daouidi v Bootes Plus SL and Others*:**
long-term nature of impairment, 81–83
personal scope of Equality Framework Directive, 81–83
democratic deficit:
NGOs' positive impact upon, 37–38, 39
democratic legitimacy, 50–51, 117
global governance and, 37–38
direct discrimination:
Coleman case, 92–94, 95
control of one's financial affairs, 30–31
Equality Framework Directive, 60–61
sameness model of equality, 5
Disabled Peoples International (DPI), 42
duty to provide reasonable accommodation:
adaption of working hours, 70–71, 89–90
associative discrimination, 95–96
Chacón Navas case, 66–67
disproportionate or undue burden defence, 18–19
Equality Framework Directive, 62–63, 66–67, 154–55
functional/individualised accommodations, 156–57
gender and disability discrimination, 103
HM v Sweden, 16–17
non-discrimination requirement, 17–19
Ring and Skouboe Werge case, 70–71, 75–76, 89–90
State's duties, 19
substantive model of equality, 8
disproportionate or undue burden defence, 18–19
HM v Sweden, 16–17
non-discrimination requirement, 17–19
State's duties, 19
Z v A Government Department, 103

Equality Framework Directive, 60
associative discrimination, 93–94
direct discrimination, 60–61
duty to provide reasonable accommodation, 62–63, 66–67, 154–55
gender and disability discrimination, 104
indirect discrimination, 61–62, 89–90, 153–55
medical model of disability, 66–67
obesity as grounds for disability, 78–79
personal scope
Chacón Navas case, 66–67
Daouidi case, 81–83
Kaltoft case, 76–81, 89
reasonable accommodation, 62–63
Chacón Navas case, 66–67
Z v A Government Department, 104
equality principle, 3
equality under and before the law, 15
inclusive model of equality, 14–15, 155
see also inclusive model of equality
international law, 4
ECtHR, 4–5
sameness/symmetrical approach, 5–7, 57
see also sameness model of equality
substantive equality, 8–12
see also substantive model of equality
see also non-discrimination principle
EU Charter of Fundamental Rights (EUCFR), 27
discrimination on the base of disability, 14–15
human rights model of equality, 14–15, 88–89
inclusive model of equality, 14–15, 88–89
Kaltoft case, 78
non-discrimination principle, 56–57, 77, 78
participatory democracy, 50–52
Wolfgang Glatzel case, 85, 88–89
EU implementation of CRPD:
EU Independent Framework, *see* EU Independent Framework
legal status of CRPD, 155–56, 157–58
monitoring CRPD implementation, 46, 116–17
experimentalist governance regime, 117–18, 125–26
monitoring framework, 123–24
open method of coordination, 118–19
participatory democracy, 48–50
CRPD good practice, 52–54
EUCFR, adoption of, 50–52
improvement, 52–54
EU Independent Framework:
civil society organisations, 159
coordination mechanisms with member states, 121–23
European Commission, 114–15, 121–23, 138–39
internal coordination, 138
vertical coordination, 138–39
EU Agency for Fundamental Rights, 133–35
European Commission, 120–21
ensuring coordination, 114–15, 121–23
experimentalist approach, 125–26
external policy representation, 115–16

negotiation and drafting of CRPD, 113–14
ratification of CRPD, 111
European Disability Forum, 135–38
European Ombudsman, 130–31
limited nature of mandate, 132–33
Ombudsman initiatives, 131–32
European Parliament, 159
Disability Intergroup, 130
PETI, 127–29, 141–42, 148
protection of disability rights, 126–30
limitations
Commission withdrawal from Framework, 139–41
European Parliament's role, 141–42
OMC, appropriateness of, 144–49
OMC, relationship with, 144–49, 158
proposals to upgrade, 148–49
reform, 159–60
good governance, 160–61
key recommendations, 160
participatory democracy, 160–61
European Commission:
ensuring coordination, 114–15
external policy representation, 115–16
experimentalist approach, 125–26
ratification of CRPD, 111
negotiation and drafting, 112–14
White Paper on European Governance, 49–50, 118, 125–26, 137
European Convention on Human Rights (ECHR), 57–58
sameness model of equality, 6, 7, 57
European Court of Human Rights (ECtHR), 4–5, 57–58
substantive model of equality, 10
European Disability Forum (EDF), 42, 52, 59, 114, 148
EU Independent Framework, 135–38, 142
European Employment Strategy (EES), 141
European Ombudsman:
accountability, 133
EU Independent Framework, 130–31
limited nature of mandate, 132–33
Ombudsman initiatives, 131–32
European Parliament:
EU Independent Framework, 141–42, 159
Disability Intergroup, 130
PETI, 127–29, 141–42, 148
protection of disability rights, 126–30
protection of disability rights, 126–28
Disability Intergroup, 130
PETI, 127–29, 141–42, 148
European Parliament's Petitions Committee (PETI), 127–29, 141–42, 148
European Structural and Investment Fund (ESI), 132
European Union:
disability, approach to, 63
Chacón Navas case, 63–64, 66–67, 73–74, 82, 89, 151
CJEU as a promoter of disability rights, 89–90
CJEU definition of disability, 65–66
Daouidi case, 81–83
Kaltoft case, 76–81
Ring and Skouboe Werge case, 67–76, 89–90
Ruiz Conejero case, 83–85, 151
sickness and disability distinguished, 63–64
Wolfgang Glatzel case, 85–89, 152
disability rights
CJEU as a promoter of disability rights, 89–90
EDF, 42, 52, 59, 114, 135–38, 142, 148
HELIOS I, 59
HELIOS II, 59
mainstreaming disability policy, 59
Treaty of Amsterdam, 58–59
Equality Framework Directive, *see* Equality Framework Directive
EU Independent Framework, *see* EU Independent Framework
external policy representation, 115–16
implementation of CRPD, *see* EU implementation of CRPD
improving interpretation of equality norms
accommodation of different characteristics, 156
adoption of functional/individualised accommodations, 156–57
recognition of intersectional and multiple discrimination, 157
intersectional and multiple discrimination
Odar case, 99–101
Surjit Singh Bedi case, 101
Z v A Government Department, 102–10, 151–52
see also intersectional and multiple discrimination
legal status of CRPD, 155–56, 157–58
negotiation and drafting of CRPD, 112–14

participatory democracy, 48–50
CRPD good practice, 52–54
EUCFR, adoption of, 50–52
improvement, 52–54
see also participatory democracy
ratification of CRPD, 111, 155
European Union Agency for Fundamental Rights (FRA):
EU Independent Framework, 133–35, 146, 148

Fag og arbejde v Kommunernes landsforening, *see* ***Kaltoft v Municipality of Billund*** **(2014)**

gender and disability discrimination:
Z v A Government Department, 102–10
CJEU findings, 103–4
duty to provide reasonable accommodation, 103
EU and international law, relationship between, 106–8
EU anti-discrimination law, 105
factual background, 102
human rights model of equality, failure to apply, 106, 151–52
inappropriateness of CJEU response, 108–10
interpretation of disability, 103
surrogacy and pregnancy distinguished, 103
validity of Equality Framework Directive, 104
global governance:
decision-making
NGOs' impact, 37–38
mistrust of institutions
EU, 48–50
participatory democracy, 37, 38, 39–43
EU, 49–50
role of civil society, 35–37
transparency
NGOs' impact, 38–39
see also EU implementation of CRPD; national implementation of CRPD
good governance, 118
EU, 48, 51–52, 54, 125–26, 159, 160–61
NGOs' role, 38
participatory democracy
EU, 48, 51–52, 54, 160–61
White Paper of the Commission on European Governance, 49–50, 118, 125–26, 137
High Level Group on Disability (HLGD), 121–23, 125, 139, 140, 144–46
HM v Sweden, 16–17
human dignity, 2–3, 15, 17, 25, 28, 41, 47, 55, 92–94, 112, 114, 136
human diversity, 2–3, 25–26, 49, 135
see also substantive equality
human rights:
accessibility, 33–34
civil and political rights v socio-economic rights
CRPD, 28–29
justiciability and non-justiciability, 26–27, 29–30
Nyusti & Takacs case, 30–33
right to control one's financial affairs, 30–33
traditional theory, 26–27, 29–30
duties of restraint, 26
justiciability and non-justiciability, 26–27, 29–30
Nyusti & Takacs case, 30–33
right to control one's financial affairs, 30–33
see also justiciability of disability rights
positive duties, 26
see also EU Charter of Fundamental Rights; European Convention on Human Rights; International Covenant on Civil and Political Rights; International Covenant on Economic, Social and Cultural Rights
human rights model of disability, 25–26, 79–80, 86–87, 89–90, 161
EUCFR, 14–15, 88–89
failure to apply
Ruiz Conejero case, 151
Z v A Government Department, 106, 151–52
gender and disability discrimination, 106, 151–52

inclusive model of equality, 155, 156–57, 161
EUCFR, 14–15, 88–89
HM v Sweden, 16–17
participatory democracy, 49–50, 118
substantive content, 17–19
indirect discrimination:
Coleman case, 93–94
Equality Framework Directive, 60, 61–62, 89–90, 153–55
EUCFR, 15

Odar case, 99
reasonable accommodation, relationship with, 153–55
Ring and Skouboe Werge case, 71–72, 74–75, 154
legitimate aim, 72–73
necessity, 72–73
proportionality, 72–73
Ruiz Conejero case, 84, 85
Surjit Singh Bedi case, 101
Z v A Government Department, 103
see also duty to make reasonable accommodation
International Convention on the Elimination of all Forms of Racial Discrimination (ICERD):
affirmative action, 11, 13
de facto equality, 11
identification of specific groups, 10–11
intersectionality, 21–22
legitimacy of positive/affirmative action, 11
margin of discretion, 11–12
levelling-down, 13
single-ground approach, 21–22
substantive model of equality, 9, 10–11, 12
International Covenant on Civil and Political Rights (ICCPR), 26
sameness model of equality, 6, 7
substantive model of equality, 9–10
International Covenant on Economic, Social and Cultural Rights (ICESCR), 26
sameness model of equality, 6, 7
intersectional and multiple discrimination, 19–20, 98
compound discrimination, 20–21
EU recognition of, 157
evolution of concept of intersectionality, 21
CEDAW, 22
CESCR, 22
ICERD, 21–22
importance of, 97–99
inadequacy of CJEU approach, 152–53
NGOs, recognition by, 43
Odar case, 99–101
Surjit Singh Bedi case, 101
women and children with disabilities, 22–23
Z v A Government Department, 102–10, 151–52

justiciability of disability rights, 17–18, 26–27, 29–30
accessibility, 33–34
right to control one's financial affairs
Nyusti & Takacs case, 30–33

***Kaltoft v Municipality of Billund*:**
non-discrimination principle
labour market and, 77–78
obesity, 77
obesity as grounds for disability, 76–77, 80–81, 151
Equality Framework Directive, 78–79
personal scope of Equality Framework Directive, 76–81, 89, 97

legal capacity, 15, 53, 81–82, 83, 144

medical model of disability, 1–2, 24, 43
Chacón Navas case, 63–64, 66–67, 73–74, 82, 89, 151
outdated nature of, 80–81, 86, 89, 106, 151–52, 156
Ring and Skouboe Werge case, 69, 86
monitoring CRPD implementation, 46, 116–17
coordination mechanisms with member states, 121–23
European Commission, 114–15, 121–23, 138–39
internal coordination, 138
vertical coordination, 138–39
EU Agency for Fundamental Rights, 133–35
European Commission, 120–21
ensuring coordination, 114–15, 121–23
experimentalist approach, 125–26
external policy representation, 115–16
negotiation and drafting of CRPD, 113–14
ratification of CRPD, 111
European Disability Forum, 135–38
European Ombudsman, 130–31
limited nature of mandate, 132–33
Ombudsman initiatives, 131–32
European Parliament
Disability Intergroup, 130
PETI, 127–29, 141–42, 148
protection of disability rights, 126–30
experimentalist governance regime, 117–18
European Commission, 125–26
open method of coordination, 118–19
see also EU implementation of CRPD

multiple discrimination, *see* **intersectional and multiple discrimination**

national implementation of CRPD:
civic education, 47–48
coordination mechanisms with EU, 121–23
harmonisation of legislation, 45
NGOs' role, 44–45
awareness raising, 47–48
national human rights institutions, 45–47
participation of disabled people, 45–46
public awareness, 47–48
see also EU implementation of CRPD
non-discrimination principle, 3
ECHR, 57–58
ECtHR, 4–5
EU law
EUCFR, 56–57
Mangold case, 56
secondary law, 56
TEU, 55
TFEU, 55–56
substantive model of equality, 17–18
duties on state parties, 18
reasonable accommodation defined, 18–19
see also equality principle
non-governmental organisations (NGOs):
decision-making, impact on, 37–38
mainstreaming disability, 39–40
participatory democracy, 40–43
monitoring procedures, 46
national implementation of CRPD, 44–45, 47
awareness raising, 47–48
harmonisation of legislation, 45
national human rights institutions, 45–47
participation of disabled people, 45–46
open method of coordination, 118–19
participatory democracy, impact on, 37, 38
rising importance, 35–37
transparency, impact on, 38–39
United Nations and, 36

obesity as grounds for disability, 76–77, 80–81
Equality Framework Directive, 78–79
non-discrimination principle, 77
personal scope of Equality Framework Directive, 76–81
Odar **case:**
disability and age discrimination, 99–101
indirect discrimination, 99
intersectional and multiple discrimination, 99–101

open method of coordination (OMC):
decentralised learning, 119
monitoring CRPD implementation
NGOs and civil societies, 118–19
participation, emphasis on, 119
whether appropriate, 144
reporting mechanisms, 144–46
sanctioning mechanisms, lack of, 146–47

participatory democracy, 37, 38
EU Independent Framework, 160–61
European Union, 48–50
CRPD good practice, 52–54
EUCFR, adoption of, 50–52
improvement, 52–54
inclusive model of equality, 49–50, 118
mainstreaming disability, 39–40
Ad Hoc Committee participation, 40–42
Working Group participation, 42
NGOs' role, 43
national human rights institutions' role, 43
national implementation of CRPD, 45–46
personal autonomy, *see* **autonomy**
positive action, *see* **affirmative action**
positive rights and duties:
integration of persons with disabilities, 88–89
lack of, 99
proportionality:
burden on employers, 75–76, 85, 154, 156–57
duty of reasonable accommodation, 18–19, 62, 75–76, 95–96, 156–57
HM v Sweden, 16–17
indirect discrimination, 71–73
public v private interests, 72–73, 85, 154, 156–57
Ruiz Conejero case, 84, 85

reasonable accommodation, *see* **duty to provide reasonable accommodation**
Rehabilitation International, 42
Ring and Skouboe Werge **case:**
concept of disability, 67–68
disability defined, 69–70
factual background, 68–69
impact of the case, 73
balancing public and private interests, 74–75
interpretation of reasonable accommodation obligation, 75–76
justification test, 74–75

shortened periods of notice, 74–75
socio-contextual model of disability, application of, 73–74
indirect discrimination, 71–72, 154
legitimate aim, 72–73
necessity, 72–73
proportionality, 72–73
personal scope of Equality Framework Directive, 69–70
reasonable accommodation
adaption of working hours, 70–71, 89–90
Ruiz Conejero v Ferroser Servicios Auxiliares SA and Ministerio Fiscal, 83–85
concept of disability, 83–84
factual background, 83–84
human rights model of equality, failure to apply, 151
sickness and disability distinguished, 84–85

sameness model of equality, 5, 8
consistency of treatment, 5–6
direct discrimination, 5
ECHR, 6, 7, 57
equality comparator, 8
failures of, 8
HM v Sweden, 16–17
ICCPR, 6, 7
ICESCR, 6, 7
principle of levelling-down, 6
procedural justice, 5–6
substantive model of equality, *see* substantive model of equality
UDHR, 6
single-ground approach to discrimination, 21
EU law, 97–98, 104, 157
ICERD, 21–22
inadequacy of, 104, 152–53, 157
see also intersectional and multiple discrimination
social construct of disability, 24–25, 150–51, 156
subsidiarity principle, 49
substantive model of equality, 1–2, 4, 12–14
associative discrimination, 96–97
CEDAW, 10, 12
Coleman case, 93, 96–97
development, 9, 109–10, 113–14, 155, 157–58
duty to provide reasonable accommodation
disproportionate or undue burden defence, 18–19
HM v Sweden, 16–17
non-discrimination requirement, 17–19
State's duties, 19
ECtHR, 10
evolution towards, 9
ICCPR, 9–10
ICERD, 10–11
indirect discrimination, 61–62, 74–75
intersectionality, relationship with, 23
non-discrimination requirement, 17–19
social construct of disability, 24–25
Surjit Singh Bedi v Bundesrepublik Deutschland:
disability and age discrimination, 101
intersectional and multiple discrimination, 101
symmetrical model of equality, *see* **sameness model of equality**

transparency, 37–38, 38–39
EUCFR, 50–51
European Commission, 140, 141
European Ombudsman, 131–32
HLGD, 140
Treaty on European Union (TEU), 55, 57–58, 77, 100, 134
Treaty on the Functioning of the European Union (TFEU):
duty for reasonable accommodation, 97
EU and international law, relationship between, 106–7
negotiation of international treaties, 111–12, 115–16
European Ombudsman, 130–31
human dignity, 92–93
intersectional and multiple discrimination, 97–98
non-discrimination principle, 55–56, 92–93, 113
obesity as grounds for discrimination, 77, 79
participatory democracy, 50, 54
personal autonomy, 92–93
PETI, 126–27

UN Conference on Environment and Development (UNCED), 37
UN Convention on the Elimination of All Forms of Discrimination Against Women (CEDAW), 9
affirmative action measures, 12, 12–13
de facto equality, 12
identification of specific groups, 10–11

intersectionality, 22
substantive model of equality, 10, 12
UN Convention on the Rights of Persons with Disabilities (CRPD), 1–2
duty to provide reasonable accommodation, *see* duty to provide reasonable accommodation
European Commission, *see* European Commission
European Union, *see* EU implementation of CRPD; European Union
inclusive model of equality, 14–15
intersectional discrimination, *see* intersectional discrimination
national implementation of CRPD, *see* national implementation of CRPD
participatory democracy, 45–46, 52–54
substantive model of equality, *see* substantive model of equality
UN Convention on the Rights of the Child (CRC), 9, 13–14
discrimination on the base of disability, 14–15
inclusive model of equality, 14–15
United Nations Economic and Social Council (ECOSOC), 36
Universal Declaration of Human Rights (UDHR):
sameness model of equality, 6–7
see also International Covenant on Civil and Political Rights; International Covenant on Economic, Social

White Paper of the Commission on European Governance, 49–50, 118, 125–26, 137
***Wolfgang Glatzel v Freistaat Bayern* (2006):**
concept of disability, 86–87
CPRD and EU law, relationship between, 87–88
discrimination beyond the workplace, 85–86
EUCFR, 88–89
inconsistency within CJEU, 87
women with disabilities:
CRPD, 22–23
see also UN Convention on the Elimination of All Forms of Discrimination Against Women
World Trade Organization (WTO):
democratic deficit, 38

Z v A Government Department:
disability and gender discrimination, 102–10
CJEU findings, 103–4
duty to provide reasonable accommodation, 103
EU and international law, relationship between, 106–8
EU anti-discrimination law, 105
factual background, 102
human rights model of equality, failure to apply, 106, 151–52
inappropriateness of CJEU response, 108–10
interpretation of disability, 103
surrogacy and pregnancy distinguished, 103
validity of Equality Framework Directive, 104
intersectional and multiple discrimination, 102–10

Lightning Source UK Ltd.
Milton Keynes UK
UKHW020255090422
401309UK00003BA/117

9 781509 945146